MIGHTY OPPOSITES

ROBERT GRUDIN

Mighty Opposites

SHAKESPEARE

AND RENAISSANCE

CONTRARIETY

UNIVERSITY OF CALIFORNIA PRESS

Berkeley · Los Angeles · London

TO MY PARENTS

University of California Press
Berkeley and Los Angeles, California
University of California Press, Ltd.
London, England
Copyright © 1979 by
The Regents of the University of California
ISBN 0-520-03666-2
Library of Congress Catalog Card Number: 78-51753

1 2 3 4 5 6 7 8 9

CONTENTS

Acknowledgments   vi

1. Shakespeare and the Function
of Contraries   1
Notes   11

2. The Infant Rind: Contrariety and
Shakespeare's Intellectual Milieu   13
Notes   44

3. Shakespeare and Ethical Tradition: Hazard and
Justice in *The Merchant of Venice*   51
Notes   72

4. Contrariety as Disease and Cure:
The Problem Comedies   75
Notes   115

5. Contrariety as Structure:
The Later Tragedies   119
Notes   179

6. *The Tempest*: Prospero as Hero
of Contraries   185
Notes   208

Index   213

ACKNOWLEDGMENTS

Work on this book began during a year spent in Cambridge, England. I am grateful to the National Endowment for the Humanities and to the Office of Scientific and Scholarly Research at the University of Oregon for the funds that made this year possible, and to the president and fellows of Wolfson College, Professor E. J. Kenney of Peterhouse, and Mrs. Ali Richter, Mr. and Mrs. David Crompton, and Mr. and Mrs. Peter Raby of Swaffham Bulbeck, Cambridgeshire, for helping to make it happy and productive.

I wish to thank my colleagues at the University of Oregon, Thelma Greenfield, Gloria Johnson, and Waldo McNeir; and Norman Rabkin and Hugh Richmond, of the University of California at Berkeley, for their invaluable encouragement and counsel. Thanks are also due to my colleagues, Robert Albrecht, Lawrence Owens, Gordon Rockett, Richard Stevenson, Richard Stein, and Oliver Willard; my students, Patricia Olson, Jeffrey Porter, and Linda Robertson; and my friends, Alan Hager and David Sweet, for miscellaneous assistance and illumination. C. L. Barber, of the University of California at Santa Cruz, and R. W. Dent, of the University of California at Los Angeles, who read the manuscript for the University of California Press, provided dozens of valuable suggestions for revision. My wife, Michaela Paasche Grudin, favored me with numerous stylistic judgments which were at once benevolent and severe.

Chapter 3 of this book was presented at the International Shakespeare Congress in Washington D.C., in April, 1976. Parts of Chapters 4 and 6 are taken from essays which appeared in *Anglia* and the *South Atlantic Quarterly*, respectively. I wish to thank the editors of these journals for permission to reprint this material. For all quotations from and references to the works of Shakespeare, I have followed (unless otherwise stated) the text of G. Blakemore Evans in *The Riverside Shakespeare*, 2 vols. (Boston: Houghton Mifflin Company, 1974).

CHAPTER 1

Shakespeare and the Function of Contraries

In Act III of *Othello*, while the Moor is still happy with Desdemona, he calls her "Excellent wretch!" (iii.90) This paradox, a sudden glimpse of white against black, is like an image of the play itself. The soldier's phrase of affection carries dramatic irony: Desdemona *is* excellent, and she will be wretched indeed. It is easy to take this disproportion between her merits and her rewards as a measure of the play's tragic power. But persistent ambiguities tempt us to question this interpretation and, in so doing, to reexamine Shakespeare's attitude towards paradox as a means of expression. Is Desdemona wretched in spite of her excellence, or wretched because of it? The absoluteness and rigidity of her virtue, her lack of vision, her insistent vulnerability, and her passivity in the face of injustice all argue that the second alternative be considered as seriously as the first. This impression deepens when we consider Desdemona's fiendish enemy, Iago. His character is webbed around with paradox. His epithets are "precious villain" and "Spartan dog" (V.ii. 235, 361); he conceives of a "Divinity of Hell," and his motto is, "I am not what I am" (II.iii.350, I.i.65). He is vigorous and creative; his goals are terrible and corrupt. Does his obvious strength of character exist in spite of his evil, or because of it? Here again, we have reason to suppose that the relationship between the apparent opposites may be positive as well as negative. Iago's wit and managerial genius neither transcend nor survive the necessities of his malice. His virtue and his evil do not hamper each other but rather unite in an unfamiliar harmony. Both Iago and Desdemona derive their psychological force from the mingling and interdependence of contraries; in a larger sense, the play owes its power to the interplay of these characters' morally irreconcilable, but dramatically correlated, personalities. This mystery of alliance and opposition is typical of Shakespeare's mature tragedy. For Shakespeare, as we will see, paradox is a concise embodiment of the tragic fact—a specific and radical observation about the workings of nature.

Paradox, or some related theme, is where most philosophical discussions of Shakespeare normally leave off. Until recently, it was seen as the boundary-line of his thought, where relative certainty ended and hopeless obscurity began. It made critics conclude, and students assume, that Shakespeare was unphilosophical, or that he was a relativist, or that he saw experience as absurd. Facing the problem more thoughtfully, Norman Rabkin has portrayed Shakespeare's world as one of "complementarity," where ideas exist in tandem with their polar opposites, and we are caught between assertions of two conflicting extremes. Rabkin's analysis has made it possible for us to see Shakespearean contrariety as an element of conscious aesthetic design. Experience born of oppositions is neither chaotic nor inscrutable; it is merely contrary, obeying predictable rules and revealing its secrets to those who are aware of its basic structure. Contraries, moreover, need not annul each other; instead, they may be corresponsive and even mutually enhancing. Thanks to Rabkin and studies like his, we may now examine Shakespearean contrariety as an accurate expression of meaning, and speculate upon the principles which form its basis.[1]

What follows is an attempt to reconstruct these principles. It is the first attempt to do so not only through a reconsideration of Shakespeare's development as a playwright but also through an analysis of trends in sixteenth-century intellectual history which clarify his attitude towards contraries. Philosophical reliance on contrariety is by no means unique to Shakespeare. His work parallels and, in some cases, may derive from doctrines which were propounded energetically by several of his predecessors and contemporaries. Chief among the spokesmen available to Shakespeare were Baldassare Castiglione, Paracelsus, Giordano Bruno, and Montaigne. Though their expression differs widely in subject and style, they are united in the belief that the interaction of contraries is one of the primary forces of experience, that contrariety can be a positive and regenerative principle, and that the only coherent response to experience, in theory or practice, lies in the acceptance of contrariety and the application of its special power. Shakespeare's relationship to these backgrounds will be in part the subject of this study. More importantly, however, I wish to show how, in case after case, an acquaintance with Renaissance contrariety can deepen our awareness of what happens in Shakespearean drama.

This exploration will necessarily involve almost every aspect of Shakespeare's art. Drama consistently dwells upon conflict and debate; but few dramatists have tested the potential of contraries as profoundly as Shakespeare, or employed them in such a wide variety of ways. He is well known for having used and even coined a large number of words whose meaning is inwardly opposed, such as those beginning with un- or ending with -less.[2] He loves to use paradox and such related figures as oxymoron, litotes, antithesis, synoeciosis, syncrisis, and inter se pugnantia.[3] His language is alive with words and phrases suggesting the extreme limits of perception (hyperbole) and the sharpest oppositions of meaning. What is remarkable about these figures is their appropriateness and their success. Shakespeare's sense of balance and his uncanny poetic aptness keep his verbal extravagances from becoming excessive, achieving instead an expression of normally unrealized tensions and contradictions in experience. By stretching and contorting language, Shakespeare expresses meanings that are otherwise beyond the reach of language, drawing us out into the margin between the end of logic and the limit of feeling. At their best, his tropes are a testing of boundaries, an attempt to tease and bully words into conformity with a deeply unconventional truth.

The fascination with extremes and opposites is expressed with equal emphasis in Shakespeare's treatment of character. His exploration of human psychology results in a series of figures—Hamlet, Othello, Macbeth, Antony, Timon, and others—whose experience is figured in terms of conflicting extremes. The innate correlation between Shakespeare's poetics and his treatment of psychology is evident in the fact that, to present these mental oppositions, he frequently relies on the hyperbolical and paradoxical figures of speech listed above. Othello's "Excellent wretch!" is the phrase of someone whose view of love is already unstable and strained; its ambiguity is echoed immediately by an oath and an assertion which are both figures of contrariety:

> Perdition catch my soul
> But I do love thee! And when I love thee not,
> Chaos is come again.
> (*Othello*, III.iii.90–92)

Othello's lines are, of course, an unconscious prophecy of dark things to come. Ironically, the drama will justify all his hyperbole and all his paradox. Yet Othello's very words reveal the psychology that will make this tragedy possible. The almost boyish penchant for absolutes, the compulsive positing of extreme alternatives suggest the flaw in his self-confidence, the fragility of his world.

In *Hamlet*, the hero's characteristic uncertainty is manifested not through timid hedgings but rather through radical assertions of contrary ideas. He shuns Ophelia, yet later assures Laertes he loved her immeasurably (V.i.269–271); he sees death either as a balm or an utter calamity (III.i.55–87); man is at once a near-divinity and an epitome of dust (II.ii.303–308). In their totality, these uneven assertions, like Othello's, comprise a form of psychological revelation. They are less expressive of honest doubt than of chronic posturing, of a mind whose repeated appeal to the absolute is in fact a compulsive evasion of the real. They suggest that Hamlet is less afraid to act than afraid to accept the terrible ambiguity of the truth. Apemantus' remark to Timon, the hero of the later play *Timon of Athens*, "The middle of humanity thou never knewest, but the extremity of both ends" (IV.iii.300–301), may be applied to Hamlet and Othello as well.

The relationship between verbal paradox and mental conflict is exploited with equal subtlety in Shakespeare's treatment of the young lover Troilus. Early in *Troilus and Cressida* he tells Pandarus,

> I am mad
> In Cressid's love. Thou answer'st she is fair,
> Pour'st in the open ulcer of my heart
> Her eyes, her hair, her cheek, her gait, her voice;
> Handlest in thy discourse, O, that her hand,
> In whose comparison all whites are ink,
> Writing their own reproach; to whose soft seizure
> The cygnet's down is harsh, and spirit of sense
> Hard as the palm of plowman. This thou tell'st me,
> As true thou tell'st me, when I say I love her;
> But, saying thus, instead of oil or balm,
> Thou lay'st in every gash that love hath given me
> The knife that made it.
>
> (*Troilus and Cressida*, I.i.51–63)

Here psychological disharmony is expressed through the systematic exaggeration of Renaissance love rhetoric. Hyperbole is stretched into a paradoxical denial of the basic qualities of nature. Swan's down is harsh; sensibility itself is hard; white becomes guilty black. The tired paradox of love as disease ("ulcer") and wound ("gash") is intensified until the element of morbidity overpowers the element of sweetness. Through a coherent distortion of style, Troilus' 'madness' loses its power as a metaphorical extension of love. The final impression—to be borne out by the action that follows—is not of the intensity of the thing described but of the pathological complexity of the speaker.

Contrariety in Shakespeare extends beyond language and psychology into larger patterns of experience. Characters repeatedly describe important aspects of life in paradoxical terms. Adversity, whether divinely imposed or brought about by men, is seen as something good:

> [Jupiter:] Whom best I love I cross; to make my gift
> The more delay'd, delighted.
> > (*Cymbeline*, V.iv.101–102)

> Sweet are the uses of adversity,
> Which like the toad, ugly and venomous,
> Wears yet a precious jewel in his head;
> > (*As You Like It*, II.i.12–14)

> But I will keep her ignorant of her good,
> To make her heavenly comforts of despair,
> When it is least expected.
> > (*Measure for Measure*, IV.iii.109–111)

Prosperity, on the other hand, can have ill effects and may even need a purgation of violence:

> Plenty and peace breeds cowards; hardness ever
> Of hardiness is mother.
> > (*Cymbeline*, III.vi.21–22)

> [To Mars (War):]
> O great corrector of enormous times,
> Shaker of o'er-rank states, . . .
> > . . . that heal'st with blood
> The earth when it is sick, and cur'st the world
> O' th' plurisy of people!
> > (*The Two Noble Kinsmen*, V.i.62–66)

Evil and goodness are often closely related and sometimes even generate each other:

> Within the infant rind of this fair flower
> Poison hath residence and medicine power;
> > (*Romeo and Juliet*, II.iii.23–24)

> . . . and my trust,
> Like a good parent, did beget of him
> A falsehood in its contrary, as great
> As my trust was, . . .
> > (*The Tempest*, I.ii.93–96)

> There is some soul of goodness in things evil,
> Would men observingly distill it out;
> > (*Henry V*, IV.i.4–5)

Evil, moreover, can work against evil, goodness against goodness:

> But from the inward motion to deliver
> Sweet, sweet, sweet poison for the age's tooth,
> Which though I will not practice to deceive,
> Yet to avoid deceit, I mean to learn;
> > (*King John*, I.i.212–215)

> O cunning enemy, that to catch a saint,
> With saints dost bait thy hook!
> > (*Measure for Measure*, II.ii.179–180)

More generally, likes can destroy likes, contraries support contraries:

> Tut, man, one fire burns out another's burning, . . .
> > (*Romeo and Juliet*, I.ii.45)

> O, the fierce wretchedness that glory brings us!
> > (*Timon of Athens*, IV.ii.30)

> In poison there is physic, . . .
> > (*Henry IV (2)*, I.i.137)

Especially in the middle and late plays, this form of statement through contradiction can occur in amazing profusion.

The technique plays a large part in establishing the tone of *King Lear*.[4] In *Antony and Cleopatra*, paradoxical tropes occur more than one hundred times. Where they do occur, moreover, it is not to brighten an otherwise dull moment but rather to reveal an important facet of character or experience.[5] Here as elsewhere, there are strong links between the poetic technique and the vision underlying it.

The fascination with contrariety asserts itself with equal intensity on the structural levels of Shakespearean drama. From *Venus and Adonis* and *The Rape of Lucrece* to *The Tempest* and *Henry VIII*, Shakespeare repeatedly uses characters as the opposed embodiments of extremes. In contrasts like those between Desdemona and Iago or Cleopatra and Octavius, the contrast is so extreme and so indelible as to impress us with the inevitability of the tragic action. In other plays, like *Measure for Measure* and *The Tempest*, opposites form the boundaries of a dialectic which in turn tempers and qualifies them. Some of these characters have been compared to figures in a morality play;[6] but this explanation ignores the dramatic and psychological realism that gives them form. Characters like Cordelia and her sisters, or Caliban and Miranda are not abstract ideas so much as discoveries resulting from an unprecedented exploration of human nature. They are radically contradictory, yet unnervingly familiar. The most irreconcilable extremes in Shakespeare, be they wonderful or terrible, are no further from each other than two arms' breadth.

Finally, Shakespeare's treatment of theme and ideology is frequently structured in terms of contraries. This aspect of his drama has been variously documented. A. C. Bradley's analysis of Shakespearean tragedy as the dialectical interaction of opposed natural forces is a milestone in the philosophical interpretation of literature.[7] In one of the earliest thematic studies of Shakespeare, G. Wilson Knight analyzed *Troilus and Cressida* with emphasis on the contrasting themes of love and war and the opposed qualities of the

Trojans and the Greeks.[8] More recently, Northrop Frye has seen Shakespearean comedy as based on the antithesis between two distinct geographical and psychological frames of reference;[9] to some extent (for example, in *King Lear* and *Antony and Cleopatra*), a similar method is developed in the Tragedies. In the Lancastrian Tetralogy, Hal's progress towards maturity is plotted amidst an interplay of disjunctive ethical and political modalities represented in word and action by Henry IV, Hotspur, and Falstaff. In equally subtle plays like *Measure for Measure* and *The Tempest*, single characters pass through meaningfully contradictory stages of vision.[10] Shakespeare consistently presents ideology not as conclusion but as process. He sees an intellectual world in which statements generate their own opposites, a social world in which actions are repeatedly modified by the responses they evoke. The study of this attitude has led modern critics to characterize Shakespeare as a master of dialectic, and he has been very aptly compared to Plato.[11]

Understanding this pattern of ideas can bring us closer to Shakespeare's 'metaphysics'—the profound but elusive order that seems to underlie much of his drama. We would be wrong, however, to approach his work as a single piece. Shakespeare's treatment of drama and poetry changed with time; and our substantial knowledge of his chronology enables us to speculate on the course of his intellectual development. We will see that his interest in contrariety originated during a comprehensive arraignment of internal contradictions in established ethical norms. Two relatively early plays, *Romeo and Juliet* and *The Merchant of Venice*, betray an ironic attitude towards traditional interpretations of experience; they suggest that Shakespeare is appraising contrariety as a possible alternative. The Problem Comedies, *Troilus and Cressida*, *All's Well that Ends Well*, and *Measure for Measure*, are franker and more derisive in their moral satire. Here, questions that were gracefully submerged in the earlier plays become explicit, and specific emphasis is placed on contradictions latent in psychological and social phenomena. It should be noted, however, that in these plays Shakespeare is not only posing problems but suggesting revolutionary solutions to them—complex and paradoxical solutions whose nature partakes of the problems themselves. These radical responses and the problems they address have a documentable relationship to theories of Renaissance contrariety, and particular use is made of the terms and doctrines of Paracelsus and his followers.

After this period, and perhaps by means of this expression, Shakespeare concerns himself no more with 'problems' or their solutions. The mature Tragedies, *Othello*, *King Lear*, *Macbeth*, and *Antony and Cleopatra*, establish a new cosmology of the human universe, exploring the limits of passion, suffering, and expression. Here, principles of contrariety are woven far more deeply into the aesthetic fabric, beyond language and behavior into the basic structures of character, time, and causality. This deepened sense of conflict, superficially different from the more immediate concerns of the Problem Comedies, nonetheless suggests the roots of these concerns—contradictions so profound that they can only be experienced briefly, never effectively controlled. It is as though Homer had written his *Iliad* after his *Odyssey*, as though the titanic excursions of will were possible only after the ripening of prudence.

The final plays follow the Tragedies as an almost organic consequence. While the Tragedies posit experience as derived from inexorable forces of conflict, the final plays review these forces as necessary to a regenerative cycle of challenge and growth. This last period is crowned by the figure of Prospero, a true hero of contraries, whose unique power depends upon the temporary control of otherwise chaotic extremes. Prospero's dramatic position—correlative to Shakespeare's—as planner and director of the play's action is here most important. It implies the integration of contrariety, not only into basic patterns of experience, but into the realm of creative imagination. Over a period of fifteen years, Shakespeare moved from a baffling dilemma to a philosophy of contraries broad enough to include the artist himself.

Notes to Chapter One

1 Norman Rabkin, *Shakespeare and the Common Understanding* (New York: The Free Press; London: Collier-Macmillan, 1967); see below, p. 13.

2 Sister Miriam Joseph, C.S.C., *Shakespeare's Use of the Arts of Language* (New York: Columbia University Press, 1947), pp. 133–34.

3 Ibid., pp. 130–41.

4 Constructions of this kind are used throughout *King Lear* to emphasize paradoxical relationships between appearance and reality, madness and reason, prosperity and adversity. See especially III.iv, III.vi, IV.iv, and Brian Vickers, *"King Lear* and Renaissance Paradoxes," *Modern Language Review* 63 (1968): 305–14.

5 These devices are heavily clustered at the play's beginning and at its end. See Act I, passim; V.ii; and below, pp. 165–69 and Chapter 5, n.26.

6 See, for example, Colin Still, *Shakespeare's Mystery Play: A Study of The Tempest* (London: C. Palmer, 1921; enlarged version published as *The Timeless Theme*, London: I. Nicholson and Watson, 1936), and Kenneth Muir, *"King Lear,"* in *Shakespeare: Select Bibliographical Guides,* ed. Stanley Wells (Oxford: University Press, 1973), pp. 177–79.

7 A. C. Bradley, *Shakespearean Tragedy* (New York: Macmillan Co., 1904) Lecture 1.

8 G. Wilson Knight, *The Wheel of Fire* (London: Oxford University Press, 1930), ch. 3.

9 Northrop Frye, "The Argument of Comedy," in *English Institute Essays* (New York: Columbia University Press, 1948).

10 See below, Chapters 4 and 6.

11 Rabkin, p. 11; W. R. Elton, *King Lear and the Gods* (San Marino: The Huntington Library, 1966), pp. 109–10, 282–83; Howard B. White, *Copp'd Hills Towards Heaven* (The Hague: Martinus Nijhoff, 1970), ch. I., passim; pp. 147–53. The comparison to Plato is White's.

CHAPTER 2

The Infant Rind: Contrariety and
Shakespeare's Intellectual Milieu

The modern study of contrariety in Shakespeare is founded
on three books which appeared more or less simultaneously
in America during the middle of the last decade. W. R.
Elton's *King Lear and the Gods* (1966) speaks of Shakespeare's play as a philosophical pattern in which antithetical
doctrines are interwoven dialectically, and ideas and tonalities are juxtaposed ironically. In Rosalie Colie's *Paradoxia
Epidemica* (1966), Shakespearean paradox is seen in the
context of an age which delighted in such devices, using
them as means of expression and education. Norman
Rabkin's *Shakespeare and the Common Understanding*
(1967) is an effort to come to terms with Shakespeare's
use of ideological and psychological forms of contrariety—
his technique of setting up, in plays like *Hamlet* and *Troilus
and Cressida,* dilemmas which baffle protagonists and seem
to neutralize choices. To Rabkin, Shakespeare is a classic
destroyer of certainties, whose "basic mode of vision" is
one in which "opposed elements" are "equally valid, equally desirable and equally destructive, so that the choice that
the play forces the reader to make becomes impossible."
Rabkin's argument is buttressed by an analogy to Niels Bohr's
notion of *complementarity*—the theory that a physical phenomenon may evoke two equally valid but mutually contradictory explanations.[1]

More recent critical work has expanded on some of these themes. In *Shakespearean Design* (1972), Mark Rose discusses Shakespeare's use of structure as an effective means of ordering the dramatic experience and juxtaposing ideas against each other. S. K. Heninger includes a discussion of contrariety as an element of Pythagoreanism in his *Touches of Sweet Harmony* (1974). Shakespeare's dialectical skill is examined by Howard B. White in *Copp'd Hills towards Heaven* (1972); and a like service is performed for non-Shakespearean seventeenth-century literature by Stanley E. Fish's *Self-Consuming Artifacts* (1972). Harriet Hawkins' *Likenesses of Truth in Elizabethan and Restoration Drama* (1972) approaches Shakespeare in terms of a special form of dialectic: "a clash between the moral and psychological truth of human experience and the empirical, literal, and factual truth about human experience"—both of which, she claims, operate simultaneously in Shakespeare's plays.[2]

A number of these studies have treated their subjects so appropriately and so effectively that further comment is all but unnecessary here. But, predictably, these books and others have opened up new areas of inquiry. With the exceptions of Colie and Heninger, who touch very specific aspects of the topic, scholarship has not yet treated contrariety as a scientific and philosophical phenomenon in Europe and England before 1600. Not only the general context in which contrariety developed, but also its particular relationship to Shakespeare, have been left largely untouched. These backgrounds provide, I believe, a helpful and pertinent intellectual matrix for the appreciation of Shakespearean drama. Moreover, they elaborate a pattern of thought which many members of his contemporary audiences probably shared, and to which, we may assume, he could consciously and meaningfully appeal.

Sixteenth-Century Intellectual Backgrounds

The interaction of contraries is one of the major issues of Renaissance thought. Contradictions, paradoxes, and dichotomies of all kinds are of such vital import to philosophers of this period that even those spokesmen who deny their significance are compelled to give them elaborate attention. Indeed, we are introduced to contraries in the Renaissance by the energetic negation of them. With the doctrine of the *coincidentia oppositorum*, Nicholas of Cusa (1401–1464) maintains that, just as all numbers are equal when compared with the infinite, all earthly contradictions are reconciled in the infinite unity of God. Giovanni Pico della Mirandola (1463–1494), who named himself "Princeps Concordiae," seeks to establish himself as the harmonizer of oppositions; he claims, moreover, that the great religious and philosophical doctrines of the world, with all their contradictory ideas of God and the good life, amount to more or less the same thing. Like Shakespeare's lady who did "protest too much," these writings bear witness to the urgency of the notions they deny; and the nature of this threat is relatively soon manifest in writings from the other side. Early in the sixteenth century, Cornelius Agrippa (1486–1535) points to major contradictions in human knowledge, and ridicules that classical symbol of harmony, the music of the spheres. Baldassare Castiglione (1478–1529) and Paracelsus (1494–1541) maintain that contrariety is the dominant principle of experience; they suggest, moreover, that the interaction of contraries can be a positive and healthy phenomenon. These iconoclasts are followed, through the sixteenth century and well into the seventeenth century, by numerous major writers who variously declare a commitment to the notion of strife. In 1644, when John Milton asserts that the knowledge of good and evil sprang "out of the rind of one apple tasted," that man's fate is to know "good by evil" and that, in general, "we learn by what is contrary," he makes the last notable statement of one of the liveliest and most persistent motives of Renaissance thought.[3]

Contrariety, here understood as the idea that experience derives from the interaction of opposing forces, is at odds not only with the Neoplatonists but also with Aristotle and the scholastic tradition. For Aristotle, contraries are the perimeters of thought and sensation, the extremes which define the limits of any subject, and thus set up the standards for distinctions of quality and degree. Whether these distinctions be in the physical world or the ethical world, the method of analysis seems to be the same. Hot and cold, prodigal and miserly serve as boundary-lines between which the philosopher can accurately locate the phenomena under study. Contraries exist only as standards for the measurement of being, and thus it is essential that every two contraries negate each other unequivocally. While the Neoplatonists see contraries as merging in a truth which absorbs and denies their differences, the Aristotelians see contraries as methodological tools whose value lies in their distinctness alone.[4]

Proponents of contrariety, however, invoke a tradition of even greater antiquity. When Giordano Bruno attempts to refute the Aristotelian notion of contraries, he relies on Plato and Heraclitus, who both taught that the interaction of contraries is a dynamic and kinetic process, that indeed contraries generate each other, and that their complex and symbiotic relationship is one of the basic motives of experience. Heraclitus maintains that strife is the dominant principle of being. Plato structures his works on contrariety (dialectic), and has Alcibiades, in a memorable speech, describe Socrates as a figure of contraries.[5] Bruno uses these authorities in an effort to establish contrariety as the primary function in metaphysics, epistemology, and psychology.[6]

Extreme forms of contrariety like Bruno's arise within an intellectual context which, by the second half of the sixteenth century, has become resonant with dualities and oppositions of all kinds. Contradictions in perceived phenomena, formal paradoxes, theoretical inconsistencies, psychological ambiguities, and moral dilemmas are made the foci for a variety of sharply dualistic methods of analysis. Indeed, the tendency to resolve experience into contrariety is so widespread that it may be seen as one of the primary intellectual modalities of the period. A partial list of its major manifestations reads like an index of Renaissance vogues. As Rosalie Colie has shown, during this period the paradox is not only an immensely popular mode of expression (an "epidemic") but also the outward sign of a characteristic attitude towards thought and experience. Petrarch's many followers portray erotic emotion as an unrelieved tension in which opposed elements like pain and pleasure or body and spirit struggle for supremacy. Calvin calls human nature itself a "matching of contraries"; and Sir Philip Sidney, a disciple of both Petrarch and Calvin, names these contraries the "erected wit" and the "infected will." The commonplace that life is an "interchangeable course, or variety," of contrary forces and effects, is established by writers who draw upon Heraclitus, Plato, the Stoics, the Pythagoreans, and Hermes Trismegistus. The skeptic doctrine, that the ascent to *ataraxia* is based on the understanding of contrarieties, is revived with great energy. Irony, the voice which simultaneously asserts and denies, becomes a popular literary strategy, championed by Agrippa, Erasmus, and Sir Thomas More. Montaigne and Bacon deliberately employ contradictory arguments to destroy their readers' preconceptions and stimulate them to active inquiry.[7] United by their radical emphasis on contrariety, and springing frequently from similar attitudes, these doctrines and techniques may all be seen as steps towards an earthly vision, efforts to bring analysis away from the realm of abstraction and into contact with the discordant messages of perceived phenomena. Shakespeare, as we will see, uses contraries to much the same effect. Here, as in so many other aspects of his art, he is not an isolated and untutored genius but rather an active and knowledgeable participant in contemporary intellectual concerns.

The radical potentialities of contrariety in the Renaissance are nowhere more evident than in the work of Baldassare Castiglione, Paracelsus, and Giordano Bruno. Castiglione, in his celebrated *Il Libro del Cortegiano* (1528), polemically asserts the dominance of contraries in the realm of ethics and the development of culture. Contrariety is a basic element of Paracelsian science, not only in its specific applications but also in its theoretical basis. Bruno, who studied Paracelsus and who draws from the same sources as Castiglione, seeks to establish contrariety as the formative principle of experience in general. The theories of Castiglione, Paracelsus, and Bruno are of particular pertinence to the study of contraries in Shakespeare, not only because a number of his dramatic, thematic, and poetic structures remind us of their ideas, but also because, more than anyone else, these three European writers exemplify the intellectual context in which Shakespeare's attitude towards contrariety took shape. Acquainting ourselves with their theories will give us easier access to some of Shakespeare's more difficult structures, and will expose more fully the intellectual raw materials upon which he worked such enduring alchemies.

Castiglione and Ethical Contrariety

The setting for Baldassare Castiglione's *Il Libro del Cortegiano* is the ducal palace at Urbino, where Castiglione had been a member of Guidobaldo da Montefeltro's court. Beyond the large reception rooms of this famous building are the elegant private apartments of the ruling family, and these are pertinent, if only by analogy, to the content and spirit of Castiglione's work. Two small, barrel-vaulted chapels, almost identical in proportions, stand side by side. One is a place of Christian worship. The other is for the celebration of pagan deities and earthly life. Together these chapels bear witness to an unusual frame of mind, an attitude which not only accepts the extremes of divine and earthly experience but seems to draw its vigor from their very polarity. In this architectural manifesto, the categorical opposition of viewpoints emerges as a source of balance and energy.[8]

Il Libro del Cortegiano partakes of a similar mixture of extremes. Read carefully, it is less a discursive handbook of courtly behavior than a classical dialogue in which diverse and sometimes radically opposed points of view are given vigorous expression. Book 3, the discussion of women, comes close to being a pitched debate. Ottaviano Fregoso, who presents the most dignified expression of the courtier's social role, begins his discourse in Book 4 by sharply criticizing everything that has been said in the first three books; in the course of his discussion he often meets with lively disagreement. In particular, Ottaviano's political ideals stand in sharp contrast to Pietro Bembo's Neoplatonism, and in even sharper contrast to the tyrannical precepts of Cesare Gonzaga.[9] Most striking of all is the general structure of the entire work, which is, in a manner reminiscent of the ducal palace itself, a deliberate counterpoise of extremes. Though the dialogue ends with Bembo's long rapture of Neoplatonic contemplation, it has for its center a massive collection of satiric anecdotes which present social experience in gross and shocking terms. Elsewhere I have argued that these anecdotes are crucial to the meaning of Castiglione's work and that their effect is to add a dimension of realism—an understanding of those unavoidable elements in life which are impure and coarse—to the otherwise refined tonality.[10] From this ironic and unrelieved balance of opposed extremes, *Il Libro del Cortegiano* derives a sense of comprehensive scope. Earthly and spiritual attitudes comment silently upon each other, and the structural implication is that the truly civilized person must keep them both in mind.

This broad awareness of extremes is justified by the moral doctrine which Castiglione presents (without *persona*) at the beginning of Book 2. In an introduction addressed to Alfonso Ariosto, he undertakes to defend his contemporary Italy from critics who attack it as vicious and corrupt. Surprisingly he begins his defense by admitting that the charge is true. Indeed there is much evil in Italy; but without evil, he goes on to say, there would be no real goodness. The wickedness of sixteenth-century Italy and its new-found greatness (in politics and the arts and sciences) are mutually dependent conditions. Indeed, there is no good without evil, and those people who are not aware of this paradoxical relationship do not know the nature of goodness.

The ways in which Castiglione supports this revolutionary contention are of critical importance here. In the first place he claims that goodness necessitates evil and vice versa because "there is no contrary without its contrary." Extreme qualities cannot be known except in terms of opposite extremes:

> Who does not know that there would not be justice in the world if there were no wrongs? No magnanimity, if none were pusillanimous? No continence, if there were no incontinence?[11]

Immediately this theory of norms expands into a theory of nature. Pleasure and pain, health and sickness, virtue and vice, and all contrary states are inseparable by the law of Creation. Moreover, "no evil is so evil as that which is born of the corrupted seed of good"; and, conversely, no man is truly good except him who is aware of his evil alternatives. Ages which, prizing "innocence," avoided evil through ignorance of it were not really good, but rather, Castiglione delightfully asserts, were "as bad as they knew how to be."[12] The argument concludes with a sweeping appraisal of history. Though earlier (late medieval) times held less corruption than sixteenth-century Italy, they were also inferior in "letters . . . paintings, statues, buildings, and everything else." However, the very best (and worst) society was that of "the worthy ancients" (*i boni antichi*):

> in the age when those more than human talents and those spirits lived who were glorious and truly divine in every virtue, many vicious men were also to be found, who, if they were alive today, would surpass our wicked men in evil deeds, even as the good men of that age would in good deeds. And to all this history bears ample witness.[13]

Castiglione has built his thesis upon a novel rendering of Aristotelian and Platonic material. In the *Nicomachean Ethics*, Aristotle examines justice, magnanimity, and continence as means between extremes of excess and defect; he also stipulates that these virtues should be considered as contraries of either extreme (5.5.17; 4, 7, passim; 2.8.1–3). In the *Republic* (491b) Socrates maintains that nothing can be as wicked as corrupted nobility of spirit; and in the *Phaedo* (60) he speaks of the interdependency of pain and pleasure and later (70–72) claims that all opposites (good and evil, just and unjust, etc.) are generated from each other. Taking these arguments out of context, Castiglione extends them to their logical extremes and combines them with a boldly non-Christian view of history. The result is a manifesto which, beyond defending its author's social and intellectual milieu, serves two highly important philosophical purposes. First, its rationale of contrariety parallels and justifies the development of the whole work, itself a grand structure of opposed yet interdependent extremes. Castiglione's moral thesis suggests that the more sublime aspects of the dialogue—the discourses of Fregoso and Bembo and the beautifully-drawn character of the Duchess (1.4)—would have no basis in reality without the viler aspects implied by the unholy jests. Second, it announces a radical morality, in which the value of innocence is wholly refuted, and worldly wisdom becomes the basis for just action. Not good will alone, but the knowledgeable choice of good over evil, and the intellectual freedom which allows of such a choice, are the qualities of true virtue. Thus, Castiglione's lively and uneven times may be seen as a school of virtue, and his heterogeneous dialogue as virtue's unexpurgated handbook.

Castiglione's doctrine of good and evil is paralleled by a number of sixteenth-century Protestant attacks on the alleged encouragement of pious ignorance by the Catholic Church. In the *Arcadia* (1590), Sir Philip Sidney formulates an arraignment of innocence which seems to derive not only from the Protestant saw that, for the Catholics, ignorance is "the mother of true devotion," but also from Castiglione's contention that innocence is, at best, a feeble hedge against corruption:

> O no; he cannot be good, that knowes not why he is good, but stands so farre good, as his fortune may keep him unassaied: but comming once to that, his rude simplicitie is either easily changed, or easily deceived: & so growes that to be the last excuse of his fault, which seemed to have been the first foundation of his faith.[14]

In the *Areopagitica*, Milton sees Book 2 of Edmund Spenser's *The Faerie Queene* (1590) as an allegorical presentation of the same idea:

> . . . our sage and serious poet Spenser, whom I dare be known to think a better teacher than Scotus or Aquinas, describing true temperance under the person of Guion, brings him in with his palmer through the cave of Mammon, and the bower of earthly bliss, that he might see and know, and yet abstain.

When, in the same passage, he shows contempt for a "cloistered" virtue, asserts we must undergo trial "by what is contrary," and attributes both good and evil to "the rind of one apple tasted," we see Christian and pagan ideas of contrariety merging in one consistent viewpoint.[15] But Elizabethans and Jacobeans wishing to speculate on paradoxical relationships between good and evil and other contraries need not have drawn their material from these sources alone. The doctrines of Paracelsus, which achieved great currency in London by the early 1590s, provide a different but equally potent endorsement of contrariety. Moreover, by a simple metaphorical extension, Paracelsus' "philosophical medicine" affords what can be seen as a novel cure for entirely nonmedical ills.

Paracelsus: *Wesen gegen Wesen*

The man who was called Paracelsus (c. 1494–1541) practiced medicine, traveled widely in Europe, and produced voluminous writings in Low German and Latin on medical, chemical, and mystical themes. His teachings, like those of his admirer Bruno, were iconoclastic and sensational; but unlike Bruno, Paracelsus attracted a strong following and significantly affected the course of science. He was a Promethean figure whose achievement, long relegated to the backgrounds of scientific history or distorted by propagandists, deserves renewed attention as part of the history of ideas.

Paracelsus' chief contributions to science lie in pathology and chemistry. First, he rejects Galen's second-century theory of humoralism, which until his time dominated Western medicine, and substitutes a view of disease which resembles our own. Walter Pagel describes this new theory as follows:

> Chief among Paracelsus' contributions to medical theory was his new concept of disease. He demolished the ancients' notion of disease as an upset of humoral balance—either an excess (*hyperballonta*) or an insufficiency (*elleiponta*)—or as a displacement or putrefaction of humors . . . .
> Paracelsus completely reversed this concept, emphasizing the external cause of a disease, its selection of a particular locus, and its consequent seat. He sought and found the causes of disease chiefly in the mineral world (notably in salts) and in the atmosphere, carrier of star-born "poisons." He considered each of these agents to be a real *ens*, a substance in its own right (as opposed to humors, or temperaments, which he regarded as fictitious). He thus interpreted disease itself as an *ens*, determined by a specific agent foreign to the body, which takes possession of one of its parts, imposing its own rules on form and function and thereby threatening life. This is the parasitic or ontological concept of disease—and essentially the modern one.
> (*Dictionary of Scientific Biography*,
> s.v. "Paracelsus")

This theory, we should note, breaks decisively not only with accepted medical thought but with scholastic cosmology as a whole. Galenic humoralism fitted well within the scholastic cosmos. In both systems, nature was seen as a fundamentally harmonious construct; disease and evil were not active forces but rather were imbalances which disrupted the larger order. By defining disease as *ens*, Paracelsus projects a wholly different sort of universe—a universe characterized by the violent interaction between contrary but equally natural forces.

Connected with his theory of disease is Paracelsus' second major scientific contribution. As specific entities, he writes, diseases require specific cures. Paracelsus sees the goal of the physician as deriving these special cures ("virtues") from the larger compounds in which they naturally occur. In this process of division and isolation, which Paracelsus not only professes but practices, lie the beginnings of modern therapeutic chemistry.[16]

It is important to understand these components of Paracelsian theory because without them we cannot account for his immense impact on the sixteenth and seventeenth centuries. (Montaigne says he has heard that Paracelsus upset "the whole order of the ancient rules" of medicine.)[17] Without them, moreover, we cannot see Paracelsus' notions of duality and contrariety in their proper context. These latter ideas, which would be more appealing to some Elizabethan writers than were Paracelsus' 'hard' achievements, are generally expressed in the form of medical, psychological, and mystical *dicta* scattered widely throughout his works. The remarkably interdisciplinary nature of these statements, and their isolated positioning, say something important about their author's method. For Paracelsus, there is no such thing as category, no inhibiting idea of relevance or irrelevance. Medicine, psychology, history, and cosmology are all part of the same science. Phenomena are so profoundly interrelated that, indeed, all science is one science. Everything in Paracelsus' world is at once an entity in itself, and a metaphor for something else. More than any other philosopher of the Renaissance, he may be seen as illustrating T. S. Eliot's idea of "the unified sensibility." His philosophy is, at very least, a comprehensive analogy to what we know as the Renaissance poetic awareness.

Paracelsus' attitude towards contrariety is directly related to his medical and cosmological theories. Man is inherently subject to the contrary forces of nature because man is a microcosm, a self-contained miniature of the universe:

> Man is the Little World . . . .
>
> The whole world surrounds man as a circle surrounds one point. From this it follows that all things are related to this one point, no differently from an apple seed which is surrounded and preserved by the fruit, and which draws its sustenance from it . . . .
>
> . . . there is nothing in heaven or in earth that is not also in man . . . .[18]

The contrariety in human nature stems from the competitive and potentially destructive relationship between the heavenly and earthly forces which operate within each individual:

> . . . a contradiction dwells in man . . . . Namely, the stars in him have a different disposition, a different orientation than the lower elements . . . . For instance, the elemental, material body wants to live in luxury and lewdness; the stars, the ethereal body, the inner counterpart of the upper sphere, want to study, learn, pursue arts, and so forth. As a result there arises an antinomy in man himself. The visible, material body wants one thing, they do not want the same thing . . . . Therefore there dwells in each of these bodies an urge to exceed what is given it, and neither wants to follow a middle course and act with measure. Both strive to exceed their bounds, and each wants to expel the other; thus enmity arises between them. For everything that exceeds its measure brings destruction in its train.[19]

This dualism is of course age-old; but what is worth noting about Paracelsus' version of it is that, unlike his Neoplatonic antecedents, he does not believe the matter/spirit dichotomy capable of full resolution, nor does he prescribe the subjugation of the earthly body by its astral competitor. The earthly body is inferior but has, so to speak, equal seniority; and thus the goal of moral philosophy is not transcendence but rather measure. Paracelsus would limit the aspirations of both forces. He sees wisdom as a governing awareness of the tension between the two contrary powers.

Like his psychology, Paracelsus' natural philosophy in general emphasizes nature's universal potentiality for both good and evil and the perennial need for measure:

> In all things there is a poison, and there is nothing without a poison. It depends only on the dose whether a poison is poison or not.

Conversely, all things, including poisons, can be cures:

> He who despises poison does not know what is hidden in it; for the arcanum that is contained in the poison is so blessed that the poison can neither detract from nor harm it.[20]

His is a dynamic and mysterious world, where good and evil are separable not by essence but only by proportion. In this environment, physical and moral relationships are paradoxical and often violent:

> The remedy should operate in the body like a fire . . . .

> If a war breaks out, the cause of it is that God sends a punishment upon a country in order by such a punishment to renew the world.

> Decay is the beginning of all birth . . . . It brings about the birth and rebirth of forms a thousand times improved . . . . And this is the highest and greatest mysterium of God, the deepest mystery and miracle that he has revealed to mortal man.

> There where diseases arise, there also can one find the roots of health.[21]

Natural forces which so chronically generate their opposites must necessarily respond negatively to their "likes." Allied with Paracelsus' general view of nature is one of his most original doctrines,[22] the theory of the homeopathic cure:

> When a medicine is found in accordance with the star, when hot is supplied against hot, and cold against cold, all this accords with the arcanum. For in administering medicines we must always set

entity against entity (*Wesen gegen Wesen*), so that each becomes in a sense the wife or husband of the other.[23]

For the Galenist theory of treatment, *Contraria contrariis curantur*, Paracelsus offers a radical alternative, *Similia similibus curantur*. This formula, which will become a Paracelsian battle cry, is the logical medical retort to the paradoxical universe he describes. *Curantur* here means "are cured" or "are annulled." If contraries, like war and renewal, or decay and generation, invigorate and encourage each other, then likes (*similia*) should weaken and deplete each other.

Paracelsus, finally, deserves mention as one of his century's most extreme adherents to the idea of free will. Here as elsewhere his precepts are dualistic and are wholly in conformity with his general view of nature. He claims that freedom and fate coexist simultaneously as correlatives, respectively, of the astral and earthly principles in man:

> The stars are subject to the philosopher; they must follow him, and not he them. Only the man who is still animal is governed and mastered, compelled and driven by the stars, so that he has no choice but to follow them—just as the thief cannot escape the gallows, the murderer the wheel, the fish the fisherman, the bird the snare, or the game the hunter. But the reason for all this is that such a man does not know himself and does not know how to use the energies hidden within him, nor does he know that he carries the stars within himself, that he is the microcosm and carries within him the whole firmament with all its influences. Therefore he can rightly be abused as stupid and unwise, and must live in dire servitude to all that is earthly and mortal.[24]

Paracelsus conceives of a dual causality, a natural determinism whose baleful power can be transcended by individuals who possess self-knowledge. This doctrine is unusual if not revolutionary in terms of its own times. None of Paracelsus' contemporaries or immediate predecessors—not Machiavelli or even Ficino or Pico della Mirandola—allow of such scope in human volition, while the majority, like Pomponazzi, Valla, Luther, and Calvin, think quite otherwise.[25] The

Paracelsian theory of the will, with its implied equation of freedom with science, is undeniably positivistic, anticipating Bacon and reminding us of our own times. Equally striking and pertinent also are analogies between this dualistic view of causality and the structures of certain Shakespearean tragedies. *Romeo and Juliet* and *Macbeth*, for example, contain elements which have puzzled many readers because they seem to suggest the simultaneous existence of fluid and determined causalities—of freedom and fate. As we will see below, an understanding of Paracelsian theory can go far in making these and other ambiguities less troublesome to students of Shakespeare.

The doctrines of Paracelsus came to Elizabethan and early Jacobean England in a variety of forms: complete texts, individual works, writings by the master's disciples, and, in at least one notable case, the immigration of a Paracelsian physician from the Continent.[26] During the 1580s and 1590s, Paracelsian material appeared in English in the form of translations, a compendium, and a number of pamphlets.[27] English interest in Paracelsianism, among both scientists and laymen, is noticeable in many areas. John Dee owned over 100 works by Paracelsus and, most probably, instructed Sir Philip Sidney and Sir Edward Dyer about some of the principles contained therein.[28] John Hester dedicates his *A Hundred and Fourteen Experiments of Paracelsus* (1596) to Sir Walter Raleigh. Ben Jonson and Thomas Middleton mention Paracelsus, and Robert Burton's Paracelsian references are so frequent that they overflow the index of the modern edition of *The Anatomy of Melancholy*.[29] George Puttenham and John Donne invoke Paracelsus in wholly nonscientific contexts. In *The Arte of English Poesie* (1589) Puttenham describes the psychological effect of the lament, suggesting that a sad poem can in fact relieve sadness:

> Therefore of death and burials, and of th' adversities by warres, and of true love lost or ill bestowed, are th' onely sorrows that

> the noble Poets sought by their arte to remove or appease, not
> with any medicament of a contrary temper, as the Galenistes use
> to cure [*contraria contrariis*] but as the Paracelsians, who cure
> [*similia similibus*] making one dolour to expell another, and in
> this case, one short sorrowing the remedie of a long and grieuous
> sorrow.[30]

Donne makes less serious use of the same idea in his early
Paradoxes and Problems. Here he argues that the loss of virginity is, in effect, a homeopathic cure for earthly mortality:

> femal *Virgins* by a discreet marriage should swallow down into
> their *Virginity* another *Virginity*, and devour such a life and spirit
> into their womb, that it might make them, as it were, immortall
> here on earth, besides their perfect immortality in heaven;...[31]

Donne is not always so kindly towards Paracelsus. In *Ignatius his Conclave* (1611) he presents him satirically as a
denizen of Hell.[32] Nonetheless, Donne's and Puttenham's
remarks are a partial index of the degree to which the
Elizabethan literary world was acquainted with Paracelsian
theories and could translate them from their original context into other frames of reference.

Of the English Paracelsian texts we know, the one by far
most likely to have attracted the attention of nonscientific
Elizabethan readers is R. B.'s (R. Bostocke's) *The Difference between the auncient Phisicke and the latter Phisicke*
(1585).[33] Bostocke's compendium of Paracelsian theory is
nontechnical, compact, gracefully written, and relatively
inclusive. It is a defense of Paracelsus based on the argument that his theories ("Chimical" medicine) represent the
true science of the ancients and, indeed, comprise the truly
Christian science, while Galenic ("Ethnicke") medicine is
nothing but a heathen interloper. He furnishes his treatise
with a helpful table of contents and provides, particularly
within the first eight chapters, an introduction to most
of Paracelsus' major ideas, including man as microcosm
(chs. 1 and 4), man's dual nature ("contrariety," ch. 2),
disease as a specific and active agent (ch. 8), the specific

cure or "vertue" (ch. 2), the homeopathic principal (ch. 5), the interdependency of good and evil (ch. 2), life and death (ch. 20), and contraries in general:

> . . . everything hath his impure seed joined with his pure, and death to his life . . . .
>
> (ch. 2, sig. B v [r])

> *contrarius ortu contrariorum fit, ita ut contrario ortu contrariorum, unde hoc ortum est pereat*: as death followeth life, and of death, life riseth, and of *esse*, cometh *non esse*, and of *non esse* riseth *esse*, likewise of *quies* riseth *motus*, and of *motus, quies*.
>
> (ch. 20, sig. J viii [v])

Bostocke attacks humoralism (ch. 5), speaks of poison as medicine (ch. 2), maintains that Adam and Eve fell into duality and contrariety, and calls their tempter "Binarius" (ch. 2). He judiciously admits his master's two notorious failings, alcoholism and poor Latin (ch. 24), but characterizes him as a man "whose pains were intollerable in searching out the secrets of Nature" (ch. 19, sig. H vii [v]). He ranks Paracelsus with Luther, Zwingli, Calvin, and Copernicus as a restorer of ancient knowledge rather than a modern revolutionary (ch. 19). His treatise rings with the conviction that Paracelsian philosophy, cognate with true Christianity and the wisdom of the ancients, is a coherent doctrine of nature whose implications extend beyond medicine to the human condition as a whole.

Giordano Bruno:
Contrariety as Metaphysics and Epistemology

The theory of nature as the operation of opposed yet interdependent principles, implicit in the work of Castiglione and Paracelsus, is expressed most comprehensively by Giordano Bruno (1548–1600). Bruno is the great synthesizer of contrariety; his goal is to compress his own insights and the diverse thought of his predecessors into an inclusive philosophy of being. He studied the writing of Paracelsus at Wittenberg and praises him highly, in his *Valedictory Oration* (1588) and in *De la causa, principio, et Uno* (*Concerning the Cause, Principle, and One*, 1585). In this latter work, he adopts Paracelsus' doctrine of the elements and reiterates with Paracelsus the Hermetic idea of the interdependency of decay and generation.[34] We may be fairly certain (from Bruno's use of the cognate *teriaca* for the German *thyriak* [treacle]) that another of his paradoxical examples—the notion of the medicinal value of poison—is directly from Paracelsus:

> [Paracelsus:]
> *Ir wissent das thyriak von der schlangen thyro gemacht wird: warumb scheltet ir nicht auch eueren thyriak, dieweil das gift dieser schlangen in ime ist?*

> [Bruno:]
> *Da onde piu comodamente cerca l'antidoto il medico, che dal veleno? Chi porge meglior teriaca, che la vipera?*[35]

In *Degli eroici furori* (*The Heroic Frenzies*, 1585), Bruno (perhaps following Machiavelli) uses the story of the Jews in Egypt as proof of the theory that adversity generates virtue.[36] Like Castiglione, he takes up the Platonic doctrine that sensation derives from contrariety:

> [Castiglione:]
> . . . we know that we can never enjoy any Pleasure if something unpleasant does not precede it. Who can appreciate rest without first feeling the weight of fatigue?

> [Bruno:]
> . . . if it were not for the bitter in things, there would not be delight, just as hard labor makes us feel delight in rest; . . .[37]

Bruno seeks also to incorporate into his thought the earlier reconciliatory theories of Nicholas of Cusa.[38] He uses these borrowings in an effort to abstract and justify a general doctrine of contraries; he would raise contrariety from the level of sense perception, morality, and applied science to the level of epistemology and metaphysics:

> ... all things are made of contraries ....

> The end of one contrary is the beginning of the other ....

> ... extreme mutations of things are known to take place between similar and dissimilar and between one contrary disposition and the other ....

> ... everything results from contrary principles ....

> In conclusion, he who wishes to know the greatest secrets of nature should regard and contemplate the minimum and maximum of contraries and opposites.[39]

According to Bruno, the interaction of opposites is simply and categorically the nature of things, the dynamic principle which arbitrates experience and organizes change.

The attainment of wisdom in a world of contraries is the subject of Bruno's *De gli eroici furori*. The work is characteristic of the man. In style and content it is energetic, complex, disjointed, allusive, extravagant, and obscure. Its varied modes of expression include direct exposition, dialogue, poetry, exegesis, motto, and the description and interpretation of emblems. In an effort to show that the ascent to light is an emotional as well as an intellectual experience, Bruno appropriates, along with the sonnet form, the attitude of the Petrarchan lover and the Petrarchan oxymoron:

> Dear, gentle and revered wound of that sweet dart, which love ever chooses; lofty, gracious, and precious ardor, which makes the soul toss in ever burning delight,

> what virtue of herb, or force of magic art, will ever release you from the center of my heart, since the fresh onslaught which strikes there at every hour, delights me the more it torments me?

> My sweet pain, new in the world and rare, when shall I ever escape from your burden, since the remedy is weariness to me, and the pain delight?

Eyes, flames, and bow of my lord, two-fold fire in the soul,
and arrows in the heart, because the languishing is sweet to me,
and the fire is dear.[40]

Here, however, the beloved is not a Petrarchan female, but
Truth itself; the Petrarchan format encloses something akin
to the Socratic love of Plato's *Symposium*. The lover's pain,
moreover, is not born of the classic tension between desire
and possession; it is rather a philosophical parallel of this
tension, the mind's struggle to reconcile within itself the
contrary principles of form and matter. As Bruno's modern
editor, Paul E. Memmo, puts it,

> The Petrarchan dialectic of contraries expressing the warring pas-
> sions of the lover as he burns and freezes, fears and hopes, is es-
> pecially useful to Bruno. It is made to reflect his concept of the
> soul as an entity in which the material and the formal principles
> struggle for mastery. Bruno brings, as a matter of fact, the Pet-
> rarchan dialectic to its metaphysical end.[41]

Bruno sees the form/matter distinction in terms of its traditional Platonic associations. With form are connected the
intellect and the spirit as aspiring to the realization of the
ideal. With matter are allied the will, the body, and immediate reality.[42] Bruno postulates a struggle between these
contraries at all but the highest level of knowledge. What
complicates this struggle, and stimulates the progression
towards truth, is the interdependency of these warring contraries. The lure of the ideal provokes the material principle
of will or desire; material phenomena, at the same time,
suggest ideal form. The process of learning thus becomes
another union of contraries, a dynamic state of simultaneous appetite and satiety:

Esuries satiata, satietas esuriens.[43]

This state, and the inner struggle it entails, justify Bruno's
use of the term, *eroici furori*. It is here that he deviates
most sharply from his Platonic forebears. Like Plato and
the Neoplatonists, Bruno postulates an ascent towards truth

which progresses from the particular to the general, from the material to the formal. But while the Platonic tradition sharply distinguishes between the insatiable longings of material love and the ordered pleasure of the philosopher, Bruno turns the principle of longing and torment into a metaphor for his whole epistemology.[44] He identifies his dialectic with a conception of love which his philosophical predecessors had discredited as slavish and bestial. Moreover, he sees wisdom not as a denial of the material principle but rather (like Paracelsus) as a balanced awareness of the formal and material extremes.[45] Like the philosophers of contrariety before him, he uses the dialectic of opposites as a means of admitting previously degraded forces of disorder into a comprehensive doctrine of nature and growth.

According to Bruno, the philosophical ascent culminates in a vision of Diana—the attainment of a realm of perception where contraries are ultimately reconciled. Fittingly, however, Diana is herself described in paradoxical terms, as the "unity" which is

> distinct in that which is generated and that which generates, or that which produces and that which is produced.[46]

It is to be questioned whether Diana really represents a transcendent philosophical goal or is rather the symbolic embodiment of the dialectic itself. In any case, *De gli eroici furori* is devoted substantially much more to process than to achievement. Life itself is seen as the friction of great forces in conflict, and our understanding is not complete until this conflict is internalized in a torment of awareness. It is this inner fury that at once animates and glorifies the philosophical quest.

Although Bruno lived in London (1583–1585), wrote, published six books, and proclaimed his genius there, his influence on Elizabethan letters was rather modest.[47] Several modern scholars have drawn attention to parallels between Bruno and Shakespeare; and to this inconclusive but intriguing number of possible connections I intend to add a few of my own.[48] Influence and parallels aside, however, there is ample reason for including Bruno in this survey. He is the lion of Renaissance contrariety, not only because he asserts its tenets most absolutely, but because he weaves together many of its earlier strands, showing a common denominator in the thought of his various predecessors. Bruno deserves attention here, moreover, because he develops ideas of contrariety into a view of psychology already implicit in the work of Castiglione and Paracelsus. All three writers accept the classical duality between the "higher" and "lower" mental principles, speaking of these as good and evil (Castiglione), astral and material (Paracelsus), and god and beast (Bruno). However, all three insist quite unconventionally that health and wisdom lie in remaining in touch with both extremes of this duality rather than in unilaterally submerging the lower half, or aiming at some kind of mean. In so doing, they break sharply with the Christian, Neoplatonic, and Aristotelian doctrines which lie behind them. Instead, they posit a dialectical concept of psychology, in which an understanding of the tension between opposed polarities becomes both a source of positive energy and a guide to wisdom. Shakespearean drama, as we will see, develops towards, and ultimately adopts, a similar point of view.

Shakespeare and Contrariety: the Early Period

Shakespeare's earliest significant allusions to contrariety occur in *Romeo and Juliet* and in Sonnet 94. These works show his ability to adopt ideas about the interaction of contraries—sometimes from more than one tradition—and integrate them into dramatic structures and poetic images of impressive power and grace. In both the play and the poem, however, the notion of contrariety is still viewed tentatively, as a possible solution to moral dilemmas, or a fascinating but obscure kind of wisdom.

Romeo and Juliet

In Act II of *Romeo and Juliet* (1595–1596), Friar Law-rence appears alone with a basket of herbs. He meditates aloud on the herb's ability to cure or kill, and compares this quality with the bifold potentiality for good or evil in the human spirit:

> I must up-fill this osier cage of ours
> With baleful weeds and precious-juiced flowers.
> The earth that's nature's mother is her tomb;
> What is her burying grave, that is her womb; 10
> And from her womb children of divers kind
> We sucking on her natural bosom find:
> Many for many virtues excellent,
> None but for some, and yet all different.
> O, mickle is the powerful grace that lies 15
> In plants, herbs, stones, and their true qualities;
> For nought so vile that on the earth doth live
> But to the earth some special good doth give;
> Nor aught so good but, strain'd from that fair use,
> Revolts from true birth, stumbling on abuse. 20
> Virtue itself turns vice, being misapplied,
> And vice sometime by action dignified.
>
> *Enter Romeo*
>
> Within the infant rind of this weak flower
> Poison hath residence and medicine power;
> For this, being smelt, with that part cheers each part, 25
> Being tasted, stays all senses with the heart.
> Two such opposed kings encamp them still
> In man as well as herbs, grace and rude will;
> And where the worser is predominant,
> Full soon the canker death eats up that plant. 30
> (II.iii.7–30)

Except for his use of the Galenist term, "qualities" (line 16), Lawrence's doctrine of medicine, nature, and psychology is conspicuously Paracelsian. Lines 9–10 echo Paracelsus' idea of the interdependency of life and death (Bostocke: ". . . death followeth life, and of death, life riseth . . . .") and his notion of the earth as womb (*matrix*).[49] Lawrence's use of the word "virtues" (line 13) in a pharmaceutical context, as giving "some special good" (line 18), evokes the major Paracelsian theory that each disease is a discrete entity (*ens*) requiring a special cure, and that such cures are virtues of larger compounds. Bostocke uses the same word in the same context:

> . . . some good thing and pure which hath *vertue* and power to cure . . .
>
> (ch. 2, sig. B vi [r]. My italics.)

The belief in the curative power of stones (line 16) is Paracelsian,[50] and the thesis that plants, herbs, and stones can all be therapeutic is like Paracelsus' aphorism, "All nature is like one single apothecary's shop."[51]

The ethical and psychological parallels between Lawrence and Paracelsus are equally impressive. The informing idea of the speech—a comparison of man and plant as creatures containing the double potentiality for good and evil (lines 21–22, 27–30)—is a key Paracelsian tenet:

> Every man is like a field, neither entirely good, nor entirely bad, but of uncertain kind . . . .[52]

When Lawrence says the same thing about good and evil in "plants, herbs, stones," his expression is like a paraphrase of Bostocke:

> [Lawrence:]
> For nought so vile that on the earth does live
> But to the earth some special good doth give;
> Nor aught so good but, strain'd from that fair use,
> Revolts from true birth, stumbling on abuse.
> (II.iii.17–20)

> [Bostocke:]
> . . . there is nothing so good, but it hath in it also some impure thing and unwholesome, . . . so also there is nothing so unwholesome, perilous and venemous, but it hath also in it some good thing and pure.
> (ch. 2, sig. B v [r])

Lawrence's final postulation of two psychological forces, one spiritual and one earthly, struggling for mastery of man (lines 27–30), resembles Paracelsus' theory of the presence in man of earthly and astral "bodies" which exist in an "antinomy" that can turn to destructive conflict.[53] Admittedly, this and a number of Lawrence's other sentiments were also available to Shakespeare through a variety of non-Paracelsian traditions. But the almost exclusive presence of so many of Paracelsus' notions in so brief a passage argues rather convincingly that Lawrence's speech is Paracelsian theory, seen clearly and at close range, poeticized and adapted for Shakespeare's thematic purposes.

What these purposes are may be seen by taking a broader view of the play. Serious readers of *Romeo and Juliet* are aware that the action poses a nice problem in causality. Is the tragedy fated? The Prologue, which calls the lovers "star-cross'd" and "death-mark'd," as well as characters who relate the catastrophe to "inauspicious stars" and "a greater power" (V.iii.111, 153), would argue yes. The plot, in which young lovers are caught and destroyed by a web of seemingly gratuitous events, would also support this interpretation. There are good reasons, however, for understanding the action altogether differently. The opening scenes contain elements which are comic and vividly satirical, both of the feud itself (the servants in I.i.1–65) and of the excesses of Petrarchan eroticism (Mercutio, passim). The play's characters, from the harebrained Tybalt to the disappointingly skittish Friar Lawrence, are violent, headstrong, impulsive, whimsical, or otherwise undependable. These unstable elements, in disordered combination like the escalating feud and the imperfect elopement scheme, produce events which may be seen not as destined catastrophes but rather as accidents inherent in disordered societies and common among irresponsible individuals. Thus it can be argued that the play's passions, whether noble or base, render their possessors so subject to fortune that they become at once its victims and its agents. Romeo's impulsiveness, his pessimism and his Neo-Petrarchan vision of love as torment and chaos[54] add to our sense of the connection between character and destiny—or rather, between warped character and the myth of a malignant fate.

As if to underline this, and to suggest a method of interpretation alternative to the popular theory of the Prologue, Shakespeare has given us the speech of Friar Lawrence. Lawrence's philosophy has nothing to do with the stars or fate. It suggests a free causality in which elements of health and disease, virtue and vice, are inherent in the individual and entrusted to his control. Grace itself (line 28) is not predestined or dependent on divinity but is rather (as in Paracelsus[55]) inborn. Shakespeare's phrase, "Revolts from true birth, stumbling on abuse" (line 20), recalls the idea of the Fall; but the implication is that here the Fall is not a single event governing all mankind so much as a disaster latent in each individual. Lawrence emphasizes the moral implications of his Paracelsian source when he repeats the word "virtue," intending it the second time not as a physical endowment but as a moral attribute: "Virtue itself turns vice, being misapplied,/And vice sometime by action dignified." (lines 21–22). Not man's inherent properties alone, but these properties in conjunction with his own self-direction, make him good or evil. Without measure and wisdom the healthiest and finest things—a flower or a pair of noble lovers—are prey to the canker death. Such a philosophy of coexistent destiny and freedom was, as we have seen, made explicit by Paracelsus himself:

> The stars are subject to the philosopher; they must follow him, and not he them. Only the man who is still animal is governed and mastered, compelled and driven by the stars.[56]

Shakespeare's whole structure of causality in *Romeo and Juliet* is strikingly similar to the Paracelsian doctrine of the will. Considering the abundant presence of other Paracelsian material in the text, there is reason to believe that the resemblance is not coincidental.

Lawrence's theory is at once borne out and qualified by his role in the dramatic action. He severely criticizes Romeo's passionate behavior, and his counsel to both lovers throughout the play emphasizes their free will and responsibility as individuals. When this counsel fails, Lawrence decides to assist in the elopement, devising a stratagem which, like his philosophy in general, has a Paracelsian tone. His description of the sleeping potion he will give Juliet is of a "remedy" which "cop'st with death itself to scape from it."[57] Like Paracelsus, Lawrence will set "entity against entity;" he will induce in Juliet a state resembling death in order to save her from the death by suicide which she has threatened. His potion works, but through an "accident" the plan fails; and to compound the failure Lawrence almost unaccountably ("I dare no longer stay" [V.iii.159]) leaves Juliet alone in the tomb to discover the dead Romeo. Faced with the tragic consequence of this error, Lawrence abandons his philosophy of free will and ascribes the disaster to "A greater power than we can contradict" (V.iii.153). His apparent recantation throws the problem of causality into doubt again. Does it invalidate free will and prove the doctrine of predestination? A Paracelsian might contend that the Friar is an unworthy executor of his own theories—that by succumbing to fear he defaults from freedom and becomes the unwitting object of his own earlier criticism. His failure, nonetheless, turns the play as a whole into a closed circle of misdirected scheming and self-defeating action. The Paracelsian alternative moves uneasily within the dramatic structure, haunting it like an unfulfilled promise of freedom and order.

Sonnet 94

Elements of Friar Lawrence's doctrine are combined with other paradoxical notions in the fascinating but obscure Sonnet 94:

They that have pow'r to hurt and will do none,
That do not do the thing they most do show,
Who, moving others, are themselves as stone,
Unmoved, cold, and to temptation slow,   (4)
They rightly do inherit heaven's graces
And husband nature's riches from expense;
They are the lords and owners of their faces,
Others but stewards of their excellence.   (8)
The summer's flow'r is to the summer sweet,
Though to itself it only live and die;
But if that flow'r with base infection meet
The basest weed outbraves his dignity:
    For sweetest things turn sourest by their deeds;
    Lilies that fester smell far worse than weeds.

This sonnet is of major importance in an understanding of Shakespeare's developing attitude towards moral philosophy. The poetry is difficult both in content and in design. The basic metaphor—"They," "as stone," "flow'r," "weed," "Lilies," "weed"—is so distended that, for the reader, the connection is easily lost. The progression is meaning from the solution of a problem—how to husband nature's riches from expense (lines 1–8)—to a statement of the problem (lines 9–14) frustrates our expectation of seeing a problem presented before it is solved. The poem's content, moreover, is almost brutally paradoxical. What Christian moralist would twice (lines 2 and 7) glorify dishonesty? How can grace lie in "the power to hurt"? What sensible poet of the Renaissance would set weeds above flowers, and prefer stone to both?

The second of these problems to some extent explains the first. Writers wishing to be doctrinally irregular have often chosen to write obscurely. The meaning will be there for those who care to look for it. In this poem the meaning is based on a conventional life/garden metaphor that is given a new twist. Shakespeare habitually uses "flowers" to represent those elements of society that are beautiful and fragile, and "weeds" to represent those elements that are appetitive and gross. A famous example of this is the Gardener's speech in *Richard II*, with its "noisesome weeds which without profit suck/The soil's fertility from wholesome flowers" (III.iv.38–39). Here as elsewhere Shakespeare capitalizes on the ironic potential of the weed/flower distinction: flowers, superior to weeds in beauty, are inferior to them in the natural virtues which insure survival and growth. In Sonnet 94 this irony becomes sharper and more complex. The flower's downfall—the fatal flaw of the merely "good" person—is seen in terms of a lack of self-knowledge. Though valuable to society ("to the summer sweet"), he has no awareness of himself ("to itself it only live and die"). This flaw renders him vulnerable to "base infection"; he is likely to "fester" and come off worse than a dynamic rogue ("Lilies that fester smell far worse than weeds"). Innocent goodness, facing the infection of evil, cannot translate itself into positive action. The noble man, if he lacks a virtue which surpasses and comprehends mere nobility, may be rendered helpless or corrupted or destroyed.

The mysterious "They" of the octave are posed as the solution to the woes of the garden. Their duty is explicitly one of husbandry, and the object of this duty is "nature's riches"—the fragile beauty of flowers and, just possibly, the boundless vitality of weeds. They can fulfill this husbandry only by being radically different from flowers or weeds: "as stone," immune to the passions that corrupt flowers, and goad weeds to aggression. That "They" have the self-knowledge lacked by flowers is implied by the first and most important line. The power to hurt and the will to do none imply a high standard of virtue indeed: goodness based not on innocence but on a knowledge of all the possible moral alternatives. Moreover, theirs is an active virtue: it shows, moves, husbands, owns. Their wise action reclaims errant nature and earns the blessings of heaven. How do they avoid the pitfalls of flowers, remaining invulnerable to disease and evil? The implied answer is so important that it is stated twice: they characteristically practice deceit (lines 2 and 7). Strength, self-knowledge, mercy and dissemblance, in an irreducible combination, are proposed as the components of active wisdom.

Sonnet 94 reflects a broader acquaintance with sixteenth-century thought than is implied by the basically Paracelsian theory of Friar Lawrence. The sonnet retains Lawrence's botanical metaphor and the related idea of the dual potentiality for good and evil in all created forms. It echoes Lawrence's statement that unwise action can turn apparent goodness into evil:

[Lawrence:]
Virtue itself turns vice, being misapplied, . . .

Sonnet 94:
For sweetest things turn sourest by their deeds; . . .

In the sonnet, however, Shakespeare ranges beyond Paracelsus for his description of the elusive "They." He takes from Castiglione or from Protestant humanism the idea that a man can know goodness only when he is aware of his evil alternatives. The recommendation of deceitful ways is Machiavellian, though the goal of this deceit ("husbandry") obviously is not. The unmoved mover, who is "as stone, . . . cold and to temptation slow," and who inherits "heaven's graces," partakes of classical virtue and the Christian tradition. But more impressive than the variety of ideas brought together is their underlying uniformity. All of them are rich in contrariety. In fact, the sonnet is a dense composite of paradoxes whose effect is to press meaning beyond good and evil to a realm where moral substances can be weighed and balanced dispassionately. Here as in Lawrence's speech there is a tone of positivism, expressed in the intimation of an imperial science which responds to nature's outrageous paradoxes with paradoxes of its own.

Conclusion

It should be clear now that when John Milton uses contrariety to defend postlapsarian knowledge in the *Areopa-*

gitica he is taking advantage of a familiar and well-defined pattern of Renaissance discourse. Indeed, when he describes good and evil as springing from "the rind of one apple tasted," he may be thinking not only of Castiglione but of Shakespeare's Paracelsian Friar Lawrence, whose "infant rind" is also a symbol of the interdependency of good and evil.[58] Shakespeare's acquaintance with the major tenets of contrariety, and his early dramatic and poetic use of them, have been in part the subject of this chapter. In later chapters we will see Shakespeare fleshing out these ideas, testing them against backgrounds of psychology and action, and ultimately incorporating them as structural principles in the composition of his drama.

Notes to Chapter Two

1 W. R. Elton, *King Lear and the Gods* (San Marino: The Huntington Library, 1966); Rosalie Colie, *Paradoxia Epidemica* (Princeton: Princeton University Press, 1966); Norman Rabkin, *Shakespeare and the Common Understanding* (New York: The Free Press; London: Collier-Macmillan, 1967). Also worth noting is Marion Smith, *Dualities in Shakespeare* (Toronto: University of Toronto Press, 1966).

2 Mark Rose, *Shakespearean Design* (Cambridge, Mass.: Harvard University Press, Belknap Press, 1972); S. K. Heninger, Jr., *Touches of Sweet Harmony* (San Marino: The Huntington Library, 1974); Howard B. White, *Copp'd Hills Towards Heaven* (The Hague: Martinus Nijhoff, 1970); Stanley E. Fish, *Self-Consuming Artifacts* (Berkeley, Los Angeles, and London: University of California Press, 1972): Harriet Hawkins, *Likenesses of Truth in Elizabethan and Restoration Drama* (Oxford: Clarendon Press, 1972). Also see Michael McCanles, *Dialectical Criticism and Renaissance Literature* (Berkeley, Los Angeles, and London: University of California Press, 1975).

3 Nicholas of Cusa *De docta ignorantia* (1440), especially 1.4, 12, 13, 22, and 26. Giovanni Pico della Mirandola *Oratio* 136r; *Heptaplus* 7, proem; *Conclusiones paradoxae numero LXXI*, no. 15. Agrippa calls "the Vertues themselves" contradictory in ch. 54 of *De Vanitate* (1530); he mocks the harmony of the spheres in ch. 17 of the same work. John Milton, *Areopagitica*, in *Works*, Frank Allen Patterson et

al., eds. (New York: Columbia University Press, 1931–38), 2:514–15. For Castiglione and Paracelsus, see below, pp. 18–30.

4 Aristotle *Physics* 1.5, 6; *Nicomachean Ethics* 2.8.1–3; 4, passim; 5.5.17; 7, passim. In both works Aristotle sees each pair of contraries as being accompanied by a third principle, which functions as mean (*Ethics*) or defining agent (*Physics* 1.6). Basically, however, his view of contraries seems congruent with our normal literary or conversational understanding of them. See *Metaphysics* 986, and *De Interpretatione*, passim. In the sixteenth century, the view that, "Of opposites, from the one affirmed is the other denied," is essential both to scholastic and Ramist logicians. See Perry Miller, *The New England Mind: The Seventeenth Century* (New York: Macmillan Co., 1939), pp. 126, 137. Also see below, p. 21.

5 Plato *Symposium* 215–18.

6 For Heraclitus on contraries, see particularly fragmts. 25, 45, 46, 62, and 104, in John Burnet, *Early Greek Philosophy* (London: A. and C. Black, 1920). Plato deals more fully with contrariety than any other classical writer. In the *Parmenides*, passim, Being itself is manifested to the young Socrates as a concept susceptible to wholly contradictory interpretations. In the *Philebus* 46–47, Socrates maintains that contrariety is a necessary element of certain forms of pleasure. "Guardians" in the *Republic* 343–54, 416 must have a nature which is both fierce and gentle; similar elements are woven together in the *polis* of the *Statesman* 309–11. We read in the *Phaedrus* 253–54 and the *Laws* 626 that human nature itself is based on oppositions. In the *Euthyphro* 7–16, contraries are used as a teaching device. In the *Phaedo* 70–72 and the *Lysis* 215, Socrates teaches that opposites generate each other. Also see *Gorgias* 496–97; *Phaedo* 60; *Protagoras* 332; *Laws* 816; *Symposium* 187. Bruno refers specifically to Heraclitus and Plato in *De la causa* Fifth Dialogue; also see below, pp. 30–34.

7 Colie, *Paradoxia*. Calvin's statement is from his commentary on Psalms 8.4, in *The Psalmes of David and Others*, trans. Arthur Golding (1571); also see G. F. Waller, " 'This Matching of Contraries': Bruno, Calvin, and the Sidney Circle," *Neophilologus* 56 (1972): 331–43. Sir Philip Sidney's remark is from *The Defence of Poesie*, in *Prose Works*, ed. Albert Feuillerat (Cambridge: Cambridge University Press, 1912–26), 3:8–9. Heraclitan contrariety was available to Shakespeare's generation in Philemon Holland's translation of Plutarch's *Moralia*, (1603), pp. 1305–06 ("Of Isis and Osirus"). For Castiglione's debt to Plato, see below, p. 21. For Stoic teachings concerning contrariety, see Epictetus 1.12, 16; here the view is that contraries like "summer and winter, plenty and poverty," contribute to

the harmony of the whole. The phrase "interchangeable course, or variety," is from Robert Ashley's 1594 translation of Louis LeRoy, *Of the interchangeable course, or variety of things in the whole world;* in particular, see fol. 5v. S. K. Heninger treats this and other Pythagorean statements of contrariety in *Touches of Sweet Harmony*, pp. 149–51. Hermes teaches that "all things must needs be composed of opposites and contraries," and that these oppositions unite in a "friendship" (*Corpus Hermeticum* 10.10a, 11 [2] 7, in *Hermetica*, ed. Walter Scott [Oxford: Clarendon Press, 1924], pp. 192–95, 212–13). This Neoplatonic doctrine became the basis for the *discordia concors* of Ficino and Pico della Mirandola. Ficino, we should remember, translated Hermes and Plotinus, as well as Plato, into Latin for the Medici. See Edgar Wind, *Pagan Mysteries of the Renaissance* (1958; rev., reprint ed., New York: Norton, 1968), chs. 3–6. For the skeptic theory of contrariety, see Sextus Empiricus, *Outlines of Pyrrhonism*, trans. R. G. Bury (London and New York: Loeb Classical Library, 1933), 1.4; also see Richard H. Popkin, *The History of Skepticism from Erasmus to Descartes*, rev. ed., (New York: Harper and Row, Harper Torchbooks, 1964), pp. xii, 17. Erasmus maintains an ironic tone throughout *The Praise of Folly*, as does More (though less openly) throughout the *Utopia*. For irony in Cornelius Agrippa, see Peter French, *John Dee: The World of an Elizabethan Magus* (London: Routledge and Kegan Paul, 1972), pp. 52–53, 144. For an example of Montaigne's use of deliberate self-contradiction, see the first essay of bk. 1. Bacon employs a similar method in his first essay (1625), "Of Truth." In his scientific writings he breaks with the Aristotelians and the Ramists, criticizing their assumption that contraries are necessarily mutually exclusive:

> Men of this sort torture things with their laws of nature, and whatever does not conveniently fall in these dichotomies, they either omit or pervert beyond nature, so that, so to speak, when the seeds and kernels of science are springing forth, they gather so many dry and empty husks. (*De Augmentis*, 7.2., *Works*, ed. Spedding, Ellis, and Heath [London, 1857–74], 9:121–22)

In *De Augmentis* 7.3, Bacon presents forty-seven sets of contraries, suggesting the complexity of experience through the divergency of plausible interpretations. See Francis Bacon, *A Selection of his Works*, ed. Sidney Warhaft (New York: The Odyssey Press, 1965), intro., pp. 5–7.

8 For a discussion of the chapels and their significance in the larger design of the ducal palace, see Pasquale Rotondi, *The Ducal Palace of Urbino: Its Architecture and Decoration* (New York: Transatlantic Arts, 1969), pp. 10, 77–95 and figs. 226, 237. Rotondi's

thesis is that these two chapels are meant to be seen as part of a triad, which also includes the humanistic *Studiolo* on the floor above.

9 Baldassare Castiglione, *Il Libro del Cortegiano* 4.18, 36–41, 51ff.; *The Book of the Courtier*, trans. Charles Singleton (Garden City, N.Y.: Doubleday Anchor Books, 1959), pp. 301–03, 319–25, 336ff.

10 "Renaissance Laughter: The Jests in Castiglione's *Il Corte-giano*," *Neophilologus* 58 (1974): 199–204.

11 Castiglione, *Il Cortegiano*, 2.2; Singleton, p. 92.

12 Castiglione, *Il Cortegiano*, 2.3; Singleton, p. 93.

13 Castiglione, *Il Cortegiano*, 2.3; Singleton, p. 94.

14 Sidney, *Prose Works*, 1:25–26. The passage occurs also in the original version (4:5). For some Protestant attacks on ignorant piety, see Morris Palmer Tilley, *A Dictionary of Proverbs in England in the Sixteenth and Seventeenth Centuries* (Ann Arbor: University of Michigan Press, 1950), I17.

15 Milton, *Works*, 2:514–16.

16 On these contributions, see Walter Pagel, *Paracelsus: An Intro-duction to Philosophical Medicine in the Era of the Renaissance* (Basel and New York: S. Karger, 1958), pp. 54–55, 104–06, 141–43, 347–50.

17 Montaigne *Essais* 2.12; in *The Complete Essays of Montaigne*, trans. Donald M. Frame (Stanford: Stanford University Press, 1965), pp. 429–30. See also p. 586 (2.37).

18 I am using Norbert Guterman's translations from Paracelsus: *Selected Writings*, ed. Jolande Jacobi (New York: Pantheon Books, 1951). For English quotations from Paracelsus, I give page references both to this edition and to the standard German edition, Paracelsus: *Sämtliche Werke*, ed. Karl Sudhoff and Wilhelm Matthiessen, pt. 1, 14 vols. (vols. 6–9, Munich: O. W. Barth, 1922–25; vols. 1–5, 10–14, Munich and Berlin: R. Oldenbourg, 1928–33). Jacobi, p. 110, Sudhoff and Matthiessen, 9:178; Jacobi, p. 112, Sudhoff and Matthi-essen, 12:164; Jacobi, p. 119, Sudhoff and Matthiessen, 9:219–20. Also see Pagel, *Paracelsus: An Introduction*, pp. 65–66, 204–10.

19 Jacobi, p. 115; Sudhoff and Matthiessen, 12:62–63.

20 Jacobi, p. 169; Sudhoff and Matthiessen, 11:136–37.

21 Jacobi, p. 163; Sudhoff and Matthiessen, 7:300–301. Jacobi, p. 244; Sudhoff and Matthiessen, 12:280. Jacobi, pp. 217–18, Sud-hoff and Matthiessen, 11:312–13. Jacobi, p. 152; Sudhoff and Mat-thiessen, 9:226.

22 Pagel's extensive researches into Paracelsus' sources yield little on this subject. See his *Paracelsus: An Introduction*, pp. 217 (n. 59), 257.

23 Jacobi, p. 170; Sudhoff and Matthiessen, 7:107. And see

Pagel, *Paracelsus: An Introduction*, pp. 146–48.

24   Jacobi, p. 228; Sudhoff and Matthiessen, 9:378.

25   See Charles Trinkaus, "The Problem of Free Will in the Renaissance and Reformation," in *Renaissance Essays*, ed. Paul Oskar Kristeller and Philip P. Wiener (New York: Harper and Row, 1968), pp. 187–98.

26   The Paracelsian immigrant was Theodore Turquet de Mayerne (1572–1655) who became physician to the Queen in 1606, and chief physician to the royal household in 1610. See Allen G. Debus, *The English Paracelsians* (London: Oldbourne, 1965; New York: Franklin Watts, 1966), pp. 150–56.

27   Debus, *English Paracelsians*, ch. 2.

28   French, *John Dee*, pp. 52, 61, 78, 128–36; and Charlotte Fell-Smith, *John Dee* (London: Constable, 1909), pp. 221–22.

29   Ben Jonson *The Alchemist* II.1; Thomas Middleton *A Fair Quarrel* II.2; Robert Burton, *The Anatomy of Melancholy*, ed. Floyd Dell and Paul Jordan-Smith (New York: Tudor, 1938).

30   George Puttenham, *The Arte of English Poesie* (1589; 1906; reprint ed., Kent, Ohio: Kent State University Press, 1970), 1.23, p. 63.

31   Twelfth Paradox (not included in the work until the edition of 1652). Cf. *All's Well that Ends Well*, I.i. 110–65, where Parolles launches a similar attack.

32   *Ignatius his Conclave*, in John Donne, *Complete Poetry and Selected Prose*, ed. John Hayward (Bloomsbury: Nonesuch Press, 1929), pp. 366–69. On Donne's attitude towards Paracelsus, see W. A. Murray, "Donne and Paracelsus: An Essay in Interpretation," *Review of English Studies* 25 (1949): 115–23, and R. C. Bald, *Donne: A Life* (New York and Oxford: Oxford University Press, 1970), p. 532.

33   Published by Robert Walley. STC 1064.

34   Giordano Bruno *Valedictory Oration* (Wittenberg), *Op. Lat* 1.1.17; *De la causa, principio, et Uno* (London: John Charlewood, 1584); *Concerning the Cause, Principle, and One*, trans. Sidney Greenberg, in *The Infinite in Giordano Bruno* (New York: King's Crown Press, 1950), Third Dialogue, pp. 126, 129; Dorothea Waley Singer, *Giordano Bruno: His Life and Thought* (New York: Henry Schuman, 1950), pp. 69, 141. Greenberg, *Concerning the Cause*, Third Dialogue, pp. 128–29; Fifth Dialogue, p. 172.

35   Sudhoff and Matthiessen, 11:138; Bruno's Italian is from the *Opere di Bruno e di Campanella*, ed. Augusto Guzzo and Romano Amerio (Milano, Napoli: Riccardo Ricciardi, n. d.), p. 415; Greenberg, *Concerning the Cause*, Fifth Dialogue, p. 172.

36   Machiavelli, *The Prince*, opening of ch. 26; Giordano Bruno, *De gli eroici furori* (London: John Charlewood, 1585); *The Heroic Frenzies*, trans. Paul Eugene Memmo (Chapel Hill: University of North Carolina Press, 1964), p. 182.

37   Castiglione, *Il Cortegiano* 2.2; Memmo, *The Heroic Frenzies*, p. 98.

38   Greenberg, *Concerning the Cause*, Fifth Dialogue, pp. 169–73; *de l'Infinito Universo e Mondi*, Fifth Dialogue; and see Singer, *Bruno*, pp. 54–59, 80–84.

39   Memmo, *The Heroic Frenzies*, pp. 98, 99, 179, 187; Greenberg, *Concerning the Cause*, Fifth Dialogue, p. 172.

40   Memmo, *The Heroic Frenzies*, p. 90.

41   Ibid., p. 45.

42   Memmo, *The Heroic Frenzies*. See especially "The Argument of the Nolan," pp. 66–69; the Third and Fourth Dialogues of the First Part, Memmo's intro., pp. 32–46, and his notes on pp. 228, 232, 234, and 235.

43   Ibid., p. 240.

44   Cf. Plato *Gorgias* 492–98; Plotinus *Enneads* 1.3; *Corpus Hermeticum* 4.6b–9; and Bembo's speech in *Il Cortegiano* 4.53, 62, 64, and 66.

45   Memmo, *The Heroic Frenzies*, pp. 121–22, 134–37, 226–27, and Memmo's Introduction, pp. 39–43.

46   Ibid., p. 226.

47   See Singer, *Bruno*, pp. 181–88.

48   Singer, *Bruno*, pp. 29–30; Memmo, *The Heroic Frenzies*, p. 36, n. 15; p. 239, n. 14. Memmo calls these parallels "analogies" without claiming any direct link between Bruno and Shakespeare. Also see below, Chapter 5, n. 17.

49   *[Matrix] ist die welt microcosmi, wie himel und erden Adae matrix war und wie der microcosmus in matrice ligt, also lag Adam in matrice quatuor elementorum.* Sudhoff and Matthiessen, 8:355. Also see A. A. Barb, "Diva Matrix," *Journal of the Warburg and Courtauld Institutes* 16 (1953): pp. 203–04 and nn. 161–64.

50   Pagel, *Paracelsus: An Introduction*, p. 147.

51   Jacobi, pp. 160, 164–65; Sudhoff and Matthiessen, 2:430, 8:84–85, 11:195.

52   Jacobi, p. 103; Sudhoff and Matthiessen, pt. 2 (Munich: O. W. Barth, 1923), 1:69; Bostocke, ch. 2.

53   Jacobi, pp. 115–16; Sudhoff and Matthiessen, 12:62–63; Bostocke, ch. 2.

54   For Romeo's pessimism, see I.iv.106–111, II.vi.3–8, and III.iii.68–70; for his Petrarchanism, see I.i.171–194 and II.iv.38–43.

55   See Pagel, *Paracelsus: An Introduction*, pp. 204–207; Jacobi, p. 119; Sudhoff and Matthiessen, 9:219-20.

56   Jacobi, p. 228; Sudhoff and Matthiessen, 2:378; and see above, p. 27.

57   IV.i.75. I am here using the Q1 reading.

58   See above, p. 36, line 23.

CHAPTER 3

Shakespeare and Ethical Tradition: Hazard and
Justice in *The Merchant of Venice*

Shakespeare's increasingly complicated view of morality and
active virtue, as manifested in *Romeo and Juliet* and Sonnet
94, is also evident in a work of the same period, *The Merchant of Venice* (1596–1597). Here sharply satirical elements
are not only framed in language, character, and plot but are
set up against a context that is heavy with classical and
Christian interpretations of good and evil. Aspects of contrariety reminiscent of the two other works are apparent, as
we will see, in the central action, the thematic substructure,
and the figure of Portia; but, in general, the play is important in Shakespeare's development less as an intimation of
new ideas than as an artful and persistent demolition of traditional notions of order. *The Merchant of Venice* is a well
of unsatisfied intellectual energy, unified in intention but
resonant with irony and doubt.

Few plays are at once more evocative and less overtly
systematic. Beneath the brilliant surface waits a congregation of structural and thematic difficulties. The distinction
between the comic and the tragic receives rough treatment.
The hinge of the plot and the basis for comic justice, Portia's
treatment of Shylock, seems cruel and mechanical; and Portia adds to the confusion by putting Bassanio and Gratiano
through minor agonies with the deception of the rings. The
final act includes a hymn to music and the heavens whose

thematic significance has never been fully defined. And yet the result of this seemingly heterogeneous mixture has enthralled not only readers but countless audiences. The language, the themes, and even the varied body of experience give, throughout, an elusive sense of unity and design.

Scholarship has tried to find the source of the play's success in some coherent principle of meaning. The spice of variety is a central idea, and Shakespeare's preeminence lies partly in his ability to endow his plays with ideas which subtly and musically reverberate upon themselves. With *The Merchant of Venice* the question of unified meaning has long been associated with the relationship between the two main sections of the story: the loan-plot, set in Venice and culminating in Portia's legal battle with Shylock; and the love-plot, set in Belmont and including the trial by casket and the episode of the rings. Using this relationship as a point of departure, I shall attempt to show how the whole structure gains unity when seen against its Elizabethan background, and how it reflects Shakespeare's fruitfully ironic attitude towards the intellectual concerns of his day.

What is the theme of *The Merchant of Venice*? If by theme we mean dominant subject of interest or implicit concern, then the play's theme is certainly the virtue of justice.[1] The climactic events both at Belmont and at Venice are the trials of Acts III and IV, and these trials are not merely necessary events but subjects for lengthy analysis or controversy by most of the characters concerned. Of course these trials differ vastly in purpose, but we shall see that even this difference unites them as integral parts of the Elizabethan idea of the general subject. Moreover, the plot is interlaced with numerous obligations and contracts: not only those having to do with the trials, but also several others. Jessica violates civil law and filial piety when she plunders Shylock's treasury and elopes with Lorenzo. Bassanio and Gratiano bind themselves in the oath of the rings when they marry Portia and Nerissa, and later they fulfill an obligation when they give these rings to the same women in disguise.

Even Launcelot Gobbo manages a substantial though foggy exposition of the theme of the bond when, early on, he ponders whether or not to desert his master Shylock:

> Certainly my conscience will serve me to run from this Jew my master. The fiend is at my elbow and tempts me, saying to me, "Gobbo, Launcelot Gobbo, good Launcelot," or "good Gobbo," or "good Launcelot Gobbo, use your legs, take the start, run away." My conscience says, "No; take heed, honest Launcelot, take heed, honest Gobbo," or, as aforesaid, "honest Launcelot Gobbo, do not run, scorn running with thy heels."

> . . . to be ruled by my conscience, I should stay with the Jew my master, who, God bless the mark, is a kind of devil; and, to run away from the Jew, I should be ruled by the fiend, who, saving your reverence, is the devil himself.
> (II.ii.1–9, 22–27)

Launcelot's words are the comic setting forth of a general situation. Throughout the play characters are judged, or judge themselves, by the extent to which they live up to legal or otherwise conventional obligations. The theme of justice, in its individual social manifestations, dominates the play. It should be no surprise that Act V is rich in the eulogy of music and the heavens; music and the heavens were the Elizabethan symbols of justice and order.[2]

But what do we mean by justice? If challenged on this point, an educated man of the sixteenth century would have been likely to cite Aristotle,[3] and the theory would not be wholly familiar to modern ears. Unlike modern justice, whose function is primarily corrective, Aristotelian justice is bipartite. It is divided into commutative justice, which concerns transactions (including crimes) between private parties or between individuals and institutions, and distributive justice, which concerns the bestowal of wealth and honor. Sir Thomas Elyot presents this distinction in *The Book Named the Governor*:

> Justice all though it be one entier virtue, yet is it described in two kinds or spices. The one is named justice distributive, which

is in distribution of honor, benefit, or other things semblable; the other is called commutative or by exchange, and of Aristotle it is named in Greeke *Diorthotice*, which is in English corrective. And that part of justice is contained in intermeddling, and sometime is voluntary, sometime involuntary intermeddling. Voluntary is buying and selling, love, surety, letting and taking and all other thing wherein is mutual consent at the beginning. Intermeddling involuntary sometime is prively done, as stealing, avoutery, poisoning, falsehood, deceit, secret murder, false witness and perjury; sometime it is violent, as battery, open murder and manslaughter, robber, open reproach and other like. Justice distributive hath regard to the person; justice commutative hath no regard to the person, but only considering the inequality whereby the one thing exceedeth the other, endevoreth to bring them both to an equality.[4]

While modern justice leaves 'the pursuit of happiness' to the private realm, Aristotelian justice supposes a system of rewards as well as a system of punishments. With its partial "regard to the person," Aristotelian justice recognizes and encourages inequalities among men. For this reason it was compatible with the English aristocratic tradition and its cherished principle that men or families could, through their own merits, rise to positions of greater honor. The bestowal of titles, properties, annuities, and honorary sinecures was seen not as undemocratic preferment but as the right and duty of good government, and could be interpreted, moreover, as an attempt to establish in society the same sort of hierarchy of virtue that was seen to exist in nature and in the heavens.[5]

The thematic unity of *The Merchant of Venice* lies partly in the fact that the play's action illuminates both aspects of the Aristotelian theory of justice. The loan-plot, which revolves around Antonio's bond to Shylock and Shylock's attempt to destroy Antonio, illustrates the workings of commutative justice. The merchant's agreement with the Jew is an example of voluntary "intermeddling" in which there is "mutual consent at the beginning." Conversely, the love-plot concerns the workings of distributive justice. Portia's father's will stipulates that a reward—Portia and her riches—be granted to the man "who you shall rightly love" (I.ii.32-33)—who, in other words, possesses a virtue not shared by other men. The justice of Venice, treating all Venetians in the same way, "hath no regard to the person"; the justice of Belmont is, on the other hand, a testament to basic inequalities of character. Venice is concerned with what is due men as citizens; Belmont, with what men may aspire to as individuals. In the trial of the bond and the trial of the caskets we thus find a presentation of the two main problems of right action.

Solving the problem of unity in *The Merchant of Venice* is important because it leads us to a deeper problem: the nature of the play's own operative justice, as it applies to all the major characters and is ultimately administered by Portia. How does Shakespeare present the distinction between distributive and commutative justice, and how do these concepts connect with the overall dramatic justice which, as playwright, he is destined to confer? In examining these questions we must realize, first of all, that the correlation between commutative and distributive justice is not a simple one. In the stress of practical politics, one principle may infringe upon the other. To what extent should justice reflect or deny the inequalities of nature? In the combination of the commutative and distributive principles resides the potential friction between democracy and aristocracy, between the politics of equality and the politics of virtue. Shakespeare, who will embody this problem tragically in *Coriolanus*, here presents a treatment that is less massive but no less subtle. His method is to play upon the distinctions between commutative and distributive justice and, more precisely, to throw commutative justice into a deliberately distorted light. As the action of *The Merchant of Venice* evolves, the commutative justice of Venice is subverted, and the distributive justice of Belmont, personified by Portia, takes full control. The justice of equality is abandoned, to be replaced by the justice of virtue.

The principle of justice at work throughout the play is set forth in the trial by casket (II.vii, II.ix, and III.ii). Here the presence of moral meaning is emphatic, evidenced in symbol (the caskets and their contents), discourse (the speeches of Morocco, Arragon, and Bassanio), and epigram ("All that glisters is not gold," II.vii,65, etc.). This heavy moral atmosphere, together with the manifest success of Bassanio's decision to "give and hazard all he hath" (II.vii.16 and II.ix.21), has led critics to view the scene as embodying a highly traditional moral, and, in turn, to see this moral as animating the play as a whole:

> When Portia and Shylock face each other in the trial scene, they are representatives not only of justice and mercy, but also of possessiveness and generosity, of those who get as much as they deserve and those who, for love, will give and hazard all they have.
>
> In the scramble of give and take, when appearance and reality are hard to distinguish, one thing seems certain: that giving is the most important part—giving prodigally, without thought for the taking.[6]

Attractive as they may appear, interpretations like this do not do full justice to the play. To give and to hazard are two different things. To give is to be generous in the Christian sense; to hazard is to wager for future profit. The motto on the leaden casket implies that both of these functions are necessary to the virtuous man. The larger context, moreover, reflects ironically on the value of undiluted giving. How can the philosophy of "giving prodigally, without thought for the taking" be reconciled with Jessica's larceny? How does it apply to Portia who, although generous, is cautious, skeptical, and zealous in her own interests? The only character who really gives prodigally is Antonio the merchant; and far from being the hero of the play or even an attractive secondary figure, Antonio is faded, anemic, and inert. He is less a possessor of virtue than a helpless ward of the virtuous. We must look more closely at the casket scenes, with specific emphasis on the meaning of "hazard."

Of the two unsuccessful suitors, Arragon is at once the more important and the more difficult to interpret. Morocco, who speaks patent bombast and is such a dunce that he believes he is participating in a game of chance (II.i.31–38), chooses the golden casket and "what many men desire" (II.vii.37). He chooses, in other words, with the multitude; and when he is eliminated, so is the vulgar conception of value and justice. Arragon is another matter altogether. He is less boisterous and more intelligent. He rightly avoids the golden illusion (refusing to "jump with common spirits" II.ix.32) and banks confidently on his own worth, which is not inconsiderable, especially to an audience whose royal family had married an Aragon and a Castile. His scorning of the leaden casket also would not have seemed unreasonable to an age whose spokesmen taught that true value should be garbed in suitable magnificence.[7] Arragon chooses the silver casket and "as much as he deserves" (II.ix.50). He is surprised to discover a fool's head and a diploma of folly. His Elizabethan audience, we may assume, were equally surprised. In the overthrow of Arragon's criteria they might have sensed an attack on their own.

The puzzlement is not wholly cleared up by Bassanio's choice of the proper casket in III.ii. After speaking at length against "outward shows," he turns to his task:

> Therefore then, thou gaudy gold,
> Hard food for Midas, I will none of thee;
> Nor none of thee, thou pale and common drudge
> 'Tween man and man: but thou, thou meagre lead
> Which rather threaten'st than doth promise aught,
> Thy plainness[8] moves me more than eloquence,
> And here choose I. Joy be the consequence!
> (III.ii.101–107)

Bassanio's paradoxical choice of lead over gold, threat over promise and plainness over eloquence evokes echoes of other paradoxical actions and utterances from Shakespeare's work of this period: of Friar Lawrence, who would cope "with death itself to 'scape from it," and of Sonnet 94, with its surprising preference for stone over flowers.[9] But Bassanio offers little or no rationale for his unconventional choice. Indeed, he seems to choose more by a process of elimination than by a doctrine of positive value. He justifies neither his rejection of the silver notion of just deserts nor his espousal of a principle which "rather threaten'st than doth promise aught." The result is dissatisfying. We cannot be sure that Bassanio has acted prudently, if he has not acted intelligibly.

The only credible solution to this puzzle lies in the larger context and, more specifically, in the contrast between Bassanio's fortunate choice and Arragon's remarkable failure. Seen in context, Arragon's downfall constitutes a radical moral thesis. In choosing "as much as he deserves," Arragon, like Morocco, misconceives the nature of the competition and the justice that controls it. His choice is folly, not because he is mistaken about his own merits but because he assumes that men "deserve" anything at all. His choice implies that right is guaranteed; his context, however, arbitrates that it is not. He mistakes a problem in distributive justice, where honor is actively won, for a commutative problem of investments and returns. His choice of silver, the "common drudge/'Tween man and man," emphasizes the tendency to see life and love in terms of regulated commerce.

Bassanio's choice of the leaden casket, then, is more than a gesture of generosity and a rejection of false allurements. The triumph of the suitor who chooses "to give and hazard" constitutes the Shakespearean avowal of a perilously disordered human reality—a reality unshackled by ethical guarantees. The established supports of society and tradition are rejected; the individual is left to compete on his own. The prize, if won at all, will be won at the expense of safety and certainty. The specific implication here, of course, is that these are the conditions that apply in real courtship, trial or no trial. Portia's later actions will show that, in her opinion at least, the same conditions apply during marriage itself. But far more disturbing than either of these suggestions is the effect that hazard will have on Venice and on the supposed rule of law.

The lesson of Belmont is that success will be accorded to him who best understands the real meaning of the competition, and that the most important element in this meaning is the absence of traditional standards and safeguards. The trial at Venice accords faithfully if alarmingly to this lesson. The readers who over many generations have debated Shylock's rightness or Portia's fairness have failed to see the link between Belmont and Venice. More importantly, they have evaluated the action in terms of an abstract justice of their own rather than seeing the trial, more realistically, as a critical essay on justice as conceived by man and practiced in court.

The dilemma in Venice is one which, though fairly simple, reduces the practical application of law to an absurdity. The Duke cannot release Antonio without the forfeiture of a legal bond. He cannot satisfy Shylock without tacitly assisting in the murder of a citizen. The commutative principles of civil and criminal law (or, as Elyot would call them, voluntary and involuntary intermeddling) focus conflictingly on the same point. The root of the problem, which might otherwise be cleared up through compromise, is Shylock. For reasons we will analyze later, Shylock sets the letter of the law (enforcement of the bond) against the spirit of the law (safety for common profit). Shylock is not just a malicious litigant. He is a renegade who, by flaunting the spirit of the law, would destroy the very basis of litigation. His presence, therefore, breaks the unstated covenant of shared interests—the only atmosphere in which law can operate effectively.

In the trial scene (IV.i) this predicament is painstakingly realized over the 160 lines leading up to Portia's entrance and indeed beyond. Shylock's dominating barbarism gets a fierce presentation. Antonio, Bassanio, and even the Duke, who all devoutly accept Venetian law, are like so many endangered sheep (Antonio calls himself "a tainted wether of the flock," line 114). Portia appears in disguise and, over an almost equal number of lines, eloquently rehearses the useless claims and appeals. When all else has failed, she abruptly looks aslant the law and confronts Shylock with two obvious quiddities:

> Tarry a little, there is something else,
> This bond doth give thee here no jot of blood,
> The words expressly are "a pound of flesh"
>
> . . . nor cut thou less nor more
> But just a pound of flesh: if thou tak'st more
> Or less than a just pound, be it but so much
> As makes it light or heavy in the substance
> Or the division of the twentith part
> Of one poor scruple, nay, if the scale do turn
> But in the estimation of a hair,
> Thou diest, and all thy goods are confiscate.
> (IV.i.305–307, 325–332)

Portia has another argument that is superior both legally and morally: the consequence of the forfeiture of the bond must also be seen as a case of attempted murder; and in this latter case, Shylock would become the defendant. Yet this more powerful and serious argument is saved for later (IV.i.346–363). It is not Portia's genuine legal reasoning, but her fallacious exploitation of the law that is given emphasis; and this disproportion, though only temporary, casts doubts on Portia's legal methods and their underlying morality.

We begin to understand why this is when we examine the trial scene in terms of the play's larger structures. The casket trial and the bond trial are developed in much the same way. In each trial the basic problem is subjected to a long preamble of false solutions which rely upon, and ultimately exhaust, all the traditional avenues of approach. In each trial the practical value of conventional ideas of right is questioned. Like Arragon, Antonio cannot obtain the justice he "deserves." In each trial the predicament is developed and ripened towards a solution that is strikingly unconventional. Bassanio's choice of the leaden casket is unconventional because of its implied rejection of the dominant assumptions concerning aesthetic and moral values. Portia's brief in Venice is unconventional because of its implied cynicism towards established legality. Both trials develop the same doctrine. Like the motto on the leaden casket, Portia's brief suggests an unstable, if not lawless, world of hazard, where known standards are radically limited and nothing is assured, where the prize falls to the enterprising contestant rather than to him who, like Antonio, is merely honest and deserving. The commutative justice of Venice, with its emphasis on equality and its refusal to regard "the person," is shown to be the false justice. The distributive justice of Belmont, with its emphatic regard for inequalities in virtue, energy, and understanding, is shown to be the active principle.

The other side of this emphasis is the satire of particular social norms and the 'rational' order of society in general. This satire not only underlies both trials but reverberates through many other actions and speeches. The number of bonds and obligations woven through the plot is remarkable; but even more remarkable is the extent to which the keeping of these contracts is painful, odious, or simply impossible. Some characters bravely face unpleasant obligations. Portia obeys the stern demands of her father's will. The defeated suitors are bound "Never to speak to lady afterward/In way of marriage" (II.i.41–42). The Duke feels himself to be under the legal necessity of authorizing Antonio's death. Other characters, Jessica and Launcelot, default outright from obligations they consider unfair. Still others find their contracts impossible to fulfill. Antonio cannot repay his loan. Bassanio and Gratiano are tricked into giving up the wedding rings they have promised to keep forever. Large and small events like these, together with the two trial-episodes, give the play an insistent unity. In *The Merchant of Venice* society asserts its order and control through a pattern of obligations. The relationship between this general pattern and the wills of individuals is seen, however, as one of uncomfortable, if not dangerous, stress. The philosopher of this comprehensive turmoil is Portia, whose very first long speech is a satire on social order and on reason in general:

> If to do were as easy as to know what were good to do, chapels had been churches, and poor men's cottages princes' palaces. It is a good divine that follows his own instructions; I can easier teach twenty what were good to be done, than be one of the twenty to follow mine own teaching. The brain may devise laws for the blood, but a hot temper leaps o'er a cold decree—such a hare is madness the youth, to skip o'er the meshes of good counsel the cripple . . . .
> (I.ii.12–21)

She conceives of the world as not only unstable but positively wicked:

> By my troth, Nerissa, my little body is aweary
> of this great world.
>
> O these naughty times
> Put bars between the owners and their rights!
>
> So shines a good deed in a naughty world.
> (I.ii.1–2, III.ii.18–19, V.i.91)

Portia's attitude throughout is consistently critical, her view of experience consistently problematic. Her spirit dominates a play that can be read as a satire on human pretensions to stability.

This satire is deepened and justified by the figure of Shylock. His malicious enthusiasm, his fury that is at once psychologically unimpeachable and politically odious, give a full mandate to the play's skepticism about the orderly relationship between society and the individual. Shylock may indeed be an alien, a stranger no less to comic decorum than to Christian social order. But, if so, he is a stranger from within, a pilgrim from the heart, whose message is the self-righteous, childish, and arbitrary indignation, the desire for absolute expression and absolute indulgence, that dwell to some measure in all of us. It is these qualities of impenetrable individualism which, perhaps more than any other, render order unstable and justice difficult. At the trial Shylock himself suggests this factor in a highly thematic speech. When asked why he will not accept payment and free Antonio, he replies:

> But say it is my humor, is it answer'd?
> What if my house be troubled with a rat,
> And I be pleased to give ten thousand ducats
> To have it ban'd? What, are you answer'd yet?
> Some men there are love not a gaping pig;
> Some that are mad if they behold a cat;
> And others, when the bagpipe sings i' th' nose,
> Cannot contain their urine: for affection,
> [Mistress] of passion, sways it to the mood
> Of what it likes or loathes. Now for your answer:
> As there is no firm reason to be rend'red
> Why he cannot abide a gaping pig;
> Why he, a harmless necessary cat;
> Why he a woolen bagpipe, but of force
> Must yield to such inevitable shame
> As to offend himself being offended;[10]
> So can I give no reason, nor I will not,
> More than a lodg'd hate and a certain loathing . . .
> (IV.i.43–60)

Obviously Shylock is not telling the whole truth, but even so his speech is revealing. In attributing his actions to "humor," he brings up a theme that has already received important treatment in the play. Portia has lengthily satirized her suitors according to their humors (I.ii.39–99). Solanio has attributed Antonio's mysterious sadness to the fixity of temperament which has, in other cases, "fram'd strange fellows," and Gratiano has jokingly enlarged on the subject (I.i.47–56, 88–100). Both Portia and the gentlemen imply that humor is an affront to civilized behavior. In Shylock's vivid physiological language, however, the theme is deepened and made to suggest momentarily a sense of tragic isolation. Shylock's grossest metaphor is, via dramatic irony, his aptest self-description. In pressing his suit against Antonio, he indeed yields "to such inevitable shame / As to offend himself being offended." In the metaphor and the psychology it describes, are expressed the arbitrary and self-destructive nature of anger and revenge. The broader context of the speech asserts the inexplicable and rebellious characteristics of humor, affection, and passion. Shylock's attainment to tragic or near-tragic stature lies in his utter expression of these characteristics. His presence in the play, aside from its other dramatic functions, is a testament to the irrational, an element which justifies Portia's satire and underlies the errors of the other characters.

Portia's use of fallacious methods in the trial scene is thus not simply right or wrong. It is better seen as a moral adventure, a deliberate use of chaotic forms in a world of recognized disorder. As such it is reminiscent of Friar Lawrence's stratagem in *Romeo and Juliet*, the wise rulers of Sonnet 94, and the theories of contrariety which form their basis. This kind of experimentation, with its satiric implications, is continued later in the episode of the rings. Bassanio and Gratiano, who have sealed their promises of marital fidelity by accepting rings from Portia and Nerissa, are duped into giving these rings up to the same women in disguise, as payment for successful defense of Antonio. Shakespeare develops this slight material into dramatic masonry solid enough to support a whole act, and in so doing continues to enlarge on the already-established themes of the play.

Portia confronts Bassanio with a dilemma which in its own less serious way is analogous to the dilemma of the Venice trial. Her request that he pay her the ring for the legal action (IV.i.423) throws two binding obligations into conflict with each other. He cannot pay Portia without violating his marital oaths. He cannot refuse her without belittling his indebtedness to Antonio. Implicitly the two choices represent the competing interests of friendship and marriage, and under the artificial circumstances Bassanio cannot endorse one interest without seeming to reject the other. Trapped between conflicting obligations, without recognizable directives for action, Bassanio is in essentially the same kind of moral wilderness that has existed for characters throughout the play. His failure to extricate himself successfully suggests anew the ambiguity of moral action, and reiterates the satire of human constancy which, despite the prior resolution of the major plot elements, will continue to persist through Act V.

Bassanio reluctantly parts with his ring (IV.i.448–450). His punishment by Portia, and the necessary denouement, are held until the very end of the play; and when they come, they seem less a real resolution than an opportunity for further satire. Before revealing the ruse, Portia and Nerissa indulge in a diatribe against their husbands' alleged infidelity, and flatly claim to have had sexual adventures of their own:

> *Bass.* By heaven it is the same I gave the doctor!
> *Por.* I had it of him. Pardon me, Bassanio,
> For by this ring, the doctor lay with me.
> *Ner.* And pardon me, my gentle Gratiano,
> For that same scrubbed boy, the doctor's clerk,
> In lieu of this last night did lie with me.
> (V.i.257–262)

These lively equivocations, though patently comic, revive the strain of moral uncertainty that has run throughout the play. Portia's debunking mockery, evident since her earliest speeches, now invades the sanctimony of her own marriage and throws all into doubt. No matter how happy or triumphal the conclusion, the thematic emphasis remains on moral hazard and potential disorder until the very last line (itself a bawdy jest).[11] Instead of enjoying the traditional harmony of the comic conclusion, we are again reminded jibingly of the motto on the leaden casket.

The intellectual concerns of *The Merchant of Venice* are of such intensity as to assert themselves in a famous scene which, viewed casually, is nothing but harmony and delight. At the start of Act V, Shakespeare suspends the dramatic action for 125 lines and indulges in what appears to be an interlude of pure poetry. Portia's arrival at Belmont is the only event interrupting a series of nocturnal reflections on love, the stars, music, sound, and light which reach their high point in Lorenzo's praise of the heavens and music (V.i.54–88). This section, which has unity and value in itself, is also rooted dramatically and thematically in the structure of the play as a whole. Dramatically, it satisfies in part the comic expectations which, throughout the play, are otherwise teased and baffled. It concludes, though, by posing the thematic questions which give the play its discordant vitality.

The interlude is, first of all, a pleasure and a relief. Jessica and Lorenzo begin the scene with a poetic dialogue about night and lovers, and though their subjects remind us again of broken vows and unhappy loves (stories of Cressida, Dido, Medea, etc.), their jests are too elegant to be disturbing:

> *Lor.*   In such a night
> Did Jessica steal from the wealthy Jew,
> And with an unthrift love did run from Venice,
> As far as Belmont.
> *Jes.*   In such a night
> Did young Lorenzo swear he loved her well,
> Stealing her soul with many vows of faith,
> And ne'er a true one.
> *Lor.*   In such a night
> Did pretty Jessica (like a little shrew)
> Slander her love, and he forgave it her.
>   (V.i.14–22)

Messengers announce the impending return of Portia and Bassanio. After ordering Stephano to bring "music forth into the air," Lorenzo begins his discourse on the heavens. His speech is contemplative and soothing. After a long series of trials and judgments, dubious bonds, and broken agreements, the mysticism of the verse offers at last a sense of fullness and returning order:

> How sweet the moonlight sleeps upon this bank!
> Here will we sit, and let the sounds of music
> Creep in our ears. Soft stillness and the night
> Become the touches of sweet harmony:
> Sit, Jessica. Look how the floor of heaven
> Is thick inlaid with patens of bright gold,
> There's not the smallest orb which thou behold'st
> But in his motion like an angel sings,
> Still quiring to the young-ey'd cherubins;
> Such harmony is in immortal souls,
> But whilst this muddy vesture of decay
> Doth grossly close it in, we cannot hear it . . . .
>   (V.i.54–65)

In the best Platonic tradition, the harmony of the macrocosm reflects the desired balance of earthly affairs—here Antonio's successful trial and the three marriages. The dramatic effect is satisfying. The ritual promise of comedy is harmony and repose; and comedy's rougher uses—its broadness, its satire, and its threat of upheaval—are dramatically justifiable only in terms of this promise. The serenade in praise of celestial harmony reminds us of this aesthetic contract and, for the moment at least, goes some distance in fulfilling it.

The question of harmony, however, is not allowed to rest. Lorenzo concludes his speech by admitting that the concord of the spheres cannot be heard by human beings. Four lines later, Jessica announces that music makes her sad ("I am never merry when I hear sweet music"). Lorenzo's reply, that music has a "sweet power" over nature and sweetens the human spirit (lines 70–88), fails to explain the cause of her sadness. Yet the fleeting paradox of beauty and sadness is important, especially when connected with Lorenzo's recent remark that human imperfections make real harmony

unavailable to the senses. The effect of Lorenzo's remark
and Jessica's sadness is to alter the tone of the poetry from
joy to nostalgia. If music reminds us of all that is harmonious and celestial, it reminds us by contrast that we very
definitely are not. In music's perfect sweetness is a ghostly
hint of impossible happiness and a faint mockery of the
dullness native to "this muddy vesture of decay." Lorenzo
goes on to speak of men whose natures are so far distant
from real concord that they have lost all touch with it:

> The man that hath no music in himself,
> Nor is not moved with concord of sweet sounds,
> Is fit for treasons, stratagems, and spoils,
> The motions of his spirit are dull as night,
> And his affections dark as [Erebus];
> Let no such man be trusted . . . .
> (V.i.83–88)

To appreciate the profound change in tone one must note
that the image of night, which shortly before was connected
with lovers, angels, and stars, has now become the blackness
of Erebus and the medium of evil. The brief experience
of harmony is over, and attention is focused again on the
world of disorder ("treasons, stratagems, and spoils"), on
evil men and, by implication, on the syndrome of Shylock
(who has indeed betrayed a hatred of music).

As though to punctuate the alteration in tone, Portia and
Nerissa appear, and Portia immediately turns light and music into subjects for a concentration of satiric conceits. Portia remarks at the brightness of a distant candle and compares its light in the darkness to "a good deed in a naughty
world" (line 91). Nerissa replies, "When the moon shone we
did not see the candle," giving Portia the chance to expand
on her first comment:

> So doth the greater glory dim the less:
> A substitute shines brightly as a king
> Until a king be by, and then his state
> Empties itself, as doth an inland brook
> Into the main of waters. Music, hark!

Ner. It is your music, madam, of the house.
Por. Nothing is good, I see, without respect;
Methinks it sounds much sweeter than by day.
(V.i.93–100)

Portia expands on the unreliability of human perception. Candles, kings, music, even birds (102–110) are unavailable to our judgment in themselves and can be evaluated only by "respect" or contrast. Even morality ("a good deed in a naughty world") seems governed by the doctrine of relativity. Nothing is absolute or safe. Portia's remarks dispel the stardust and bring back the dominant skepticism of the play. Light and music—the same images which inspired Lorenzo's outburst of idealism—evoke in Portia a commentary on the uncertain business of living and a realization of the muddy vesture which prevents real knowledge. Portia, whose life onstage has been an education in irony and realism, rejects the deceptive messages of sense and language as she has rejected the false security of law. Her gentle, almost contemplative satire on perception and value reflects not only on the society around her but also on her own morally ambiguous efforts to correct its uncertain course.

We have seen that while justice is the structurally unifying theme of *The Merchant of Venice*, its treatment is complex and ironic. Formal justice breaks down in Venice, undermined by Shylock's barbarous misuse of it; and this satire is, if anything, intensified by Portia's enlightened travesty of civil law. On the level of individual action, characters in Belmont as well as Venice are repeatedly unable to judge correctly or to adhere to choices once made. Man's chronic moral vagrancy is the subject of Portia's first speech, and remains throughout the object of her pedagogical attention. In the implied comparison between commutative and distributive justice, the former, with its emphasis on equality and social stability, is given short shrift; while the latter, with its hazard, doubt, conflicting interests, and endless competition, is allowed to govern the play's action. In the complicated development of Act V, the satire is broadened beyond justice to include sexuality and human cognition.

We are speaking now of what seems very near the accepted conception of the Problem Comedy. Certainly two of the elements which characterize *Troilus and Cressida*, *All's Well that Ends Well*, and *Measure for Measure*—the pervasive spirit of satire and the emphasis on moral ambiguity—are richly present in *The Merchant of Venice*. A third element, less obvious but equally important, is also present. From the viewpoint of causality, The Problem Comedies resemble the mature Tragedies in their spirit of autonomy—their refusal to honor institutional structures like law, or cosmic hypotheses like Providence or Fate. These plays do not suggest the assertion of social order or the working out of a supernatural design, but rather the unalloyed interaction of separate wills. In the Romantic Comedies, the rôle of Providence as a spiritual force and principle of dramatic structure is most clearly evident in the emphasis on coincidence and the stress on total resolution. In the Problem Comedies and the mature Tragedies, on the other hand, human freedom and individual responsibility function as givens. While this factor adds vitality to language, psychology, and action, it also creates a feeling of loneliness, the sense of an emptiness to which there is no appeal. We may see some of the earliest landmarks of this world in *The Merchant of Venice*, whose action is compounded of wit and will alone, and whose characters receive not what they are 'destined' to receive, or even what they 'deserve,' but rather what by their actions they win or lose. The play's satire on social law is matched, in other words, by the implied absence or noninvolvement of cosmic law. *The Merchant of Venice* may thus be seen as marking a decisive break with traditional schemes of order and morality.

With the middle period a new sort of Shakespearean character appears, notable less for particular traits of personality than for the extent to which his compelling motives revolve upon themselves, forbidding him communication with the characters around him.[12] In this respect, as in others, *The Merchant of Venice* may be seen as prologue to the more 'serious' plays which follow. Shylock's presence, radiating bitterness and despair, is socially irresolvable. His fierce energy and radical moral isolation suggest at once the limitations of civil law and the glibness of the comic formula. As representative of a chaotic inner world, he defines a new law of experience and dramatic reality. In part, this consideration explains the ungentle treatment he finally receives at the trial in Venice. If Shakespeare allowed Shylock to be freely pardoned, he would be blurring his central theme. If we forgave Shylock, we could forget him. Because it disappoints our comic expectations and offends our sense of justice, Shylock's unreconciled suffering remains in accord with his author's iconoclastic intention.

Portia is equally necessary to the meaningfully disordered context which is developed in *The Merchant of Venice*. Indeed, her character exists in a kind of symmetrical opposition to Shylock's. Shylock tries to force a chaotic vision into the mold of law and convention; Portia subverts convention and uses the forces of disorder in an effort to restore a workable harmony. Her character reminds us that, in a world in motion, balance may be maintained only by artful imbalancing. If Shylock's function is to embody chronically disruptive elements of experience, Portia's is to suggest a civilized response to them. Seen in this light, both characters reflect significantly on the ideas of contrariety discussed in Chapter 2 above. Like *Romeo and Juliet* and Sonnet 94, but much more extensively and specifically, *The Merchant of Venice* discloses a world of paradox, in which good, evil, and other opposites are alarmingly interdependent, traditional systems of value are undermined, and justice is available only through the reversal of accepted modalities. This world admits of only one potential master: a figure who understands the discordant propensities of experience and uses them against themselves to effect a temporary peace. Friar Lawrence and the "They" of Sonnet 94 are prototypes of this figure; Portia, the first complete representative. Descendants of Portia inhabit all the Problem Comedies, and interesting variations on this type can be found in the mature Tragedies.

Notes to Chapter Three

1   For a review of scholarship before 1955, see John Russell Brown's Introduction to the Arden edition. For interpretations of the theme of the bond, see Muriel Bradbrook, *Shakespeare and Elizabethan Poetry* (London: Chatto and Windus, 1951), pp. 170–79; S. Burckhardt, *"The Merchant of Venice:* The Gentle Bond," *English Literary History*, 29 (1962): 239–62; R. Hapgood, "Portia and *The Merchant of Venice*," *Modern Language Quarterly*, 28 (1967): 19–32; and J. P. Sisk, "Bondage and Release in *The Merchant of Venice*," *Shakespeare Quarterly* 20 (1969):   217–23.   As will be seen, I agree with the emphasis put by these writers on bonds in *The Merchant of Venice*, but maintain that bonds are themselves part of a broad thematic structure which concerns justice in general.

2   See, for example, E. M. W. Tillyard, *The Elizabethan World Picture* (London: Chatto and Windus, 1943), ch. 5; Theodore Spencer, *Shakespeare and the Nature of Man* (1942; reprint ed., New York and London: Collier-Macmillan, 1966), ch. 1; and S. K. Heninger, Jr., *Touches of Sweet Harmony* (San Marino: The Huntington Library, 1974), ch. 5.

3   The original statement is in Aristotle *Nicomachean Ethics* 5.2–5. The tradition is carried on by Thomas Aquinas *Summa Theologica* Secunda Secundae, Question 61.   In the sixteenth century, see Robert Recorde, *The Whetstone of Wit* (1557), p. 192, and Pierre de la Primaudaye, *The French Academie* (1586), 1:370.   Commutative and distributive justice are personified strikingly in the *Buon Governo* (1338–40), a painting by Ambrogio Lorenzetti in the Palazzo Pubblico at Siena.

4   Sir Thomas Elyot, *The Book Named the Governor* (1531; reprint ed., London: Dent and New York: Dutton, both 1962), pp. 159–60 (3.1).

5   See Elyot, *The Governor* 1.1.

6   John Russell Brown, Introduction to the Arden edition of *The Merchant of Venice*, pp. xvii, xviii.

7   See Elyot, *The Governor* 2.3; Baldassare Castiglione *Il Libro del Cortegiano* 2.28; *The Book of the Courtier*, trans. Charles Singleton (Garden City, New York: Doubleday Anchor Books, 1959), pp. 123–24; and George Puttenham *The Arte of English Poesie* (1589) 3.1.

8   I am here reading "plainness" (Theobald's emendation) for the established "paleness." "Plainness/Eloquence" is a decorous antithesis; and Shakespeare was too careful a writer to describe lead in the same way that, three lines above, he describes silver.

9   See pp. 35–43 above.

10   Here I am using the very respectable reading of F1 and Q1. If a comma belongs within this line at all, the sense demands that it come after "himself" rather than after "offend" (where most editors put it).

11   See Eric Partridge, *Shakespeare's Bawdy* (1948; reprint ed., New York: E. P. Dutton & Co., 1960), p. 179.

12   Walter Kaufmann, in *From Shakespeare to Existentialism* (Garden City, N.Y.: Doubleday Anchor, 1960), ch. 3, makes a similar point about Shakespeare's tragic heroes. But figures like Shylock, Troilus, and Angelo show that a character need not be of strictly heroic stature to be, in Kaufmann's words, "marked and set apart" (p. 40).

CHAPTER 4

Contrariety as Disease and Cure:
The Problem Comedies

Shakespeare's Problem Comedies are notable for their thematic emphasis on sickness and doctors. Throughout his career Shakespeare makes effective use of metaphors drawn from disease and medicine, but in these middle plays the metaphors are intensified and given a wholly new dimension. Images of diseases and wounds abound, and these images are tributary to central themes of psychological and social disorder. But in addition to this, each play hinges on the activities of a real or metaphorical doctor who knowledgeably employs the medical metaphor, and who sees herself or himself as a purveyor of 'cures.' In the lengthy expository scene of *Troilus and Cressida* (1601–1602), Ulysses speaks of the Greek enterprise as "sick," describes cosmic order in terms of medicine, and uses the same sort of language to characterize his own political strategy.[1] Helena of *All's Well that Ends Well* (1602–1603), herself a doctor, performs a revolutionary cure and uses medical language in expounding her own philosophy of life.[2] In *Measure for Measure* (1604), the Duke speaks of a "fever of goodness" and of his major actions as a "remedy" that he will "apply"; Isabella describes his scheme as "a physic/That's bitter to sweet end."[3] These comedies, then, concern themselves with both diagnosis and treatment. Seen more concretely, they are at once moral satires and moral experiments.

It is perhaps typical of our age that criticism now seems to focus more on the diagnostic (satiric) side of the Problem Comedies than on their curative side. Granted, there is some justification for this bias. While Shakespeare characterizes the diseases themselves with remarkable vividness and conviction, the 'cures'—stratagems carried out in turn by Ulysses, Helena, and the Duke of Vienna—strike us as being mean and toneless. They savor more of reason and practicality than of psychological revelation; they tend to result either in failure or, at best, mechanical success, rather than in growth or deepened understanding. The 'medicine' seems less a cure than a placebo, the 'doctors' less enlightened leaders than well-meaning charlatans.

These critical considerations should not, however, cause us to ignore the importance of the medical metaphor in the development of Shakespeare's thematic concerns. When so inclined, Shakespeare could describe the subjects here seen as 'disease'—ungovernable passion, corrupt convention, and political upheaval—with radically different patterns of imagery. In the Lancastrian Tetralogy, for example, these subjects are linked with the Fall of Man; in *King Lear* they are connected with the functions of animals. In contrast with these thematic structures, the disease/medicine idea is more scientific and more optimistic. No frail mortal can redeem the Fall or teach manners to a sea monster. But mortals can study diseases, adopt treatments, and sometimes produce remedies. The use of the medical metaphor suggests that Shakespeare is attempting a positive approach to problems which, at other times in his career, are presented as being inscrutable. Indeed, the customary discomfort felt by audiences and readers of these plays may be less the result of a pessimistic or disenchanted creative approach than the natural response to an ambitious moral enterprise.

There are topical considerations as well. The Problem Comedies (1601/02–1604) are contemporaneous with a major outbreak of the Plague. Faced with this massive and destructive force, Londoners were debating the comparative effectiveness of medical treatments, and the Galenico-Paracelsian controversy (see Chapter 2 above) was at its height. The Problem Comedies reflect these issues and, as I will show, project them into broader areas of experience.

Troilus and Cressida

Ulysses, the "physician" of *Troilus and Cressida*, is also to a large extent the play's intellectual touchstone. This is true not so much because he is lionized in the plot—indeed he turns out to be a rather sorry failure—as because his comments often approximate our own response to the dramatic action. During the first three acts, prolonged displays of acuteness, eloquence, and, above all, irony make him our window into the play, our guide to what would otherwise be a closed circle of satiric foils. He is also the only authoritative spokesman in the lengthy and discordant political colloquia which consume much of the early dialogue. Specifically, his famous speech on degree supplies a doctrinal framework in which much of the later action can be understood. For this reason we should study his speech and its context with some care.

In I.iii we are introduced to the camp of the frustrated and divided Greek army. Agamemnon and Nestor, acknowledged receptacles of authority and wisdom, lecture the sour-faced generals, encouraging them to renew their hitherto unsuccessful military effort. Their speeches are redolent with Stoic sentences and other incitements to classical virtue. Agamemnon maintains that adversity is natural to great causes and then, somewhat reversing himself, claims that it is,

> But the protractive trials of great Jove
> To find persistive constancy in men.
> (I.iii.20–21)

Nestor 'applies' Agamemnon's speech by translating it into a series of lively metaphors. Both speeches are, in a practical sense, unavailing, for both leaders fail to explain the real cause of the adversity that keeps their forces from victory. Indeed, this lack of effectiveness and understanding is a sign of their limitations as general and counselor. Ulysses shows an awareness of this when he takes the floor after them. His opening words to Agamemnon and Nestor perform their intended function of formal praise, but are tinged with persistent ambiguities:

> Agamemnon,
> Thou great commander, *nerves and bone of Greece*,
> Heart of our numbers, soul and only sprite
> In whom the tempers and the minds of all
> *Should be shut up*, hear what Ulysses speaks.
> Besides th'applause and approbation
> The which, [to Agamemnon] *most mighty for thy place and sway*,
> [To Nestor.] And thou *most reverend for [thy] stretch'd-out life*,
> I give to both your speeches, which were such
> As Agamemnon and the hand of Greece
> Should hold up high in brass, and such again
> As venerable Nestor, hatch'd in silver,
> Should with *a bond of air strong as the axle-tree*
> *On which heaven rides*, knit all the Greekish ears
> To his experience'd tongue, yet let it please both,
> Thou great, and wise, to hear Ulysses speak.
> (I.iii.54–69. My italics.)

Ulysses identifies Agamemnon physically with an army he will shortly describe as disordered and corrupt. He praises the commander-in-chief for what he "should be" rather than for what he is. He honors Agamemnon and Nestor, respectively, for their authority and old age—qualities that have more to do with circumstance than with virtue. The remark that Nestor's strength lies in air suggests wind or vanity; and the connection between Nestor and the heavens comes just prior to a speech in which Ulysses will describe the heavens in chaos. Ulysses has at once fulfilled a formal obligation and ironically suggested the emptiness of that obligation. Without openly insulting either character, he has implied a negative opinion about their speeches and their leadership in general.

Ulysses now proceeds to inform the Greek leaders that degree or subordination is necessary to all things natural and political, and that the lack of degree in the Greek camp is responsible for the Greeks' lack of success in the siege of Troy:

> The specialty of rule hath been neglected,
> And look how many Grecian tents do stand
> Hollow upon this plain, so many hollow factions.
> (lines 78–80)

Using a complex metaphor woven from astronomy and medicine, he asserts that degree is a cosmic phenomenon, and that its shaking is a universal disaster:

> The heavens themselves, the planets, and this centre
> Observe degree, priority, and place,
> Insisture, course, proportion, season, form,
> Office, and custom, in all line of order;
> And therefore is the glorious planet Sol
> In noble eminence enthron'd and spher'd
> Amidst the other; whose med'cinable eye
> Corrects the [ill aspects] of [planets evil],
> And posts like the commandment of a king,
> Sans check, to good and bad. But when the planets
> In evil mixture to disorder wander,
> What plagues and what portents, what mutiny!
> What raging of the sea, shaking of earth!
> Commotion in the winds! frights, changes, horrors
> Divert and crack, rend and deracinate
> The unity and married calm of states
> Quite from their fixture! O, when degree is shak'd,
> Which is the ladder of all high designs,
> The enterprise is sick.
> (lines 85–103)

Ulysses goes on to strengthen the analogy between cosmic and social disorder. He paints a memorably disquieting picture of total anarchy:

> Then everything include itself in power,
> Power into will, will into appetite,
> And appetite, an universal wolf
> (So doubly seconded with will and power),

     Must make perforce an universal prey,
     And last eat up himself.
                  (lines 119–124)

Ulysses' famous speech has long been regarded as a classic statement of the medieval idea of order as expressed by the scholastics and handed on by Tudor conservatives like Elyot and Hooker.[4] To understand why this interpretation is palpably inaccurate, we must look at the context and consider the speech with the care that Shakespeare's earliest editors said his work deserves.[5] We should note, first of all, that Ulysses' speech establishes him by common consent as the dominant voice in the reform of the Greek forces. Henceforth he will politely but very firmly call the plays.[6] The result of his oration is thus the reverse of his manifest argument. Ulysses explicitly praises subordination and authority, but the effect of his words is to undermine subordination and authority by taking the control of the army away from its recognized general. In effect he stages what modern journalists would call a bloodless coup. Does this revolutionary action contradict his words on order? A close reading of the speech suggests that, on the contrary, his words themselves imply the necessity for his radical action.

Ulysses' idea of degree is expressed on two analogous levels: the cosmic (planets and earth, lines 85–101) and the social (states, communities, etc., lines 103–124). The meaning of the speech is wrapped up in the ironic implications of the analogy. On the cosmic level, Ulysses describes two very different sets of conditions. First there is the normal, orderly course of things (lines 85–94). The peaceful heavens are presided over by Sol, whose rule is emphatically monarchic ("enthron'd," "like the commandment of a king"). Sol's function as monarch is particularly important with regard to individual evil planets, whose "ill aspects" he "corrects." Like a doctor ("med'cinable eye") Sol works to keep the universe healthy and peaceful. His medicine is not preventive; it is curative ("corrects"). Ulysses does not say what the illness is—what makes evil planets evil; apparently that is outside Sol's province. Even in good times, then, Sol's power over nature is limited.

It follows that in bad times Sol's power is more limited still. Periods of chaos occur when planets "in evil mixture to disorder wander"—when disorder becomes manifold and complex. What action Sol can take under these circumstances is not mentioned. In fact, Ulysses never mentions the benevolent sun-king again. The implication is that Sol's kind of monarchic government is not effective under conditions of extreme disorder, such as may exist, in politics, under the destructive rule of "appetite" (lines 119-124). Under such circumstances, "everything includes itself in power"—mere authority will not be heeded unless it can assert itself with superior force.

The distinction between orderly and chaotic conditions is especially important when we apply Ulysses' view of nature and government to the situation in the Greek camp. The monarchic Sol is directly analogous in his position to Agamemnon; and with this in mind we must ask which of the two alternative conditions of nature is more relevant to the state of the Greek force. Clearly, as Ulysses implies both at the beginning and at the end of his speech, the evident conditions are those of chaos or complex disorder:

> And look how many Grecian tents do stand
> Hollow upon this plain, so many hollow factions.
> (lines 79-80)

>   . . . so every step,
> Exampled by the first pace that is sick
> Of his superior, grows to an envious fever
> Of pale and bloodless emulation, . . .
> (lines 131-134)

Not just evil planets, but an "evil mixture" operates in the Greek camp, and the monarchic authority of Agamemnon is, according to the gist of Ulysses' speech, unable to deal with evil mixtures. While praising degree and formal authority, Ulysses ironically suggests that, under the circumstances, these qualities are of no avail. The conservative rhetoric conceals a radical premise—a premise which justifies Ulysses' subversion of Greek authority.

To understand the real purport of Ulysses' speech is to understand Shakespeare's developing view of social order. Ulysses' ironic arraignment of traditional government is an expression of the same attitude which provokes, in *The Merchant of Venice*, a satire on justice, and will provoke, in *All's Well that Ends Well*, a satire on language. In all three plays the relationship between man and his most treasured institutions is subjected to ironic scrutiny. Far from being a statement of the sedate and orderly "Elizabethan world picture," Ulysses' speech is a tangential departure from that philosophy. The principle of degree is seen not as the social reflection of a basically harmonious Nature, but rather as a covenant for restraining massively discordant energies. The mere 'untuning' of degree gives birth to what Hobbes will later call the state of nature:

> Strength should be lord of imbecility,
> And the rude son should strike his father dead;
> Force should be right, or rather, right and wrong
> (Between whose endless jar justice resides)
> Should lose their names, and so should justice too!
> (lines 114–118)

Ulysses is not an enemy of the traditional idea of order. He is, however, a critic of the accepted view that social order is guaranteed or made absolute by natural law. His speech and its dramatic context imply that traditional authority must occasionally be buttressed by a mode of government capable of dealing with the exigencies of an "evil mixture." If this emergency government can look to nature at all, it must confront not the placid and respectable "laws of na-

ture and of nations"[7] but rather the fearsome necessity
which condemns unrestrained lawlessness to death by self-
consumption:

> And appetite, an universal wolf . . .
> Must make perforce an universal prey,
> And last eat up himself.
> (lines 121, 123–124)

This formulation, reminiscent of *Hamlet* and prophetic of
the later Tragedies, may have significance not only as a diagnosis of Greek disorder but also as the intimation of a potential cure. It suggests that even chaos is subject to at least
one specific and predictable law. Ulysses goes on, as we will
see, to extract elements of order from the very phenomena
of upheaval—to seek a treatment within the disease itself.

When Ulysses' speech is finished, he has effectively sup-
planted Agamemnon and Sol. In his new role he is addressed
by the Greek leaders in significantly medical terms:

> *Nest.* Most wisely hath Ulysses here discover'd
> The fever whereof all our power is sick.
> *Agam.* The nature of the sickness found, Ulysses,
> What is the remedy?
> (lines 138–141)

Ulysses does not immediately say what his idea of a remedy
is. His later words and actions, however, suggest a coherent
mode of treatment. At the end of the scene he draws Nestor
aside and announces the birth of a stratagem. The chief
fomenter of the present chaos is the recalcitrant Achilles.
Achilles' own personal brand of chaos—his dominant passion—is pride ("Possess'd he is with greatness," II.iii.170).
Instead of 'correcting' (*à la* Sol) Achilles' disease, Ulysses
proposes to employ it. By snubbing Achilles and flattering
Ajax, Ulysses will make wounded pride the agency by
which the champion is drawn back into the fold:

> For that will physic the great Myrmidon,
> Who broils in loud applause, and make him fall
> His crest that prouder than blue Iris bends.
> (lines 377–379)

The paradoxical notion delights Nestor, and he ends the scene by characteristically "applying" Ulysses' idea:

> Two curs shall tame each other; pride alone
> Must [tarre] the mastiffs on, as 'twere a bone.
> (lines 389–390)

The formal outline of Ulysses' "physic" (he later calls it "derision medicinable" III.iii.44) is now clear. In the manner of a Paracelsian physician, he will use like against like. He has implied that in a chaotic world the only coherent principle is that, in the absence of all impediments, appetite will "eat up himself." He now intends artificially to encourage this principle of natural justice.

He proceeds to do exactly this. In II.iii he skillfully flatters Ajax; in III.iii he stirs Achilles to the quest for new honors. Achilles is moved by Ulysses' eloquence:

> I see my reputation is at stake,
> My fame is shrewdly gor'd.
> (III.iii.227–228)

He decides to meet Hector when the Trojans come to camp. Later, when Achilles vows to fight Hector (IV.v.230–270), we may assume that his change of heart is due to the success of Ulysses' scheme. Shortly afterwards, however, the Greek champion's resolve, and all the Ithacan's careful plotting, go down the drain. Achilles receives a letter and

> A token from . . . my fair love,
> Both taxing me and gaging me to keep
> An oath that I have sworn. I will not break it.
> Fall Greeks, fail fame, honor or go or stay,
> My major vow lies here; this I'll obey.
> (V.i.40–44)

Achilles' erotic instincts spell the downfall of Ulysses' plan. Ulysses, who wisely gauged the power of pride, has mysteriously underestimated the power of love. His eloquent boast of providence, made to Achilles in III.iii, is proven false. We last see Ulysses armed and in the midst of battle, reporting deeds he neither planned nor can control (V.v. 30–42).

The plot takes yet another ironic turn. Patroclus' death causes Achilles to change his mind again. He returns to battle and, when he cannot beat Hector fairly, has him gang-murdered (V.vi–viii). A third passion, anger, has superseded pride and love as Achilles' motivation. The sinister exploit provoked by anger is recognized as the decisive factor in the fall of Troy (V.x.4–9) and the unforeseen fruition of Ulysses original plan. Though Ulysses' specific stratagem goes awry, his general description of the laws of chaos is vindicated by the action. Chaos is bringing on its own end. The confused destructiveness of the final battle-scene, and Pandarus' epilogue, which grossly links sex with disease and death, are images of appetite's destined self-consumption.

This redoubled fictive irony leaves us in some doubt as to the theoretical implications of *Troilus and Cressida*. Shakespeare has made Ulysses the spokesman for new ideas. He has suggested that these ideas have substantial doctrinal value, but has cast severe doubt upon their specific practicability. As with Friar Lawrence in *Romeo and Juliet*, we are left with the sense of an unfinished experiment, a bold but ultimately dissatisfying ethical construct.

This sense of frustration is coherent with the experience of the whole play, which presents (as most modern readings show) a kaleidoscopic exposition of disorderly and dissatisfying relationships between reason and appetite.[8] The failure of Ulysses' plan exemplifies the failure of rational forces to come to terms with passion throughout *Troilus and Cressida*; and Ulysses himself, defender of reason and enemy of passion, may be interpreted allegorically as a rational principle which can approach, but never fully comprehend or reform, the lawless and subjective world of the affections. His later actions and speeches characterize him increasingly as an arch-rationalist who is unable to cope effectively with the chaotic manifestations of erotic experience. His master plan, we remember, fails precisely because he ignores the possible effects of love on Achilles. When the Greeks are introduced to Cressida, Ulysses rejects her with gratuitous impoliteness, describing her later as something sordid and foul (IV.v.46–63). And when, late in the play, he serves as guide to the agonized Troilus, Ulysses is amazed that love can drive a man so wild:

> May worthy Troilus be half attached
> With that which here his passion doth express?
> (V.ii.161–162)

In Troilus' world of love and rage, Ulysses is clearly on foreign soil. His godlike vision is limited by its lack of consideration for the beast; his moralistic rejection of the irrational is cognate with the limitations of his providence and the ultimate failure of his policy.

Ulysses' combination of vision and blindness, and his abrupt decline from ideological hero to helpless onlooker, are paradoxes so severe that they exceed the limits of successful satire, instead suggesting unrefined ambiguities in the attitude of the playwright himself.[9] By analogy, these psychological and dramatic irregularities suggest the reason why the medical metaphor, which, like Ulysses, connects appetite with sickness and decay, is never in the Problem Comedies a psychologically or dramatically fulfilling technique. In the two plays which follow *Troilus and Cressida*, Shakespeare will exhaust the potentialities of this metaphor and ultimately abandon it. He will do so because he will reject, profoundly and permanently, the moralistic equation of passion with disease and death.

All's Well that Ends Well

The next Problem Comedy, *All's Well that Ends Well* (1602-1603), affords an overview by which the medical elements of all three plays may be most effectively considered. It is the only one of the three plays which suggests a theoretical basis for the dominant metaphor, and the only play in which both sides of the metaphor—the medical and the moral—are united in a single doctor-heroine. Helena's two major goals—to cure the King of a "fistula" and to capture her beloved Bertram—represent respectively the medical and moral aspects of the play. In her first soliloquy she sketches the general outlines of her method and also gives some clues as to its philosophical background:

> Our remedies oft in ourselves do lie,
> Which we ascribe to heaven. The fated sky
> Gives us free scope, only doth backward pull
> Our slow designs when we ourselves are dull.
> What power is it which mounts my love so high,
> That makes me see, and cannot feed my eye?
> The mightiest space in fortune nature brings
> To join like likes, and kiss like native things.
> (I.i.216-223)

The major ideas advanced in this speech also figure prominently in the teachings of Paracelsus. Helena's theory of a dualistic causality, which allows intelligent mortals "free scope" but subjects the "dull" to destiny, is an accurate statement of the Paracelsian theory of free will and fate quoted and analyzed with reference to *Romeo and Juliet* in Chapter 2 above:

> The stars are subject to the philosopher, they must follow him, and not he them. Only the man who is still animal is governed, mastered, compelled and driven by the stars, . . . [Man] . . . carries the stars within himself, . . .[10]

Helena opines that destiny, like the Paracelsian "stars," is "in ourselves"; and Shakespeare further suggests his relationship to his source by using the medical term "remedies." Moreover, when Helena advances the notion that nature seeks "to join like likes," she is probably adapting another famous element of Paracelsian doctrine. Bostocke supports the idea of a homeopathic cure by postulating a natural force which attracts similar things to each other. Likes cure likes, because

> Such medicines for the love and liking they have to our nature af-
> flicted have a desire to be joyned and coupled together, as a hun-
> gry and thirsty man desireth meat or drink, which nourish well.

And later, more generally,

> Natura, natura delectatur et coniungi appetit.[11]

What is important to note here is not only the similarity of ideas but the fact that Shakespeare is doing something with the idea of "likes" that Paracelsus and Bostocke never made manifest. Like Puttenham and Donne[12] Shakespeare is performing intellectual alchemy on the idea—transmuting a philosophical thesis into a dramatic and literary experience. Here two Paracelsian doctrines are taken out of context and combined with each other to form a novel view of causality and ethics. By telescoping together the notion of the fate/ freedom dualism and the idea of the natural magnetism of "likes," Helena implies that we are free only when we fol- low nature (nature is the "power" of lines 220-221) and that nature's way is the attraction and interaction of similar forms. Medically, this means the interaction of a "like" cure with a "like" disease; dramatically, the interaction of a Helena with a Bertram.

Helena goes on to cure the King, and in so doing demon- strates that she is not only a Paracelsian theorist but also a Paracelsian physician. In a well-documented essay, Richard K. Stensgaard uses historical and biographical evidence and (more importantly) analysis of specific medical terminology ("manifest experience," "faculties inclusive," etc.) to draw parallels between Shakespeare and Bostocke and to make distinctions between Helena's theory of medicine and the theory of the Galenists. He also shows that Shakespeare's direct reference to Paracelsus (II.iii.11) has been seen as a slighting one only because its readers have been unfamiliar with its historical context. In her specific methods, her espousal of experience above theory and her belief in the transcendental element in medicine, Helena calls to mind the revolutionary medical doctrines which were attracting significant literary attention during Shakespeare's middle years.[13]

This complex of ethical and medical ideas must have lent *All's Well that Ends Well* a sense of newness and topicality which was available to many of Shakespeare's contemporaries but has since been lost. It was richly appropriate to pull these strains together in the figure of Helena, herself a representative not only of modernity and science but also of individual initiative and social mobility (a doctor's daughter, she is quintessentially "middle-class"). In a way which anticipates Bacon, Helena employs modern science and renews the world. Plague-ridden London and its possibly Paracelsian King would have appreciated the currentness and applauded the optimism of this graceful dramatic gesture.[14] But careful listeners and readers could find even greater cause for amusement and fruitful conjecture. Paracelsian wisdom was transmitted not only through expository writing but also through fable.[15] Bostocke claims, moreover, that his master is among those writers who

> disperse their meaning in several places, to the end they would be understode onely of the deligent and painfull reader and not of the unworthie.[16]

Those who were able to grant similar indulgences to their beloved playwright would have noticed that the sensational medical content of *All's Well that Ends Well* is turned into a metaphor which dominates the play's moral discourse.

After the cure of the King, the plot bifurcates, dealing alternately with Helena's entrapment of the errant Bertram, and the French Lords' exposure of that egregious timeserver, Parolles. These two fictions differ superficially, but structurally they resemble and illuminate each other. Both deal with the unveiling of dishonest practices. Parolles has been consistently gulling his crony Bertram. On his side, Bertram has been seeking to beguile a Florentine virgin named Diana. Both artifices are thwarted and uncovered by subtler artifices: respectively, Helena's use of the bed-trick and the Lords' concoction of a false ambush and a phony language. Both villain-victims, finally, are treated mercifully and agree to mend their ways. Bertram will accept Helena. Parolles vows an even more extensive revision of attitude. He will leave off pretending and live by being "the thing I am" (IV.iii.322). His self-degradation wins him social redemption as servant to the old Lord Lafew. The justice that operates in the play is luminously paradoxical. Truth is revealed by falsehood. Balance is regained, and things brought back to their proper places, not by an assertion of order, but rather by artful dispositions of chaos.

Considering the play's scientific content, the resemblance between this form of comic justice and the general theory of the Paracelsian cure is worth noting. The use of sin against sin, deceit against deceit, may be seen as a metaphor for the homeopathic treatment of disease. This similarity between medical and moral experience if heightened by the neat specificity of the moral cures. Bertram and Parolles are both corrected by methods which are cognate with their own particular types of waywardness. Bertram, whose failing is lawless sexual desire, is tricked into committing the sexual act with his own wife. Helena is quite explicit about the paradoxical nature of the stratagem:

> . . . wicked meaning in a lawful deed,
> And lawful meaning in a lawful act,
> Where both not sin, and yet a sinful fact.
> (III.vii.45–47)

The thorniness of this passage is significant. By using sexuality against itself, Helena is doing what she has earlier said nature does: joining like to like. This revolutionary approach results in a temporary confusion ("lawful" vs. "wicked," etc.) which may be read also as a satire on the traditional and linguistic bases of morality.

Parolles' homeopathic punishment is equally specific but much subtler. He has traduced language, and he is traduced by it. Parolles' name means "words," and he is indeed made of words. He "hath a smack of all neighboring languages," and when he boastfully announces, "I love not many words," the unheard reply is, "No more than a fish loves water" (IV. i.15–16, III.vi.84–85). To old Lafew, he is not worth "another word" (II.iii.262–263). Later he begs Lafew for "a single word"; and Lafew replies that, with a name like "Parolles," he begs for more than one (V.ii.35–40). He is not just a treacherous knave but a character whose falseness is deeply related to the phenomenon of language—specifically, to the perversion of language from a mode of communication to a medium of pretence. Parolles is a walking betrayal of the manifest intention of speech and a purveyor of its insidious potential. In him the play's implicit meaning is deepened from a satire of behavior almost to a satire of perception, a critique of that substratum of awareness at which experience is codified and verbalized. Like Shylock, though less seriously, he is a thematic entity, a common denominator of social disorder. With medical appropriateness he is unmasked, discomfited, and ultimately redeemed by a heavy dose of language. Captured and blindfolded by the French Lords and soldiers, he is subjected to a fabulous language that puts him entirely at a loss:

[2.] Lord. *Throca movousus, cargo, cargo, cargo.*
All. *Cargo, cargo, cargo, villianda par corbo, cargo.*
Par. O ransom, ransom! [*They seize him.*] Do not
hide mine eyes. [*They blindfold him.*]
[1. Sold. as] Interpreter. *Boskos thromuldo boskos.*
Par. I know you are the Muskos' regiment,
And I shall lose my life for want of language.
(IV.i.65–70)

Parolles is defeated by the absurd perfection of his own monstrosity. His misappropriation of speech is counter-acted by a total subversion of speech, a symbolic demolition of meaning itself. Importantly, his later vow to reform is phrased in terms of the thematic dichotomy between essence and appearance:

> Simply the thing I am
> Shall make me live. Who knows himself a braggart,
> Let him fear this; for it will come to pass
> That every braggart shall be found an ass.
> Rust sword, cool blushes, and, Parolles, live
> Safest in shame! Being fool'd, by foolery thrive!
> (IV.iii.333–338)

Such recantations are rare in Shakespeare, and when they do occur, they deserve scrutiny. Parolles, like the King, has been subjected to a revolutionary cure. A feigner, he has been reformed by deceit; an enemy of meaning, he has been reformed by absurdity. Like is effectively cured by like; and Parolles' testament of reformation twice emphasizes ("braggart . . . ass," "fool'd . . . foolery") the healthy rela-tionship of likes—the undistorted condition in which the essence of things is in accord with our perception of them.

What is the meaning of homeopathic morality? In Bert-ram's case the theme is left incomplete. Bertram begs "par-don" and promises to love Helena "dearly, ever, ever dearly" (V.iii.8, 15–16); but after enduring five acts of his silliness and dishonesty, we are justifiably dissatisfied with his refor-mation. Like a clumsy and ponderous comic prop, he is finally wrestled into position for the promised conclusion. Is the sense of strain and disappointment intentional? By adding ten lines of dialogue—a speech roughly equivalent to Parolles' recantation, in which Bertram displays new self-understanding and a fledgling love for his wife—Shakespeare could have brightened his comic conclusion and shown con-fidence in the regenerative potentiality of his new morality. His failure to make such an effort suggests instead an ironic attitude towards the moral implications of the comic genre and an uncertainty as to the psychological value of Helena's stratagem. Shakespeare will never write another play in which the problem of sexuality is treated solely as an exercise in strategy and tactics.

With Parolles, however, the meaning of the stratagem is deeper and more resonant. We have seen how his case is developed as a serious examination of the manifold potentialities of language. This examination and the meaningful speech which crowns it are, moreover, profoundly related to the dominant verbal themes of the play. To understand Parolles' 'cure' is to understand the aesthetic dialectic which makes *All's Well that Ends Well* very worthy of study.

The important philosophical 'problem' of *All's Well that Ends Well*—if we judge by depth of expression and coherence of concern—is not ethical but epistemological. It is not the much-discussed theme of appearance vs. reality, but a corollary and more specific theme, a question of reality vs. language. Careful readers are forced again and again to question the imprecise media by which experience is expressed; and, through this questioning, to ponder the effectiveness of the intellectual process by which experience is understood. Major characters raise the subject explicitly. When the King questions her about her identity in Act V, Helena responds,

> 'Tis but the shadow of a wife you see;
> The name, and not the thing.
> (V.iii.307–308)

Lavatch the clown rousingly mocks the social abuses of language by claiming to the Countess that there is a single answer that fits all questions:

> It is like a barber's chair that fits all buttocks: the
> pin-buttock, the quatch-buttock, the brawn-buttock, or
> any buttock.
> (II.ii.16–18)

The clown's catch-all is the exclamation, "O Lord, sir!," and he supplies his patroness with a catalogue of its applications. His praise of words is ironically a satire on words. If a single phrase fits all occasions, what is the use of language? The exclamation, with its inane flattery and stylish blasphemy, suggests the perversion of language from a means of honest communication to a blank counter in a vacuous social game.

The most absolute indictment of language belongs to the King. As he tries to convince Bertram that Bertram should love Helena for her virtue rather than for her "name" or social position, his attention turns to the question of language and meaning in general:

> If she be
> All that is virtuous—save what thou dislik'st,
> A poor physician's daughter—thou dislik'st
> *Of virtue for the name.* But do not so.

> Good alone
> Is good, *without a name*; vileness is so:
> The property by what [it] is should go,
> Not by the title. She is young, wise, fair,
> In these to nature she's immediate heir;
> And these breed honor.

> *The mere word's a slave,*
> Debosh'd on every tomb, on every grave
> A lying trophy, and as oft is dumb
> Where dust and damn'd oblivion is the tomb
> Of honor'd bones indeed.
>
> (II.iii.121–124, 128–133, 137–141. My italics.)

We can understand and sympathize with the King's dissatisfaction with language—with the desire to experience "true" qualities in their unalloyed essence. Language, especially when employed in a competitive social context, can twist the fabric of experience or even quite demolish it, substituting a synthetic arrangement of false impressions. Parolles, who is made of words, represents this perverted but credible ephemera. He uses stylish verbal constructs to conceal his own faithlessness and cowardice: to paint himself as his own opposite. Bertram, who is Parolles' gull, writes two letters in which he plays with language in a curious way:

> "I have wedded her, not bedded her, *and sworn to make the 'not' eternal.*"
>
> (III.ii.21–22)

> "When thou canst get the ring upon my finger, which never shall come off, and show me a child begotten of thy body that I am father to, then call me husband; *but in such a 'then' I write a 'never.'*"
>
> (III.ii.57–60. My italics.)

Bertram's affected witticisms suggest a thematic defect of character. His use of adverbs—"not," "then," and "never"—as nouns implies that he objectifies words, that he indeed equates "the word" with "the thing itself." His enslavement to words, and thus to the abuse of values which characterizes his whole society, is more massively suggested by his ignorant attachment to the word-man, Parolles. Together with Parolles, Helena, Lavatch, the Lords, and the King, Bertram is thus an element in a systematic attack on the social misuses of language.

But in whose name, and to what effect, can language be attacked? The King's advocacy of pure ideas is naive and self-contradictory. His defense of concepts like "good" and "vileness" against their names is itself a construct of words. Concept and sign cannot be arbitrarily divided from each other; and in seeking to achieve such a division, the King is as much a gull of language as Bertram and Parolles. If redress for impreciseness and corruptibility of language is to be found, it must be sought in language itself. The larger context seems to bear out this paradoxical implication. Helena, the philosopher-heroine, practices deceit with language. She knowledgeably subverts the function of words so that she may regain Bertram. More significantly, the trick which traps and redeems Parolles is symbolically molded of language. While the satiric content of *All's Well*

that Ends Well is an attack on language, the broader structure points toward a redemption of language.[17]

The substance of this redemption becomes clearer if we
realize that the Lords' plot against Parolles is, in operation,
quite similar to the workings of satiric art. Just as Parolles
is cured by an artful exaggeration of his own specific ail-
ment, so satire medicates to society by providing it with an
ironic concentration of its own ills. In this sense, satire is
homeopathic, a purgative whose effect depends upon its
similarity to the disease. To misappropriate a phrase of
Ulysses', satire is "derision med'cinable," a simultaneous
mocking and mending. In *All's Well that Ends Well* this
therapeutic derision is directed against the corruption of
language. The play mocks the social uses which overwork
and exploit language, which change it from a vehicle of sin-
cere communication into the currency of the marketplace,
elastic and amoral. The satire is achieved, however, through
endearing and redeeming intricacies of language. The magic
of irony and a resonant thematic structure produce a symbolic transfiguration of language: a death in use and rebirth
in art. We are taught at once to despise the mindless or selfish degradation of words and to revere their nobler potentialities. The exposure of Parolles is thus a symbol of the effect of the play as a whole—an example of the moral therapy
of verbal art. What happens to Parolles is in miniature what
should happen to the reader of the play.

To conclude our study of this play we might glance again
at its title. The thematic unity of *All's Well that Ends Well*
accords deeply with one of the most meaningful pieces of
nomenclature in Shakespeare. The phrase "All's well that
ends well" is on one level a generic definition of comedy
and an ironic arraignment of its uses. The happy 'end,' with
its aura of justice, enlightenment, and reconciliation, is what
structurally defines the genre. It supplies a promise, a pervasive sense of future bounty, which is active on audience or
reader throughout the course of the play. The misfortunes

of Viola and Sebastian, or Rosalind and Orlando, are colored by our ingrained awareness that very shortly they will be eased; the excesses of Proteus, Don John, or Duke Frederick are mitigated by the almost contractual certainty that they will soon be corrected. In a visual sense, comic characters are lit from the future; conversely, figures in tragedy are lit from the past and walk into their own shadows. But this dramatic effectiveness can also be an intellectual drawback. The dominance of futurity can rob the present of its meaning, and the realistic potentialities of art can give way to the generalized pattern of dramatic ritual. Shakespeare's growing preference for mixed genres—his use of comic elements in the Tragedies and his invention of the ambiguous Problem Comedy—reflects his desire to fulfill a context of experience whose intensity is not mitigated by the symmetry of dramatic forms. His refusal to satisfy us with the outcome of Helena's plot is also a refusal to be satisfied fully with the power of the comic formula to affect or enlighten. The effect of this is to diminish the importance of artistic "ends" and to establish the importance of art as process.

An analogous dialectic operates on the ethical level. If, dramatically speaking, "All's well that ends well" is a sentiment deriving from New Comedy, it is, ethically speaking, a modern notion whose most notable spokesman is Machiavelli. The idea that the end justifies the means is stated outright in *Il Principe* (*si guarda al fine*)[18] and implied throughout the political and dramatic works. Shakespeare plays upon the moral implications of this motto. In the sense that Helena uses "a sinful fact" to achieve "a lawful act," she is a modern who partakes of the Machiavellian tradition. Unless we accept the idea that *All's Well* is simply a bad piece of writing, we must assume that Shakespeare is treating Helena and her machinations ironically. The businesslike perfection and mathematical coldness of her scheme cause us to question the titular motto and its philosophical source. The social effectiveness of the Machiavellian idea of means and ends is admitted; what is notably absent, however, is a sense of its moral or psychological value. All may end well, but there is no feeling of people as ends—no idea of method as a vehicle for positive change. Like the bare comic formula, the bare Machiavellian formula is empty of moral meaning. In both cases, the problem seems to lie in the preoccupation with 'ends' or goals. Helena is, in a sense, punished by her own success. She wins Bertram de Rossillion, the most unredeemably boorish husband in Shakespearean literature, and the implication is that her prize is suited to her effort. Shakespeare's title is the foil to a deep questioning of modern prudence.

The implications of the Parolles-plot are different and far more positive. The artifice which beguiles Parolles is anything but cold and mechanical; indeed, his trial-by-gibberish is by far the most delightful scene in the play. The Lords' stratagem of "terrible language" which is undertaken "for love of laughter" (IV.i.3; III.vi.34, 41) is, in essence, the opposite of Helena's scheme. The Lords have no selfish goal, but rather seek only to expose the truth and to produce delight; the unexpected by-product of this activity is a positive alteration of character. If Helena demeans art into a somewhat sterile tactical device, the Lords' stratagem suggests art's nobler function—its unique capacity to kindle self-knowledge. Shakespeare will return to this theme in the play which follows *All's Well that Ends Well*, *Measure for Measure*.

Measure for Measure

Measure for Measure adheres faithfully to the 'problem' formula set up in *Troilus and Cressida* and *All's Well that Ends Well*. In all three plays, Shakespeare establishes broad patterns of social and psychological disorder. The passions (chiefly sexual) set characters at odds with themselves and with established social justice. On its own side, society is mocked for the crudeness and rigidity of its moral and intellectual constructs: for abstractions (like Ulysses' rule of

"Sol," or the French King's idea of "good" and "evil") that have little to do with psychological or political reality. Standing between these foils is the trickster-hero, who seeks, through paradoxical contrivances, to reconcile the warring elements. Each of these central figures has impressive intellectual credentials. Ulysses is a legendary personification of worldly wisdom and a practitioner of "new" politics; Helena is a sort of modern scientist. In *Measure for Measure* the Duke (disguised) proclaims himself "a scholar, a statesman, and a soldier" (III.ii.146). In the course of the play his character undergoes an evolution suggesting three definite stages, and each of these (as we will see) can be related to a specific form of Renaissance intellectuality. It is the phenomenon of these stages themselves, however, that makes *Measure for Measure* different from the two earlier plays. While Ulysses and Helena do not change notably throughout five acts, the Duke undergoes a development which puts his revealed awareness more and more in touch with his dramatic and intellectual context. *Measure for Measure* is, among other things, the story of an education, and this education is especially significant because it suggests basic changes in Shakespeare's attitude towards art and experience.

The first stage of the Duke's development is presented more or less in retrospect during the expository scenes. He presents himself as having been something of a recluse. He tells Angelo, "I love the people, / But do not like to stage me to their eyes" (I.i.67–68); and later he reminds Friar Thomas that

> none better knows than you
> How I have ever lov'd the life removed,
> And held in idle price to haunt assemblies
> Where youth, and cost, witless bravery keeps.
> (I.iii.7–10)

Even when he describes himself to Lucio as "a scholar, a statesman, and a soldier," the word-order suggests that public duty has not been his first love. The picture sketched is of a scholarly type who for fourteen years (I.iii.21) has held himself aloof from society, letting the laws of Vienna "slip." The implication is that this withdrawal is due not only to a love of studies but also to a positive distaste for society. To Angelo he deplores the people's noise and enthusiasm, suggesting that their favor is unsafe to a monarch (I.i.69–72). To the Friar he portrays Viennese high life as immature, immoderate, and witless. He even denounces that most social of phenomena, love between the sexes:

> No; holy father, throw away that thought;
> Believe not that the dribbling dart of love
> Can pierce a complete bosom.
>
> (I.iii.1–3)

That the evil in society can justify the retirement of a man who loves goodness was a thesis much disputed in Shakespeare's time. Its most notable formulations occur in Montaigne:

> The Common-wealth requireth some to betray, some to lie, and some to massaker: leave we that commission to people more obedient and more pliable.

> ... *of a thousand there is not one good* ... Contagion is very dangerous in a throng.

> Therefore it is not enough, for a man to have sequestered himself from the concourse of people: it is not sufficient to shift place, a man must also sever himself from the popular conditions, that are in us. A man must sequester and recover himselfe from himselfe ... It is the true solitarinesse, and may be enjoyed even in the frequencie of peopled Cities, and Kings courts: but it is more commodiously enjoyed apart.[19]

The parallelism between the Duke's initial philosophy and the philosophy of Montaigne extends even to Montaigne's assertion that true isolation is not complete without the purgation of "popular conditions" or social vices from within the individual. In lines that are placed emphatically at the beginning of a scene, the Duke declares that he has purified himself of the most vulgar of conditions, sexual desire. His remark that the "dribbling dart" of love cannot pierce his "complete bosom" is highly significant in context. Sexual excess is the thematic vice of *Measure for Measure*, and every major figure is defined by his or her attitude towards it. By vaunting his imperviousness to sexuality, the Duke is adopting a suspiciously arbitrary attitude towards this thematic question. His initial self-image reminds us of Shakespeare's Ulysses: a celibate arch-rationalist, who believes that his wisdom sets him above the common abuses of mankind.

The Duke's scholarly reclusiveness does not last, and his words to Friar Thomas suggest the reason why. Though philosophically justified, the Duke's retirement constitutes a political neglect of duty with strong negative effects on Vienna. As Cicero puts it, in Grimald's translation, retired philosophers,

> while they attein one kind of justice, that they hurt noman with doing of iniurie, they fall into the other. For being letted with the study of learning, they forsake them, whom they ought to defend.[20]

With someone in the Duke's official position, the injury is even worse. He admits himself that his seclusion from political affairs has made him in large part responsible for Vienna's corruption:

> We have strict statutes and most biting laws
> (The needful bits and curbs to headstrong weeds),
> Which for this fourteen years we have let slip,
> Even like an o'ergrown lion in a cave,
> That goes not out to prey. Now, as fond fathers,
> Having bound up the threat'ning twigs of birch,
> Only to stick it in their children's sight
> For terror, not to use, in time the rod
> [Becomes] more mock'd than fear'd; so our decrees,
> Dead to infliction, to themselves are dead,
> And liberty plucks justice by the nose;
> The baby beats the nurse, and quite athwart
> Goes all decorum.
>
> Sith 'twas my fault to give the people scope,
> 'Twould be my tyranny to strike and gall them
> For what I bid them do; for we bid this be done,

When evil deeds have their permissive pass,
And not the punishment.
(I.iii.19–31, 35–39)

I have quoted at length because the passage is a wonderful example of the deliberate misuse of language and logic.
The Duke's description of matters Viennese is not good
poetry but something better; it is poetics as psychological
revelation. The frenetic rush from metaphor to metaphor
(in thirteen lines, the Duke is horseman, gardener,[21] lion,
fathers, nurse, and [perhaps] lawnbowler; decrees bite and
die, and justice is plucked by the nose) achieves a complex
exposition: it describes events in Vienna but also suggests
an active mind gingerly turning over a painful thought. The
speech radiates embarrassment and uncertainty; in so doing,
it both defines and satirizes the Duke's early attitude towards political experience.

The Duke's words to Thomas are also of value because
seen in context they reflect a flawed understanding of political responsibility. He tells Thomas that he has invented
a pretext for leaving Vienna and suddenly puts his office in
the hands of the puritanical Lord Angelo. Angelo, the Duke
expects, will bring Viennese corruption to a quick and possibly violent end; he will "strike home" in "ambush" of the
Duke's name (I.iii.41). The Duke plans to cure excessive
liberty through excessive severity, and without injury to his
own conscience or reputation. He denies responsibility for
Angelo's expected cruelty. Yet in the same breath he says,
"for we bid this be done,/When evil deeds have their permissive pass" (I.iii.37–38). Clearly, if the Duke was responsible
for Viennese excesses because he let them happen, he will
be similarly responsible for any righteous outrages commit-
ted by Angelo. His failure to comprehend this analogy is
a gauge of incomplete political awareness.

If the first stage of the Duke's philosophical development
is reminiscent of Montaigne, the second stage—his deceitful
use of Angelo as minister of vengeance—is unmistakably
Machiavellian. An essay by N. N. Holland has drawn our

attention to a striking parallelism between the Duke's stratagem and the seventh chapter of *Il Principe*.[22] Here Machiavelli speaks with approval of Cesare Borgia who, finding
disorder prevalent in newly-conquered Romagna, deputes
Remirro de Orco, "a cruel and able man," to rule and pacify
the state. Remirro succeeds with brutal efficiency in providing Romagna with "good government." Cesare then resumes control, establishes a new government, and achieves
a reputation for clemency by executing Remirro for his excessive cruelty. No example more aptly illustrates Machiavelli's belief that *si guarda al fine*, or his often implied doctrine that the general disordered monstrosity of mankind
necessitates a particular, deliberate monstrosity on the part
of the ruler. The Duke of Vienna seems to partake, briefly
at least, of similar convictions. A typical intellectual, he
feels guilty about his past inactivity and seeks to make up
for it by dabbling in the modern and the extreme.

Shakespeare's use of contemporary ideas is here both
satirical and dialectical. In relating the early stages of the
Duke's development to Montaigne and Machiavelli, he is
evoking two topical sensations[23] and subjecting them to
subtle ironies. More importantly, however, he is fleshing
out two plausible views of political reality and enclosing
them in a dialectic that is compounded with ironic discourse
and fictive experience. This dialectic imposes standards
which neither Montaigne's notion of reclusiveness, nor its
cynically activist alternative, can meet. The action arbitrates
a new kind of understanding.

It is the Duke's third phase, that of secret ruler and beneficent schemer, that is most thoroughly characterized in
Measure for Measure. The Machiavellian plan is abandoned
when, in III.i, the Duke learns that Angelo intends to use
political power as the stage for his own personal atrocities.
After this, the Duke surreptitiously resumes control of his
state. Disguised as a friar, he moves subtly and surely to
save Claudio's life and Isabella's virginity, to expose Angelo
and Lucio, and to win husbands for Juliet, Mariana, and

Kate Keepdown. His words and actions in the last three acts suggest an unconventional but curiously dignified method of government. To rule without authority is to rule by energy, prudence, and art. Montaigne's reclusiveness and Machiavelli's activism are abandoned for a method which, at least temporarily, combines the moral rectitude of the former with the political effectiveness of the latter.

The title *Measure for Measure* suggests justice, and it is on justice that the Duke's attention is primarily focused. His situation demands that he save the innocent and correct the guilty. But just as his principle of rule goes beyond formal authority, his idea of justice transcends the system of restraints, punishments, and rewards with which the concept is usually associated. The Duke's early view of justice in its commutative sense is that of law and order—"decorum," as he puts it (I.iii.31). Justice, he tells Friar Thomas, is a "bit" or "curb" to keep society under control (I.iii.20). His later actions, however, suggest a more ambitious goal for justice: order and harmony in the mind of the individual citizen. To this end he employs deceits, but not such deceits as we read of in Machiavelli, or even note in the policy of Shakespeare's Ulysses. The Duke's schemes are illusions so imaginative and provoking that they savor less of politics than of drama.[24] Indeed, the Duke seeks to administer justice in Vienna through something approaching the effect of tragedy.

As in *Troilus and Cressida* and *All's Well that Ends Well*, the protagonist's method operates paradoxically. The Duke will apply "craft against vice" (III.ii.277); his remedy is "bitter to sweet end" (IV.vi.8). He characterizes his plan in lines which pit words and ideas against themselves:

> So disguise shall by th' disguised
> Pay with falsehood false exacting, . . .
> (III.ii.281–282)

The Duke's actions, like his words, show him to be a comprehensive practitioner of the moral physic previously employed by Ulysses and by Helena. The "fever on goodness" which he has first sought to shun and then to suppress, is combated with a remedy which, like a Paracelsian cure, is married to the nature of the disease. The double-dealing Angelo is himself deceived. Instead of being apprehended before the fact, he is forced to live out the potential consequences of his plan to bed Isabella and kill Claudio (almost until the play's end he believes that Claudio is dead). Through the bed-trick, the sexual act becomes, paradoxically, a cure for Angelo's sexual excess and a means of preserving Isabella's virginity. In another symbolic gesture, Lucio the womanizer is compelled to marry his whore (V.i.518–521). Vice is not attacked head on; rather it is gradually and gently turned against itself.

But if vice can nullify vice, virtue can nullify virtue. Shakespeare is very much aware of this corollary and uses it to formulate the 'problem' or moral enigma which dominates the play. The language of *Measure for Measure* suggests that the play is not only about justice as it affects good and evil but also about the nature of good and evil themselves; and that the second question is even more difficult than the first. The Duke's words about his own methods testify that good and evil are at crucial points interchangeable. Other characters discover this disturbing truth much more painfully than the Duke. As he is being taken to jail for fornication, Claudio speaks paradoxically of the relationship between freedom and restraint and, more generally, of the contradiction between will's aim and will's effects:

> *Lucio.* Why, how how, Claudio? Whence comes this restraint?
> *Claud.* From too much liberty, my Lucio, liberty:
> As surfeit is the father of much fast,
> So every scope by the immoderate use
> Turns to restraint. Our natures do pursue,
> Like rats that ravin down their proper bane,
> A thirsty evil, and when we drink we die.
> (I.ii.124–130)

Here 'good' as object desired is distinguished radically from 'good' as real benefit. What we seek is the opposite of what we need, and the fault seems to lie in our "natures."

Angelo's case suggests an even more pointed example of goodness turning against itself. Musing on his lust for Isabella, he returns again and again to the contradictory moral theme:

> [I] Do as the carrion does, not as the flow'r,
> Corrupt with virtuous season. Can it be
> That modesty may more betray our sense
> Than woman's lightness? Having waste ground enough,
> Shall we desire to raze the sanctuary
> And pitch our evils there? O fie, fie, fie!
> What dost thou? Or what art thou, Angelo?
> Dost thou desire her foully for those things
> That make her good?
>
> O cunning enemy, that to catch a saint,
> With saints dost bait thy hook!
>   (II.ii.166–174, 179–180)

Specifically, Angelo is referring to a contradiction typical in human sexual behavior. Impervious to promiscuity, he quite simply falls prey to the lure of the forbidden. A chronic self-denier, he lusts after an image of sexual denial—a prim votaress in her neat habit. His words, however, have a broader thematic meaning. Can virtue be virtue if it has the power to corrupt and to destroy? Does goodness lie in essence or in effects? Can one, as Angelo later puts it, "sin in loving virtue"? Questions of this sort were common in the Renaissance. Cornelius Agrippa, Erasmus, Machiavelli, and Montaigne all carry out lively attacks on traditional conceptions of human excellence.[25] Shakespeare's attack is subtler but no less deadly. By making Angelo take up a preposterous moral position which is in turn ironically modified by events, he suggests that radical moralism in general (including the Duke's own early avowals in I.iii) is by nature unfit to survive the shock of experience.

The pattern is complicated even further by other characters. In III.i Claudio finds himself imploring his sister to rescue him by sinning. Isabella's angry decision to let Claudio die reflects the diametrical opposition of two "vir-

tues," chastity and benevolence. Her previous phrasing of
this dichotomy is significant:

> Then, Isabel, live chaste, and, brother, die;
> More than our brother is our chastity.
> (II.iv.184–185)

We might sympathize with the position Isabella feels forced
to take. But her absolute formulation of this position is, together with her fierce anger towards Claudio, the tell-tale of
a flawed moral attitude. Absolutists do not belong to the
Shakespearean aristocracy.[26] His mixed world endures their
presence only as foils. Isabella's couplet makes us reject her
as a moral spokeswoman and throws the whole canon of
traditional virtues into doubt.

There is also noise from the other side. 'Vice,' as sex and
even as prostitution, finds zealous and sometimes moralistic
defenders. Lucio defends his dubious practices by citing the
widely-respected principle of accepted usage:

> *Pom.* I hope, sir, your good worship will be my bail.
> *Lucio.* No indeed will I not, Pompey, it is not the wear.
>
> Faith, my lord, I spoke it but according to the trick.
> (III.ii.72–75; V.i.505–506)

He argues that sexuality is natural, and jokingly implies that
because of its ancientness it has nobility:

> Yes, in good sooth, the vice is of great kindred; it is
> well allied; but it is impossible to extirp it quite, friar,
> till eating and drinking be put down.
> (III.ii.101–103)

Pompey the bawd considers himself an established trades-
man. When asked if his profession is lawful, he cannily replies, "If the law would allow it, sir" (II.i.227). Despite
threats of punishment, he persists in it magnanimously:

> Whip me? No, no, let carman whip his jade,
> The valiant heart's not whipt out of his trade.
> (II.i.255–256)

Perhaps most significant of all is the figure of Elbow. Elbow is notable for his inspired misuses of words:

> [I] do bring here before your honor two notorious *benefactors*.

> If it please your honor, I know not well what they are; but precise villains they are, that I am sure of, and void of all *profanation* in the world that good Christians ought to have.

> Marry, sir, by my wife, who, if she had been a woman *cardinally* given, might have been accus'd in fornication, adultery, and all uncleanliness there.

> Varlet, thou liest! thou liest, wicked varlet! The time is yet to come that she was ever *respected* with man, woman, or child.
>> (II.i.49–50, 53–56, 79–81, 167–169. My italics.)

In the best Renaissance tradition, Elbow's folly constitutes a negative kind of wisdom. In each case, the subject of the error is a moral concept. In each case, he says the opposite of what reason demands and the listener expects. Yet, taken literally, each error embodies a satire on the conventional morality of which Elbow, as constable, is representative and spokesman. Specifically, gentle abuse is visited on the accepted standards for virtuous action ("benefactors"), on Christian *mores*, on the chastity of Cardinals, and on the criteria by which individuals are "respected" by their peers. Elbow's errors reflect outwards as well as inwards. They imply that the reversal of values is typical of social life.

Though variously silly and corrupt, Lucio, Pompey, and Elbow are philosophical spokesmen of vital importance in the dialectic of *Measure for Measure*. If the words and experience of the figures in the main plot are structured so as to cast extreme doubt on the doctrinal bases of moral action, the figures in the subplot expand and justify this satire. Each in his own way, Lucio, Pompey, and Elbow suggest the ambiguous relationship between the formation of abstract values and the uneven needs and uses of society. They suggest that society, like a great hypocrite, makes and mars its values in the same breath; that value is the dainty garment of a gross social reality. Through them we sense an underlying unity in social experience, a burden of shared failings which turns words like "chastity" and "justice" into pale and feeble equivocations. Elbow's marvelous identification of "carnal" with "cardinal" symbolizes a dialectic which draws all elements of society, from highest to lowest, into a single soiled bundle.

The moral prescription of *Measure for Measure*—the Duke's striking reversal of traditional methods—is thus balanced by the satiric vision of a world where values are indeed reversed, where 'virtue' and other ethical abstractions are undercut by unexpected emphatic reiterations of natural lawlessness. The paradoxical symmetry of the moral action—virtue disguised as vice counteracting vice disguised as virtue—is a further elaboration of the contrariety on which theme and action in the two earlier Problem Comedies is based. Yet, *Measure for Measure* constitutes a significant departure. The schemes of Ulysses and Helena are, as we have seen, characterized by a pervasive rationality. They are the impositions of reason upon a manifestly unwilling natural context; moreover, they are imposed by characters who despise and consider themselves separate from the natural appetites they seek to bring under control.[27] This separation between mind and nature leaves us dissatisfied with the outcome of the drama and suspicious that Helena and Ulysses, as proponents of ambitious but unfulfilled theories, themselves fall partially within the boundaries of Shakespeare's unsparing satire. In *Measure for Measure*, however, the Duke's broadening awareness moves him closer and closer to a conscious identification with the human forces he seeks to govern. Like Parolles, the Duke is compelled by experience to come to terms with 'the thing he is.' The idea of moral awareness is linked emphatically with the idea of self-knowledge, and this combination allows at least for the possibility of reconciling hitherto dissonant voices of the spirit.

Shakespeare expresses the sense of psychological growth largely through a structural device employed elsewhere in the Problem Comedies[28] but seen most particularly in *Hamlet*. The stories of Fortinbras, Hamlet, and Laertes are developed in parallel. Shakespeare makes Hamlet show a sympathetic awareness of Laertes' similar predicament:

> For in the image of my cause I see
> The portraiture of his.
>   (*Hamlet*, V.ii.77-78)

In *Measure for Measure* the parallelism between Angelo and the Duke is equally apparent. Indeed, Angelo and the Duke are both aspects of the same character. Both are depicted from very early on as being celibate, moralistic, imperious, intellectual, and vain. Both avow the distinction of being immune to vulgar passions. Both hold the same political position, and both are attracted to the same woman. Having set up two would-be angels, Shakespeare makes one of them fall, and allows the other to share the knowledge of that fall. This device is used to justify a sharpening in the Duke's awareness. The Duke's growth in wisdom is announced in a carefully written and centrally located soliloquy which is valuable not only as a window into the play but also as a way-marker in Shakespeare's changing attitude towards experience.

The speech comes at a wonderfully rich moment in the course of the drama. The Duke has just learned of Angelo's misgovernment and has already hatched a scheme to thwart the deputy. He has overheard Isabella's rejection of her brother Claudio; he has met Isabella and been impressed by her beauty. Then, in a brief but compendious scene, the whole roguish pageantry of Vienna marches before him. Elbow, Pompey, Lucio, Overdone, the Provost, and the benign Escalus pointedly remind the Duke and us of every major element of plot and theme. The disguised Duke questions people about himself. He writhes with embarassment as he hears himself described by Lucio, slanderously but delightfully, as a drunkard and a lecher:

Ere he would have hang'd a man for the getting a hundred bas-
tards, he would have paid the nursing a thousand. He had some
feeling of the sport; he knew the service, and that instructed him
to mercy.

(III.ii.117–120)

Escalus informs him that the Duke was a man, "that above
all other strifes, contended especially to know himself" (III.
ii.232–233). The irony is that, until the lines which almost
immediately follow, the Duke has given evidence of no such
virtue. The condensed experience of Act III justifies and
gives psychological credibility to the revelation of a new
attitude. At last alone, the Duke declares,

> He who the sword of heaven will bear
> Should be as holy as severe;
> Pattern in himself to know,
> Grace to stand, and virtue go;
> More nor less to others paying
> Than by self-offenses weighing.
> Shame to him whose cruel striking
> Kills for faults of his own liking!
> Twice treble shame on Angelo,
> To weed my vice, and let his grow!
> O, what may man within him hide,
> Though angel on the outward side!
>
> Craft against vice I must apply.

(III.ii.261–272, 277)

We need not do much literary psychoanalysis to understand
this speech in context. A previously impenetrable character
has just been exposed to the charms of an attractive heroine,
to the hypocrisy and passion of a kindred spirit and to the
manifold waywardness of a whole city. He has been jibingly
reminded of his own potential waywardness; and his attention has been turned, in so many words, towards self-knowledge. The soliloquy is a manifesto of self-knowledge and its
political implications. It is a guide to the combination of
slyness and sympathy that will inform the Duke's later actions. It is also a brief document of intellectual history.
The doctrine expressed in the Duke's soliloquy accords

with the moral and psychological contradictions of *Measure for Measure* and is itself a manifesto of contrariety. The speech is built on a paradox so important as to be driven home four times:

sword ——————heaven
severe ——————holy
virtue ——————grace
go ——————stand

In each case an active principle is yoked to a passive principle. The "virtue" (strength) connected with swords and severity is symbolized by motion ("to go" in Elizabethan English could mean "to walk"). The "grace" connected with holiness and heaven is symbolized by stillness ("stand"). Historically this symbolic marriage of contraries suggests the reconciliation of two dominant Renaissance traditions: the classical tradition, whose sternness and emphasis on political action was evident in the Renaissance translations and in writers like Castiglione and Machiavelli; and the Christian tradition, whose emphasis on pacifism and mildness was repeatedly endorsed by Erasmus and seconded by More.[29] Many before Shakespeare had urged that the best aspects of both traditions be combined in a new order. Others, like Machiavelli and Erasmus, maintained that such an alliance was impossible. The Duke's soliloquy does not fall precisely in either camp. The repeated use of antithesis suggests that Shakespeare here is less interested in a fully harmonic unity than in a dynamic and energetically maintained balance of extremes.

The key to this difficult balance lies in the phrase, "Pattern in himself to know." The accepted interpretation of this line, "To know that the precedent for his judgments lies in his own conduct" (Arden edition *et al.*), suggests a form of self-knowledge; and with the thematic and psychological context of *Measure for Measure* in mind, we may conjecture that this self-knowledge includes an admission of the chaotic potentiality which unites all the denizens of Vienna, from Kate Keepdown to the Duke himself, in a common lot. It is this sort of self-inclusive awareness, rather than the simplistic and restrictive morality of his early speeches, that seems to guide the Duke in the later scenes. It may be seen as the philosophical substratum for his striking combination of aggressiveness and mercy, virtue and grace. The heterogeneous propensities of human nature, its insuppressible mobility between good and evil, makes such a mixture of classical and Christian attributes in a ruler both realistic and necessary.

The satire of *Measure for Measure* is thus the buttress of a new morality. We have seen that the Duke endeavors to 'cure,' rather than punish, Angelo's excess of passion. The same general method is apparent in his treatment of Claudio, Juliet, and Isabella. These petty sinners are all put through the psychologically purgative agony of believing that Claudio will be beheaded. Isabella indeed believes that her brother has been executed and does not discover that he is alive until the final moments of the play. Her plea for mercy upon Angelo (V.i.443–454) shows unexpected charity, suggesting that she, like other characters, has gained moral insight from the Duke's beneficent tormentings. The Duke's *modus operandi* is thus consistent with his paradoxical doctrine. Justice in *Measure for Measure* works through intense but wholly undestructive pain. The "sword of heaven" is not martial but surgical.

The end which crowns these innovative machinations is somewhat disappointing. The long final scene in which the Duke resumes formal control, reveals all intrigues, and grandly metes out justice to his subjects is all but devoid of the vital satire which characterizes the earlier action. Critical reformations occurring in Angelo and Isabella are expressed rather stiffly, and the Duke's enlightened descent from self-styled rational perfection to self-confessed humanity (he ends by proposing to Isabella) is itself too neat and rational to be very convincing. The moral realism of the drama pales as comic necessity, like a grinning tyrant, banishes all productive ironies and sentences the whole pack of characters to marriage.

Nonetheless, the play signals an impressive change of attitude. With the Duke's recognition of "pattern in himself," Shakespeare has for the first time created a moralist who learns to include himself within the soiled but lively condition of humanity. Manifestly similar to the wise rulers of Sonnet 94, who, "have pow'r to hurt, and will do none," "do not do the thing they most do show," and, "husband nature's riches from expense," the character of the Duke and the whole thrust of *Measure for Measure* diverge from this earlier ideal in one important way. The rulers of the Sonnet are "as stone, / Unmoved, cold and to temptation slow." Indeed, Shakespeare's virtuous deceivers from Friar Lawrence to Helena are moral purists who reject in themselves the passions they seek to bring under control in others. The Duke's transformation from purist to realist, and the brilliant psychological treatment of purists like Angelo and Isabella, show a turning away from this absolutism. In general, *Measure for Measure* suggests a rejection of "stone"[30] and godlike virtue, an end to the equation of human sensuality with disease, and an acceptance of man's chaotic propensities as irreducible principles of experience. Significantly, precedents for this new development can be found in the chief spokesmen for contrariety. Castiglione sees no wisdom in a view which does not accept and encompass the extremes of moral behavior. Paracelsus, though inimical to passion, gives it equal place with reason in human nature and makes self-knowledge the essential ingredient of freedom. Bruno again and again proclaims the necessity of recognizing and drawing vitality from the inner conflict of the formal and material extremes.[31] In the last of his Problem Comedies Shakespeare shows, for the first time, an awareness of this sort. The acceptance of the passions as natural rather than morbid elements and the concomitant rejection of stonelike virtue may be considered milestones in the artistic growth which leads to the unprecedented expressiveness of the mature Tragedies.

Notes to Chapter Four

1   I.iii.103; I.iii.91; III.iii.44.

2   See below, pp. 87–89.

3   III.ii.222–223; III.i.198; III.ii.277; IV.vi.7–8.

4   See, for example, E. M. W. Tillyard, *The Elizabethan World Picture* (London: Chatto and Windus, 1943), ch. 5.

5   I am referring to the Preface to the First Folio (1623), John Heminge and Henry Condell, "To the great Variety of Readers," F1, A3: "Reade him, therefore; and againe, and againe: And if then you doe not like him, surely you are in some manifest danger, not to understand him."

6   In II.iii.259–260 and III.iii.39–43, Ulysses makes suggestions to Agamemnon that are little short of commands.

7   See Hector's speech on a related subject, II.ii.163–193, especially lines 173–186.

8   The pioneer in this field, as in many other areas of Shakespearean thematic criticism, was G. Wilson Knight; see "The Philosophy of *Troilus and Cressida*," *The Wheel of Fire* (London: Oxford University Press, 1930).

9   For a summary of divergent views of Ulysses, see my essay, "The Soul of State: Ulyssean Irony in *Troilus and Cressida*," *Anglia* 93 (1975): 55–69. A portion of that essay has been used in the preceding analysis. The critics I listed, though disagreeing about almost everything else, seemed to agree (as I did with them) that Shakespeare's Ulysses was the product of a unified and deliberate artistic awareness. This assumption may well hold true for most Shakespearean characters, but I no longer see any reason to make it about figures who are as manifestly inconsistent as Ulysses.

10   Jacobi, p. 228; Sudhoff and Matthiessen, 2:378.

11   R. Bostocke, *The Difference between the auncient Phisicke and the latter Phisicke* (1585), ch. 5, sig. C vi (r); ch. 23, sig. L i (r). Also see ch. 8, section 14, Sig. E v (r): "In the Chymicall Medicines the Anatomie of the disease and medicine do agree and ioyne together." The idea of the mutual attraction of likes was, admittedly, proverbial before Paracelsus. See Morris Palmer Tilley, *A Dictionary of Proverbs in England in the Sixteenth and Seventeenth Centuries* (Ann Arbor: University of Michigan Press, 1950), L286.

12   See pp. 28–29 above.

13   Richard K. Stensgaard, "*All's Well that Ends Well* and the Galenico–Paracelsian Controversy," *Renaissance Quarterly* 25 (1972): 173–87.

14   The Plague was in London between 1602 and 1606. King James himself "shows a detailed knowledge of [Paracelsus' works] in his *Counterblaste to Tobacco*" (W. A. Murray, "Why Was Duncan's Blood Golden?," *Shakespeare Survey* 19 (1966): 34–44, p. 36).

15   Bostocke, ch. 16, passim; ch. 23, sig. K viii (v).

16   Bostocke, ch. 23, sig. L i (v).

17   For a Baconian attack on abstractions such as the King's, and on misuses of language in general, see *The New Organon* 1.43, 51.

18   Machiavelli, *Il Principe*, end of ch. 18. Interestingly, Shakespeare uses the Italianate *fine* to mean "end" in one of Helena's doctrinal utterances:

> All's well that ends well! still the fine's the crown;
> Whate'er the course, the end is the renown.
> (III.iv.35–36)

19   *The Essayes of Montaigne*, trans. John Florio (1603; reprint ed., New York: Modern Library, n.d.), 3.1, p. 714; 1.38, pp. 188, 190–91.

20   *De Officiis* 1.9, in Grimald's translation (1553). Cicero's work had also been translated into English in 1533 by R. Whytinton. Like Montaigne's Essay 3.1 (quoted just above), Cicero's *De Officiis* contains a prolonged examination of the distinction between the "useful" (profitable) and the "honest" (virtuous). Montaigne derives his theme and his title ("De l'Utile et de l'Honneste") from Cicero.

21   There is editorial debate as to the authenticity of "weeds" (line 20). Even if we read Theobald's "steeds," though, it would only triflingly unmix the metaphor.

22   N. N. Holland, "*Measure for Measure*: The Duke and *The Prince*," *Comparative Literature* 11 (1959): 16–20.

23   Florio's translation of Montaigne had appeared in 1603, one year before the probable composition of *Measure for Measure*.

24   See Harold Goddard, *The Meaning of Shakespeare* (Chicago and London: University of Chicago Press: 1951), 2:165–66.

25   Agrippa (*De Vanitate* ch. 54) says that the virtues may be inimical to each other. Erasmus' satire comes not only in *The Praise of Folly* but also in *The Education of a Christian Prince*, ed. Lester K. Born (New York: Columbia University Press, 1936), pp. 201–203. In the latter work, he derides the classical idea of magnanimity. Machiavelli (*Il Principe*, ch. 15) maintains that the traditionally-conceived virtues may be useless and even harmful. Montaigne (2.2; Florio, p. 306) says that there is something "sinister" about too constant virtue, and relates virtue to the passions. See also Bacon "Of Fortune."

26   In the important essay, "De l'Experience" 3.13, Montaigne claims that *"Affirmation and self-conceit, are manifest signes of foolishness"* (Florio, p. 973). Regarding this essay, see below, pp. 173–76.

27   Helena takes the side of traditional morality in the banter about virginity with Parolles in *All's Well that Ends Well*, I.i. In III.vii she refers to Bertram's suit for Diana as "wanton siege" and "important blood." She never (jokingly or otherwise) refers to any pleasure she will derive from the "sinful" act she will commit with Bertram, even though that act will be the consummation of their marriage.

28   I have shown above how Bertram and Parolles take on parallel roles (as the victims of schemes) in the final acts of *All's Well that Ends Well*. In *Troilus and Cressida*, important parallels exist between Cressida and Helen (as erotic lures to battle), between Ulysses and Hector (as voices of rationality, I.iii and II.ii), and between Agamemnon and Priam (as useless figures of authority). There is parallelism, too, in the general outlines of the Greek and Trojan plots: Troilus' seduction of Cressida, and Ulysses' winning-over of Achilles are made to occur simultaneously. On the distinction between structural forms in the Middle Plays and the mature Tragedies, see below, pp. 120–23.

29   For Erasmus' pacifism, see *The Education of a Christian Prince*, the *Querela Pacis*, and the *Dulce Bellum Inexpertis*. More's Utopians prefer to let hirelings fight for them and are excused even from the brutality of slaughtering their own cattle. See below, p. 191.

30   Shakespeare connects Angelo, not the Duke, with the image of stone (I.iii.52–53).

31   See above, pp. 25–26, 33–34.

CHAPTER 5

Contrariety as Structure: The Later Tragedies

'Tis dangerous when the baser nature comes
Between the pass and fell incensed points
Of mighty opposites.
                    Hamlet, V.ii.60–62.

When Hamlet refers to himself and Claudius heroically as
"mighty opposites," we should not take his words at face
value. Hamlet is anything but an uncompromising adversary;
rather, he is notoriously ready to see both sides of a question. Neither does he represent some isolated and radical
form of awareness. Instead he is the play's focal point, the
medium by which its major issues are sifted and interpreted.
Moreover, while these issues infallibly partake of ethical and
psychological contrariety, this contrariety is not reflected in
the construction of the play at large. Verbally, thematically,
and structurally, *Hamlet* is one of the most homogeneous of
Shakespeare's works. It is a play whose characters are all
trapped in a web of common awareness, a shared burden of
passion and crime. They are separated from each other only
by the guilt and suspicion which this burden carries with it.
This unanimity of experience is suggested by language,
characterization, thematic parallels, and repeated actions.
Hamlet and Claudius duplicate each other's sentiments without knowing it.[1] Laertes, Polonius, and Hamlet, in discrete
interviews, lecture poor Ophelia about her chastity, as the
Player-King will lecture the Player-Queen, and Hamlet will
lecture Gertrude. The pattern of universal sexual guilt is
completed when the chaste Ophelia, driven by grief into
a chaotic inner self, babbles of sex and sin. Throughout the

119

action, massive thematic parallels like that of Fortinbras-Hamlet-Pyrrhus-Laertes as avenging sons, or Old Fortinbras-Old Hamlet-Hyperion-Polonius-Claudius as ousted elders, supply a mythic undercurrent of cognate experience. The confused and self-reduplicating slaughter of the final scene, in which each of the four major characters functions simultaneously as victim, murderer, and revenger, carries the disquieting message home. All the characters, in one frightening sense, are the same character. The killer, the victim, and the revenger are all ourselves. Despite its violence and discord, *Hamlet* is built on a terrible unity. Its encompassing theme is the weight of our inner motives, intolerable yet incommunicable.

Something similar may be said of the Problem Comedies which follow *Hamlet*. In each of these plays, Shakespeare uses structural parallels and overriding themes to suggest a universally shared experience. *Troilus and Cressida* is animated by the theme of chaotic appetite, as operative in the parallel stories of Troy and the Greek camp. In *All's Well that Ends Well*, the theme of language dominates, and the plot bifurcates into the parallel deceptions of Bertram and Parolles. *Measure for Measure* is a large framework of parallels, all dealing with the psychology, ethics, and politics of sex and implying that, in these and other matters, the same laws govern all humanity. Contrariety abounds in these plays, as we have seen; but it is expressed in terms of psychological and doctrinal paradox rather than built into the plays' larger structures. It appears as a mysterious and dangerous force, naggingly implicit in experience and comprehensible only by moral experimenters like Ulysses and Helena. Contrariety is a problem submitted for scrutiny. Even in *Measure for Measure*, Shakespeare seems to be viewing it analytically, holding it at arm's length.

The unusual energy of the tragedies which follow (1604–1608) has much to do with a notable change in these psychological and aesthetic attitudes. Contradictions which were, in the Problem Comedies, subjects of satire and debate, are woven into the very fabric of *Othello, King Lear, Macbeth,* and *Antony and Cleopatra.* Indeed, contrariety becomes the metaphysics of the drama, the organizing principle of the aesthetic experience. These plays derive much of their power from extreme oppositions of character, like those between Iago and Desdemona, Edmund and Edgar, and Caesar and Cleopatra. Moreover, each play is built around a protagonist—Othello, Lear, Macbeth, and Antony—whose volition swings compulsively and fatally between opposites. Time and place are organized so as to suggest, within the confines of one work, interlocking extremes of prosperity and adversity, order and chaos. Language is heavier with paradox and antithesis than ever before. With the exception of the double plot of *King Lear,* parallel structures are rare; and, in general, the technique of setting up a shared awareness gives way to the establishment of isolated outposts of emotion and ideology. Desdemona, Iago, Cordelia, the later Macbeth, and other major characters espouse values that are absolute and non-negotiable—values which render them unavailable to communication, and set them at the very fringes of human experience. In each of the four plays, extreme modes of understanding are set destructively against each other. The breadth of the abyss is emphasized by characters who effectively touch both extremes and are destroyed in the process: either suicidally, like Othello, Lady Macbeth, and Antony; or by thought alone, like Gloucester, Lear, and Enobarbus. Through such characters Shakespeare suggests the heroic difficulty of attaining a comprehensive overview and the tragic necessity for doing so. Contrariety is at once the motive power of tragedy, and the mystery, the vague massive shape, which the tragic vision ultimately addresses.

Cognate with these aesthetic and metaphysical changes is a great liberalization of attitude towards the passions. Shakespeare's immediately preceding treatments of the tragic genre—*Romeo and Juliet, Richard II, Julius Caesar,* and *Hamlet*—are subdued and reluctant tragedies, weak in outrage and based less on flamboyant villainy than on un-fathomable ambiguities of the spirit. The later Tragedies, though hardly less subtle, are urgent, violent, and boisterous; again and again they erupt in uninhibited assertions of will. *Hamlet* and the first two Problem Comedies treat the passions as base, unwholesome things which resemble diseases. This attitude undergoes significant modification in *Measure for Measure* and *Othello*, and is all but abandoned in the three tragedies that follow. Characters like Emilia in *Othello* and Edmund in *King Lear* defend sex wittily and by no means unpleasantly. More generally, passion is seen as producing good as well as bad. Acts of goodness like Emilia's denunciation of Iago, and Edgar's exploits are often born of outrage and suffering rather than of rational discourse. Edgar's school is "known and feeling sorrow"; he is "pregnant to good pity," and this emotional education is symbolic of the whole experience of *King Lear*. Antony is "dolphin-like" in his pleasures. A remarkable sanguinity graces his passion, connecting it with the brightness and warmth of the sun and the generative aspects of nature. In Cleopatra the paradoxical encomium of passion is even more emphatic. "Vildest things become themselves in her"; her sensuality is so glittering and creative that it relates her to the mystery of Time and to poetic vision itself. Like Shylock, these characters speak an inner voice; but unlike his, their experience teaches us to accept and prosper from the uneven messages of the affections.

Shakespeare is not a systematic moralist, but the mature Tragedies nonetheless say something important about the nature and scope of moral inquiry. Their effect is to complicate the realm of experience in which things may justifiably be termed good or bad. Through language and structure we are reminded repeatedly that while the actions which result from passion are moral issues, the passions themselves, as inexhaustible inner energies, are, like birth and death, part of the common denominator; that the passions are among the intrinsic motives of life and as such are immune to ethical praise or blame. In mature Shakespear-ean tragedy, the moral world is not the central world, but rather the complex extrusion from an inner furnace of power. Goodness and badness exist in vivid profusion; but the disquieting implication is that they spring from the same source.

This vision provokes a voyage of psychological discovery that is unprecedented in the language. Macbeth is "fair and foul." He is corrupt but intensely vital. His agonized aware-ness of the increasing gap which separates him from normal humanity is one of the most striking moral phenomena in Shakespeare. Antony's good and bad propensities spring from the same charged coil of energy. 'Bad' figures like Iago and Edmund are nonetheless active, creative, and mis-chievously amusing. Conversely, characters like Desdemona and Duncan, who embody traditional forms of goodness, do so with ambiguous, if not disastrous, results. They lack the initiative and alertness of the wicked, and consequently be-come the live bait for wickedness. The regenerative pro-tagonists, Edgar and Malcolm, achieve their rare position not through practicing Christian or Stoic virtue, but rather through developing a stark awareness of the extremes of human volition. Indeed, 'virtue' in these plays ceases to be a static entity and becomes instead a dynamic force, an im-pulse towards choice and action based on a sense of the communality of human experience and a knowledge of man's terrible versatility. Through such means as these, Shakespeare elaborates in the mature Tragedies a new psy-chological and moral cosmos. The revealed laws of this universe are contrary, but not chaotic or inscrutable. We are counselled, at first tentatively and then, in *Antony and Cleopatra*, quite forcefully, to accept and value these laws.

Othello

Written at about the same time, drawn from the same source and dealing with some of the same topics as *Measure for Measure*, *Othello* is nonetheless a wholly different dra-

matic entity. The difference lies less in the obvious require-
ments of genre than in the organization of meaning through
character, language, and action. In *Measure for Measure*, as
in *Hamlet*, these elements are used structurally to reduplicate
and universalize certain aspects of meaning. In *Othello*, on
the other hand, the same elements are used to encapsulate
wholly disjunctive aspects of meaning. Each of the major
characters—Othello, Iago, and Desdemona—establishes a radically distinct tonality, compelling us into his or her unique
reading of experience. Delineated early and developed in-
tegrally until the conclusion, these patterns of awareness are
never synthesized, never reconciled. Moreover—and herein
lies the remarkable effect of the play—each of these different worlds, so vastly separate from each other, is nonetheless deeply familiar to the audience. In this, his most aggressive play, Shakespeare anatomizes our sympathies, exposing
a native dissonance.

What makes this approach effective is, first of all, the
treatment of Iago. As an element of extreme villainy Iago is
that aspect of the play's meaning most likely to be expelled
from the audience's voluntary sympathies—to be treated, as
the devil is normally treated by medieval Christianity, as
a kind of foreign invader. Shakespeare strives to prevent
this conventional reaction in two ways. First, he gives Iago
a position in the play's structure which makes a certain
amount of intellectual sympathy with him impossible to
avoid. Iago guides us through the play. He confides in us;
through his good graces we are aware of what is happening
and why he is making it happen. He is the liaison between
action and audience, and the effect of this constantly renewed communication is that, merely because of our presence in a theater or in front of a book, a part of us enters
unwillingly into his conspiracy. We become accomplices before the fact, and our anticipation of the fatal event is an
agony not only of helpless indignation but also of incipient
guilt.

Shakespeare tilts the play's axis towards evil in another and equally subtle way. He makes Iago our intellectual compatriot. Iago is the only one of the three major characters who is <u>aware of the ironic complexities of human nature</u>. He is the only major character who indulges in that innately civilized activity, the jest. He not only conceives and directs the action, but also is the play's chorus, satirist, and fool—even its minstrel. He obviously delights in his own schemes and artfully ornaments them in their execution. In short, he thoroughly reflects, on one level, the values of the dramatist and the poet. We are bound to him, and disturbed by him, because in these ways his awareness is most germane to our own.

All this would be mere dramatic sleight-of-hand, suggestive but ultimately unenlightening, if something in the larger moral pattern of *Othello* did not justify our curious confraternity with the villain. With this possibility in mind, it seems logical to pay close attention to the other limit of the play's spectrum, Desdemona. Desdemona is clearly the character in the drama most to be sympathized with. Indeed, the least painful and most popular way of appreciating *Othello* is by fully indulging this sympathy, considering the play a powerful fiction about a monstrous wrong. But this interpretation, while emotionally quite valid, does not do justice to the ironic resonances of Shakespeare's art. Just as Iago's wickedness is given ambiguous overtones by his language and position in the play's structure, Desdemona's virtue is complicated by its expression and context. The effect is one of subtle and disquieting balance. While Iago insidiously attracts our sympathy, Desdemona at times seems to repel it.

This is not to deny her immensely powerful impact. No character in secular literature is more grossly wronged than Desdemona, and no one appeals more strongly to our sense of outrage. There is a wronged child in all of us, heard from time to time, helplessly crying redress for mischiefs manifold. Desdemona evokes this voice of the spirit and prolongs its outcry painfully. Moreover, Desdemona is not just dreadfully abused; she is also intensely virtuous. Her virtue is the whiteness against which Iago's slander and Othello's brutality shimmer in black. Benevolence, innocence, chastity, and meekness unite to give her character an almost religious tone of purity. This combination of extreme outrage and extreme virtue is almost irresistibly compelling. It all but transcends our sense of justice and injustice, summoning up the power of martyrdom.

perhaps a mirror?

Yet it is for this very reason, if for none other, that Desdemona's character should receive careful scrutiny. Few forms of art or argument are as powerful, or as potentially misleading, as those which appeal to inviolable cultural sympathies. Often enough, the function of truly enlightening art (for example, Plato's) is to evoke these sympathies in contexts which perplex and qualify them. With this in mind, we may ask an apparently ridiculous question. Is Desdemona really virtuous? If so, then by whose standards?

The language in which Desdemona is characterized by others or describes herself is significant not only dramatically but in terms of its intellectual context. To Othello, she is a "pearl," a "heavenly sight" (V.ii.347, 278); to Iago's wife Emilia, she is "heavenly true," "the sweetest innocent/ That ere did lift up eye" (V.ii.135, 199–200). These Christian epithets are hallmarks of her character. Her virtue is of a traditional saintliness—a negativity towards sin so impenetrable that she cannot imagine sinful acts or verbalize sinful ideas. Speaking of adultery, she asks her friend Emilia if

> . . . there be women do abuse their husbands
> In such gross kind?
> *Emil.*   There be some such, no question.
> *Des.* Wouldst thou do such a deed for all the world?
> *Emil.* Why, would not you?
> *Des.*   No, by this heavenly light!
>   (IV.iii.62–65)

To Iago, Desdemona tenders assurances of her own fidelity in language that is even more psychologically revealing:

> If e'er my will did trespass 'gainst his love,
> Either in discourse of thought or actual deed,
> Or that mine eyes, mine ears, or any sense
> Delighted them [in] any other form; . . .
> Comfort forswear me!
>
> I cannot say "whore."
> It does abhor me now I speak the word;
> To do the act that might the addition earn,
> Not the world's mass of vanity could make me.
> (IV.ii.152–155, 159, 161–164)

Desdemona's appeal to heaven is telling; her claim that she has avoided infidelity, not only in deed but in "discourse" and "sense," parallels Christ's grave strictures against sensuality in Matt. 18:9: "If thine eye offend thee, pluck it out and cast it from thee: . . . " Her ironically self-contradictory statement that she cannot pronounce the word "whore" aspires to the absolute virtue of the saints and martyrs. Desdemona's virtue clearly stems from the medieval idea of female goodness as innocence, chastity, and fidelity. Like Chaucer's Constance or Griselda, she is a Christian heroine whose virtue lies in her imperviousness to evil—to temptation from without or passion from within.

Conversely, Desdemona's character is a testament *against* what we know as the Renaissance idea of active virtue. Othello's faithful wife would have been anathema either to Castiglione or to the line of eminent English poets who challenged the ethical validity of innocence. Castiglione's earlier-quoted remark that the innocent were not truly good but rather "as bad as they know how to be" could hardly find a more appropriate target than Othello's spotless wife; nor could Sidney's comment, made through the counselor Philanax, that innocence ("rude simplicitie") is dangerous because it can be "easily changed, or easily deceived."[2]

Much the same sentiment informs the action of Book III of Spenser's *Faerie Queene*, where Florimell, the passive heroine who merely shuns evil, is condemned to run a gamut of would-be rapists; while Britomart, the armed heroine who faces evil and battles with it, is victorious and clearly superior. Shakespeare seems to address the same sort of virtue when, in Sonnet 94, he alludes to those that "have pow'r to hurt but will do none"; and Milton, who brings this moral doctrine to a head in the *Areopagitica*, dismisses spotless innocence out of hand; he characterizes ignorance of evil as superficial goodness:

> Assuredly we bring not innocence into the world, we bring impurity much rather; that which purifies us is trial, and trial is by what is contrary. The virtue therefore which is but a youngling in the contemplation of evil, and knows not the utmost that vice promises to her followers, and rejects it, is but a blank virtue, not a pure; her whiteness is but an excremental whiteness; . . .[3]

Can moral standards of this sort be fairly applied to the experience of *Othello*? Certainly, as a line of argument popular among leading English Protestants, these ideas were available to Shakespeare and his contemporaries. The play *Othello* at times suggests a similar view. Desdemona's virtue, we should remember, is oblivious or "blank" not only to the female libido but also to Othello's incipient brutality and Iago's cancerous evil. Iago, who has himself distinguished between knowledgeable virtue and mere innocence (in II.i.151 he praises the woman who "Fled from her wish, and yet said, Now I may"), recognizes the trusting goodness of Othello and Desdemona as the perfect breeding-ground for his own wickedness:

> [Of Othello:]
> The Moor is of a free and open nature,
> That thinks men honest that but seem to be so,
> And will as tenderly be led by th' nose
> As asses are.
>
> (I.iii.399–402)

[Of Desdemona:]
So will I turn her virtue into pitch,
And out of her own goodness make the net
That shall enmesh them all.
                    (II.iii.360–362)

Emilia undercuts Desdemona's intimations of spotlessness
with an irony which suggests that her mistress' innocence of
evil is also an ignorance of the world:

Dost thou in conscience think—tell me, Emilia—
That there be women do abuse their husbands
In such gross kind?
Emil.   There be some such, no question.
Des. I do not think there is any such woman.

Emil. Yes, a dozen; . . .
                    (IV.iii.61–63, 83–84)

Emilia goes on to deliver a spirited attack on the sexual
double standard which, though it runs directly counter to
Desdemona's sentiments, nonetheless carries impressive
Renaissance credentials: similar arguments have been presented sympathetically by Castiglione himself.[4] Ironies of
this sort do little to qualify the grace and sweetness of Desdemona's character. Nonetheless they clearly outline her
limited awareness against the background of a flawed but
vivid moral reality.

The pattern of words and ideas which thus complicates
our response to Desdemona is reinforced by her dramatic
presence. The physical phenomenon of theater sets up an
unspoken aristocracy of roles in which, by their mere vol-
ume and liveliness, servants can overshadow their masters,
and devils can command more respect than saints. On this
level, Desdemona frustrates and disappoints us more than
the necessities of plot would seem to dictate. Her passivity
stands in sharp contrast not only to Iago, who is an imp of
alertness and activity, but also to the whole dramatic fabric.

In a play of constant activity—affirmations, debates, plots, passions, storms, and skirmishes—Desdemona is (except for her ill-advised defense of Cassio) significantly impoverished of deeds. In terms of stage awareness, moreover, she 'knows' less than almost any other major character in Shakespeare. Not only is she ignorant of what, for tragic purposes, she cannot know; she also shows an annoying lack of awareness of things which anyone ought to know. Othello's near-frenzy about the lost handkerchief, prolonged over sixty-five lines, leaves her totally confused (but not the sensible Emilia, who asks, "Is not this man jealous?" III.iv.99). Seeing her husband strangely overwrought, Desdemona quite insensitively continues to press him about Cassio (III. iv.86–97). Othello's pathological jealousy, obvious here and in IV.i, where he calls her devil and strikes her, is not apparent to Desdemona until he accuses her explicitly in IV.ii. These lapses may be laid to Desdemona's inexperience or the unexpected nature of Othello's rage. Nonetheless they result in a radical and potentially irritating disparity of awareness between character and audience. Her dramatic inertness has thematic overtones. It is cognate with the passive, medieval virtue she defends to Emilia. It is echoed even in the awful action of the final scene where, still ignorant of what is going on, she is isolated, enveloped, and snuffed out. Her stage presence reiterates and fulfills the ironic implications of her cloistered virtue.

I use the word "ironic" here in its most serious and disturbing sense. As Freud has reminded us, there are essential ironies in our own mentality, responses that are both profound and contradictory. Desdemona's powerful appeal to our sense of wronged innocence touches on these areas of ambivalence. As civilized creatures we wish to protect the weak; as human beings we identify with their suffering. Yet there are instincts which, in spite of these wishes, or indeed because of them, prod us to do exactly the opposite. Nothing is quite so dear as innocence; but, over a period of time, nothing can be so uniquely annoying. Like all passive and helpless creatures, Desdemona sharpens the impulse to aggression in others. Her trust is the sweet air nourishing Iago's plot; and her prim righteousness more than once exacerbates Othello's rage. Just as, in *Measure for Measure,* Isabella's ostentatious chastity is the catalyst for Angelo's lust, Desdemona's virtue is the lure to mischief. I have suggested above that, because of Iago's position as confidant and chorus, we as audience become, to some unavoidable extent, accomplices in his unholy project. Perhaps also we—or at least the sinners among us—share some of the malevolence and frustrated anger which Desdemona's character evokes onstage. This ambivalent response would explain, to some extent, the remarkable power and intimacy of the play *Othello*.

Desdemona, we must conclude, is not Shakespeare's idea of a virtuous woman. She is rather Othello's idea—the type of lamblike femininity that his assertive but insecure maleness would demand. The side of us that identifies with Desdemona, however fully and instinctively, is not necessarily our healthiest side. It is our 'good' side, the element within us that has been taught, by millenia of familial, social, and religious influences, to seek refuge and stability in moral abstractions. Shakespeare has taken this intense but partial psychological element and expressed it in a character who is, in the same way, both compelling and incomplete. He has placed her, moreover, in a dramatic context which profoundly embodies the discordant complexity of a total human spirit. *Othello* is, on one important level, a kind of psychological allegory, an aesthetic structure in which individual aspects of a single mentality are infused with character and posed dynamically against each other. It is a play in which the contrariety or psychological discord so frequently referred to and exemplified in the Problem Comedies becomes the metaphysical basis of the tragic structure.

Understanding this is the key to the mystery of Iago. We

need not speak of motive or lack of motive in Iago.[5] He is less a motivated being than he is a motive itself. His incomplete intensity parallels and reflects Desdemona's. She appeals to heaven, he to a "Divinity of Hell"; she is "Excellent wretch," he "Spartan dog"; she is a "pearl," he a "precious villain."[6] The two characters are pure opposites; but the verbal and dramatic contexts hint at a mutual necessity. The combination of opposition and balance holds a radical message. We are artfully compelled to identify with Iago so that we may become aware that he, like Desdemona, is a universal psychological presence. If Desdemona embodies the lure and agony of an absolute morality, Iago embodies the natural result of this civilizing influence, the rude will chafing against moral law. He suggests the repressed anger we feel at being good, the revenge our irrational natures take for the imposition of rational morality. To supply this element with a 'motive' or rational purpose would be to distort its essence grossly. Goodness is its reason for being. In a psychological as well as aesthetic sense, Desdemona engenders Iago. His evil takes its vitality from her goodness and cannot survive long without it.

Othello is the point of contact between these two interdependent extremes. This is true not only in the obvious dramatic sense, but also in the sense that his psychology includes both the civilized propensity for absolute ideals and the savage recalcitrance against these social constructs. Shakespeare deftly and economically makes this internal division plain. Othello is a proven leader whose first and final speeches boast of service to the state. He is a seeming miracle of self-control who twice breaks up violent altercations, and who, according to Iago, once watched impassively as in battle a cannon, "from his very arm / Puff'd his own brother" (III.iv.136–137). He prizes reason and looks down on sexual passion, asserting that he will not allow the "toys" of Cupid to blind the "speculative and offic'd instruments" of his brain (I.iii.270). But Othello is also a Moor among Venetians. In Shakespeare's hands his hero's blackness and exotic origin are less marks of social isolation than birth-marks of nature, symbolizing the untranslatable energy which waits and frets under civilized rule. As the play's action moves from Christian West to heathen East, and as the Moor's allegiance swings from his angelic wife to his base lieutenant, he says goodbye to his civil "occupation" (III.iii.357) and lapses into savagery. Significantly, the victim of his fury is the figure who quintessentially represents the abstract order and purity of the *ethos* he has abandoned.

The extent and suddenness of Othello's fall is a classic topic of debate. Can so abrupt a reversal of polarities be credible? It *can*, we may conjecture, precisely because Othello's character is founded so exclusively upon polarities—radical extremes isolated from a central reality that would give them pertinence and stability. His early attitude towards his inner energies is not harmonious, but partakes rather of the uneasy relationship that exists between jailer and prisoner:

> No, when light-wing'd toys
> Of feather'd Cupid seel with wanton dullness
> My speculative and offic'd instruments,
> That my disports corrupt and taint my business,
> Let housewives make a skillet of my helm,
> And all indign and base adversities
> Make head against my estimation!
> (I.iii.268–274)

Note the connection drawn between thought and society ("speculative and offic'd"), the unnecessarily negative evaluation of conjugal sexuality ("corrupt and taint"), the emphasis on "helm," "head". Othello aspires not to a balance between reason and emotion but rather to a hegemony of those faculties which distinguish the civil from the animal.

Psychological enterprises of this sort are common in Shakespeare. The heroes of *Love's Labour's Lost* undertake a retreat from "the huge army of the world's desires" (*Love's*

Labour's Lost, I.i.10). Henry V boasts that his passions are as subject as "our wretches fett'red in our prisons" (*Henry V*, I.ii.241–243). Hamlet, Ulysses, and the *persona* of the Sonnets speak of the passions in various tonalities of disapproval and disgust. In *Measure for Measure*, both Angelo and the Duke set themselves up as heroes of temperance. The implications of this absolutism are usually ambiguous or ironic. As we have seen, the Duke's conversion from a sterilized morality to an apparent acceptance of his own imperfect humanity shows signs of being a Shakespearean manifesto. In *Othello*, the same lesson is taught negatively, violently, and with almost mythic force. With Othello as with Angelo, the suppression of passion seems to have a causal relationship to the building of intolerable inner pressures. Very naturally, the inevitable release of these pressures results in what seems a polar reversal of attitudes. This would explain why Othello is, indeed,

> . . . one not easily jealous, but being wrought,
> Perplex'd in the extreme.
> (V.ii.345–346)

Shakespeare's treatment of this failing, and of the psychological propensities which accompany it, is organic and comprehensive. Throughout the play, Othello's language suggests again and again the compulsive polarization of experience. Even in prosperity, he ties his confidence to absolutes and dares the world to disappoint him:

> [Greeting Desdemona:] O my soul's joy!
> If after every tempest come such calms,
> May the winds blow till they have waken'd death!
>
> . . . If it were now to die,
> 'Twere now to be most happy; for I fear
> My soul hath her content so absolute
> That not another comfort like to this
> Succeeds in unknown fate.
> (II.i.184–186, 189–193)

He figuratively bases his own hopes of grace and the whole
order of Creation on the power of his love:

> Excellent wretch! Perdition catch my soul
> But I do love thee! and when I love thee not
> Chaos is come again.
>
> (III.iii.90–92)

Overcome by jealousy, he characteristically expresses his
feelings in terms of juxtaposed but mutually annulling
realities:

> But there, where I have garner'd up my heart,
> Where I must either live or bear no life;
> The fountain from the which my current runs
> Or else dries up: to be discarded thence!
> Or keep it as a cestern for foul toads
> To knot and gender in! Turn thy complexion there,
> Patience, thou young and rose-lipp'd cherubin—
> Ay, here look grim as hell!
>
> (IV.ii.57–64; and also see IV.ii.66–69, III.iii.
> 270–273, 345–347, etc.)

This fever of polarities is nothing strange or new. It is no
more than the wreckage of Othello's earlier world—a fragile
confidence propped up by absolute formulations. His furi-
ous antitheses do not suggest the loss of control so much as
the fact that control has never fully existed. The decline
from fervent absolutism to hopeless contrariety is consistently manifest in his later speeches to Desdemona. After
III.iii his picture of her is never a human one. She must be
angel, or devil, or both:

> Come, swear it, damn thyself,
> Lest being like one of heaven, the devils themselves
> Should fear to seize thee . . .

> Devil . . .

> O devil, devil!

> Cold, cold, my girl?
> Even like thy chastity. O cursed, cursed slave!
> Whip me, ye devils,
> From the possession of this heavenly sight!
>
> (IV.ii.35–37, IV.i.240, 244, V.ii.275–278)

Even Desdemona's living flesh (V.ii.4–5) becomes for Othello an image of absolute purity, and her breath is like balm. The agonizing paradox, that this ethereal body is also apparently a "cestern" of lust, will give way to an even more unbearable contrariety: that Othello has righteously murdered an angelic wife.

As upon some machine of torture, Othello's consciousness is tied to and stretched between receding extremes of feeling. This holds through the very end, the suicide:

> [Othello:] And say besides, that in Aleppo once,
> Where a malignant and a turban'd Turk
> Beat a Venetian and traduc'd the state,
> I took by th' throat the circumcised dog,
> And smote him—thus. [He stabs himself.]

In this context the remembered image is both mad and precise. Othello the Christian citizen, the rational Venetian, is executing the other Othello, the passionate, heathen renegade. The fatal psychological polarity, momentarily almost a physical presence, becomes the active image of the tragic conclusion.

Pathological idealism—the faith that builds upon absolutes and founders with them—is a diagnosis that can apply to more than one of Shakespeare's tragic heroes. What makes *Othello* uniquely disturbing, however, is that the play's whole structure tends to realize rather than contradict this radical attitude towards experience. Iago is indeed a kind of devil; Desdemona personifies angelic purity; the drama resounds, on a larger scale, with the same appalling dissonances which afflict its hero. Thus, far from being allowed to judge Othello objectively, we are lured into his world and compelled to appreciate intensely the polarities which torment him. This emotional experience is also one which teaches, compelling us to realize how much, in the larger theater of life, such opposites depend upon and engender each other. The unstable polarities of Othello's awareness, the disturbing symmetries that link Desdemona and Iago, remind us of the yoked contraries that operate in all civilized interaction: overassertiveness and inner insecurity, righteousness and loathing, excessive rationality and misdirected passion, innocence and corruption. The veneration for moral absolutes emerges as a destructive process in which extremes lead to their own opposites and rigidity degenerates into chaos. This is, of course, the same moral "message" as that of *Measure for Measure*; but the lucid intellectuality of the Duke of Vienna would look pale in a world of *Othello*'s intensity. The mature Tragedies do not inquire into experience; they recreate it. In *Othello* we are not asked to solve the Problem but rather forced to live it out.

King Lear

King Lear (1605) marks a turning-point in the development of Shakespeare's thematic concerns. The works of the five previous years—*Hamlet*, the Problem Comedies, and *Othello*—are characterized by their recurrent and sometimes almost exclusive emphasis on problems of sexuality: appetite, jealousy, and guilt. *Othello* brings this period to a close, almost as though the play's convulsive energy and completeness of expression were the breakthrough to a broader and less tormented view of experience. Sexuality is by no means ignored in *King Lear*, *Macbeth*, and *Anthony and Cleopatra*; it simply loses its status as a tyrannizing dilemma, and is relegated to a position in a significantly more comprehensive treatment of the passions. The passions, moreover, are no longer related primarily to disease and chaos but rather become dynamic aspects of the whole moral spectrum, as conducive to wonder as they are to fear. Coherent with this newly generous view of experience are the plays' massive action, expansive language, and cosmic scope. These mature dramas unveil a tragic world, not so much because they dwell upon sadness, as because only the tragic mode will accommodate their unqualified energy of character and breadth of theme.

This energy and expressiveness in no way imply the denial of form. *King Lear*, Shakespeare's most tumultuous tragedy, is also one of his most intricately contrived. Passionate or otherwise intense experience is built upon a structure of characterizations which is remarkable for its symmetry. This massive construct, set in motion by Lear's abdication, describes with almost astronomical precision a single and complete revolution in time. Language and ideas reiterate themselves with almost musical regularity. These formal intricacies constitute the play's substructure, elegantly submerged beneath compelling dramatic action. They do not hinder *King Lear*'s energy, but rather are, like the skeleton of an organism, the only means by which that energy may be held and conveyed.

Before conjecturing on the meaning of *King Lear* or upon its intellectual backgrounds, we must understand its structural basis as completely and accurately as we can. First of all, its characterizations develop a pattern of interconnecting parallels and oppositions. No major figure except the Fool is without another character who is either his correlative or his foil, and several have both. Shakespeare uses a second source[7] to parallel the conflicts inherent in Lear's female offspring with those of Gloucester's male family. Gloucester's course shadows Lear's, and Gloucester's blindness— as a paradoxical source of wisdom—is used to the same effect as Lear's madness. Edgar's feigned madness reflects Lear's genuine madness. Kent initially parallels Cordelia and France as an exponent of unadorned virtue; later he parallels Edgar as a loyal friend in disguise. Edmund's political course and the vision which underlies it parallel those of Goneril and Regan.

Contraries are just as numerous and emphatic. The extreme moral oppositions between Cordelia and her sisters, and between Edgar and Edmund, are set up very clearly at the beginning and developed coherently throughout. The King of France, who chooses to marry Cordelia because of her beauty and virtue alone, contrasts sharply with the opportunistic Duke of Burgundy. An analogous contrast may be seen between Goneril and Regan's husbands, the decent Albany and the ruthless Cornwall. The moral opposition between Kent and Oswald—the loyal courtier and the serviceable henchman—is emphasized when they come to blows twice, and is alluded to specifically by Kent:

> No contraries hold more antipathy
> Than I and such a knave.
> (II.ii.87–88)

We have seen structures of this sort before. In *Hamlet* and the Problem Comedies, Shakespeare favors the use of parallels; *Othello*, on the other hand, is based on the interaction of opposites. We have also seen that in Shakespeare these structures are developed into a connotative language with characteristic expressive functions. Parallels universalize meaning. They can serve basically intellectual purposes (like the parallel between the Duke and Angelo in *Measure for Measure*) or they can (like the Fortinbras–Hamlet–Pyrrhus–Laertes structure) suggest mythic undercurrents of feeling. Their message, be it positive, tragic, or ironic, is that certain forms of experience are universal—that there are underlying patterns in life. They establish a functional idea of human nature, a doctrine whose profound effect has to do with its subtle, almost subliminal, mode of statement. Oppositions in Shakespeare hold an equally urgent and coherent message. They express irresolvable complexities of character and experience. Contrarieties like those between Venus and Adonis, Iago and Desdemona, and Caliban and Ariel are developed so intensely and suggestively as to mirror the chronic ambiguities of the human will. In *Othello* these principles are not only formulated in characterizations but integrated into the dynamics of the hero's psychology. The effect of structural contrariety, like the effect of parallels, can be both rational and mythic. Contraries can teach us something about our own divided sympathies. They can serve to express and thus ease the mute burden of our inner feelings.

The complementary interaction of both these structural languages is one of the keys to the immense power of *King Lear*. Shakespeare uses parallels and contraries, like the parallels and meridians of a map, to order and chart an otherwise hopeless wilderness of experience. In so doing, he establishes, perhaps more than in any other work, the complexity and the universality of the motives he describes. But parallels and oppositions are by no means the only elements of psychological geometry at work in the play. Shakespeare gives his pattern of characterizations a recognizable overall shape, and we must sketch this shape before studying its function in time.

Recurring verbally and structurally throughout the play is the idea of the circle. Gloucester and Lear initially buttress their notions of reality on astronomical and astrological principles. Gloucester believes in what Edmund calls "spherical predominance," and Lear swears by "the operation of the orbs" (I.ii.123, I.i.111). Later, when his view of divine order has been demolished, Lear calls on the storm to, "Strike flat the thick rotundity of the world!" (III.ii.7). The Fool calls Lear, "an O without a figure" (I.iv.192–193), and later refers to him indirectly as, "a great wheel" running down a hill (II.iv.72). Lear himself brings up the idea of the wheel memorably and mysteriously in a late speech to Cordelia:

> You do me wrong to take me out o' th' grave;
> Thou art a soul in bliss, but I am bound
> Upon a wheel of fire, that mine own tears
> Do scald like molten lead.
>   (IV.vii.44–47)

And near the play's conclusion, the dying Edmund characterizes his own history in terms of a wheel in motion: "The

wheel is come full circle; I am here" (V.iii.175). These are
not just powerful metaphors; they have much to do with
the moral and temporal structures on which the play is built.
Lear's "wheel of fire," first of all, is a telling figuration of
the oppositions and correlations which give the play its
moral intensity. Since Lear and his companion figures,
Gloucester and the Fool, are centrally affected by the actions of all the other major characters, who are themselves
arranged as opposites, a circle is the *schema* that will most
adequately describe the total pattern (see accompanying
chart). The antagonisms between the figures at diametric
points on the circle all directly relate to Lear himself. But
curiously he and his party are isolated from the sources of
action. He, Gloucester, and the Fool are the only major
figures who have no opposite numbers. Analogously, after
Act I, none of them has a causal role in the dynamics of the
plot. Just like a prisoner on a wheel, Lear is both the center
and the sufferer.

The play's circularity is not only ethical but also temporal. As Edmund quite simply puts it, the wheel turns. It
describes one massive revolution between the beginning and
the end of *King Lear*. The play begins with Lear's conferral
of English rule upon Goneril and Regan. It proceeds through
a period of doubtful and divided rule which leads up to the
battle near Dover and the chaotic rivalry between the two
sisters. It concludes with Albany's conferral of rule upon
Kent and Edgar. On the political level, then, *King Lear* turns
a circle, moving with massive credibility from order to disorder to order. This circle of political change is reiterated
by the fortunes of the warring parties. Lear and his adherents (the Fool, Cordelia, Kent, Gloucester, and Edgar) begin
at the height of prosperity. They are forced into extremes
of agony and humiliation; but Edgar and Kent survive to become, in the end, custodians of the new order. Conversely,
the leaders of the anti-Lear party (Goneril, Regan, and Edmund) begin the play in subordinate or unexalted positions.
The sisters are less cherished than Cordelia,[8] and Edmund as

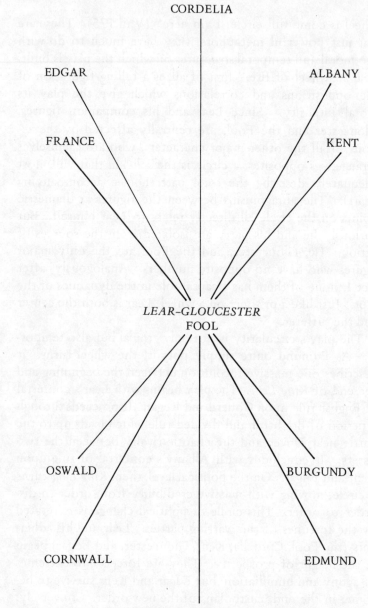

CORDELIA

EDGAR   ALBANY

FRANCE   KENT

LEAR–GLOUCESTER
FOOL

OSWALD   BURGUNDY

CORNWALL   EDMUND

GONERIL AND REGAN

a bastard is seen as inferior to Edgar. Through rhetorical initiative and brutal force, they rise to full power in the state. But they are ultimately defamed, destroyed, and even ignored.[9] In terms of power and prosperity, then, each party achieves the opposite of what it has been, and then turns back towards its beginnings with a motion as steady and irresistible as the revolution of a planet.

This revolution bears surface resemblances to the medieval Wheel of Fortune; but, in fact, its workings are very much more complicated. What drives the wheel on its course is not some divine, external, or mechanical force, but rather the heated interaction of the wheel's own polarities. These motive forces, sometimes sketched and sometimes realistically fleshed out, include the massive political conflict between Cordelia and her sisters, the dissension between Albany and Cornwall, and the strife between Edgar and Edmund. Circularity seems to function, like a demonstrable law of nature, in the phenomenon of social upheaval itself; and this implied doctrine of history is given further credibility by the fact that, in several additional instances, opposites seem to attract, and pairs repel each other. Lear's initial effort to achieve security and ease brings rampant disorder; while, conversely, he and other characters are later forced to admit that disorder and adversity can have beneficial effects.[10] The 'bad' Edmund, when first compared with his 'good' half-brother, is prepossessingly lively and witty; while 'good' qualities, like Cordelia's uncompromising honesty, Kent's integrity, Edgar's trust, and Albany's milky kindness, are initially seen as contributing to bad results. The philosophy of opportunism and license, proclaimed doctrinally by Edmund and realized in his use of sexual politics with both Goneril and Regan, rebounds negatively against itself, becoming the entropy which destroys the whole party. Extreme attitudes, be they good or bad, turn destructively upon themselves, creating a world which revolves by contrariety, and finds rebirth in its own decomposition.

The circular and paradoxical motion of time in *King Lear* is worked out in ways which are both ample and specific. It is most evident in the complex but intensely meaningful relationship between Edgar and Edmund. Here Shakespeare repeatedly uses lines of opposition and parallel to develop, more fully than ever before, a process of spiritual anguish and growth. The obvious polarity between the two brothers is clear almost from the beginning. In three early soliloquies (I.ii.1–22, 118–137, 179–184), Edmund alludes to his own alleged "baseness"—his illegitimacy and lack of preferment. He espouses a libertarian philosophy of nature and relates himself proudly to aspects of animal life and images of sexual vigor ("lusty stealth of nature," "fierce quality," "goatish disposition," "rough and lecherous"). He trusts in his own strength and imagination ("composition" and "invention") for a speedy rise ("I grow, I prosper"). Edgar, as Edmund tells us, is quite the opposite. He is "noble"—both legitimate and prosperous; he is connected not with nature but with the laws of society ("curiosity of nations"). He lacks natural energy (Edmund relates him to a "tribe of fops"), and his conventional morality makes him an easy mark for Edmund's deceits ("whose nature is so far from doing harms/That he suspects none"). To make the polarity complete, Edmund sets out to prove that, as he rises, his opposite must fall.

The events which follow, however, ironically complicate this apparently straightforward opposition of character. Edmund, first of all, slanders Edgar by ascribing to him a letter which endorses Edmund's own brand of libertarianism:

> "This policy and reverence of age makes the world
> bitter to the best of our times; keeps our fortunes from
> us till our oldness cannot relish them. I begin to find
> an idle and fond bondage in the oppression of aged tyranny,
> who sways, not as it hath power, but as it is suffer'd."
> (I.ii.46–51)

The letter refers slightingly to law and convention, the same "plague of custom" and "curiosity of nations" which Edmund has just quite frankly characterized as false (I.ii.3–4). Having laid his own treasons on the head of his half-brother, Edmund conversely adopts Edgar's tone of innocence in discussing the matter with his father:

> *Glou.* Know you the character to be your brother's?
> *Edm.* If the matter were good, my lord, I durst swear it were his; but in respect of that, I would fain it were not.
>   (I.ii.62–65)

This reversal of roles and values has ironic elegance and helps (as we will later see) to establish an important political tonality. But there is also a larger design which, unbeknownst to either half-brother, develops toward a closed circle of reversed modalities. Accused and hunted, Edgar seeks a new identity ("Edgar I nothing am" II.iii.21). He adopts the disguise of Tom o' Bedlam—a figure whom Edmund has specifically (though out of Edgar's earshot) related to himself (I.ii.135–137). He associates himself, like Edmund, with baseness and beasts:

>   Whiles I may scape
> I will preserve myself, and am bethought
> To take the *basest* and most poorest shape
> That ever penury, in contempt of man,
> Brought near to *beast*.
>   (II.iii.5–9. My italics.)

Later, when he appears on the heath, Edgar avows an identity whose similarity to Edmund's character is extraordinary:

> *Lear.* What hast thou been?
> *Edg.* A servingman! proud in heart and mind; that curl'd my hair; wore gloves in my cap; serv'd the lust of my mistress' heart, and did the act of darkness with her; swore as many oaths as I spake words, and broke them in the sweet face of heaven: one that slept in the contriving of lust, and wak'd to do it. Wine lov'd I [deeply], dice dearly; and in woman out-paramour'd the Turk. False of heart, light of ear, bloody of hand; hog in sloth, fox in stealth, wolf in greediness, dog in madness, lion in prey.
>   (III.iv.84–94)

The uncanny juxtaposition of opposites continues until the end. Disguised, Edgar puts his father through an imaginary death, while Edmund seeks his father's death in fact (IV.vi. 1–76, IV.v.11–14). Just as Edmund has used a letter to destroy his half-brother at the beginning of the play, Edgar uses a letter to topple Edmund at the end (V.i.40–47, V.iii. 108–114). The wronged Edgar, once abased, is victorious; the "base" Edmund is brought low again. The revolution of words, values, and events is complete. When Shakespeare makes the dying Edmund announce that "The wheel is come full circle," he is drawing our attention to a mysteriously symmetrical and organic function of change.

What does this radical concept of time, action, and identity mean? We must remember, first of all, that Edgar's experience throughout the play suggests a cycle of learning and growth. Like a very recent parallel, the Duke in *Measure for Measure*, he leaves a basically passive role and is drawn by dramatic necessity towards knowledge, virtuous action, and ultimate success. Both characters take up disguises, and both achieve self-awareness through a sympathetic understanding of the experience of other characters. Edgar refers to this hard-won knowledge when, in one of his disguises, he characterizes himself as

> A most poor man, made tame to fortune's blows,
> Who, by the art of known and feeling sorrows,
> Am pregnant to good pity.
> (IV.vi.221–223; and also see III.vi.102–110)

For Edgar, virtue springs from suffering and an awareness of the sufferings of others. Figuratively speaking, he falls *into* grace. But active virtue depends on more than sympathy and pity. In *Measure for Measure*, the Duke's growing effectiveness as a ruler seems to depend on his growing awareness of baseness and badness as universal propensities of mankind. Edgar's overall experience suggests a development from helpless innocence to a virtue that is knowledgeable enough in the ways of vice to beat the vicious at their own

game. His "servingman" speech, and other nearby speeches
in which he portrays himself as a specimen of haunted villainy, reiterate this development on a psychological level.
His new ability to recognize evil, identify imaginatively with
it, and accept it as part of a universal burden of nature is
emblematic of the rise to active virtue and the achievement
of heroic stature.

The magnitude of Edgar's growth, and its thematic significance, are apparent during his final episodes with his
father (IV.i,vi). On the heath the blind Gloucester asks
Tom o' Bedlam to lead him to a Dover cliff, adding dismally
that he will need no leading thence (IV.i.73–78). Edgar
takes his father to the country near Dover. He gives him
a chilling description of an imaginary cliff. He carefully
supervises a mock-suicide. Recovering from his tiny fall, the
old man is amazed to find himself alive. Edgar's admitted
motives are spiritual and medicative ("Why I do trifle thus
with his despair / Is done to cure it" IV.vi.33–34). Telling
Gloucester that his survival is "a miracle," Edgar advises him,

> therefore, thou happy father,
> Think that the clearest gods, who make them honors
> Of men's impossibilities, have preserved thee.
> (IV.vi.72–74)

And Gloucester vows new fortitude:

> Henceforth I'll bear
> Affliction till it do cry out itself
> "Enough, enough," and die.
> (IV.vi.75–77)

Gloucester's imaginary suicide powerfully evokes the sense
of juxtaposed agony and renewal which characterizes *King
Lear* as a whole. The idea of the Fortunate Fall and the
overtones of miracle and conversion add a religious feeling
to the scene and underline the significance of Edgar's role.
By directing his father's death and rebirth, Edgar temporarily transcends the dreadful enthrallment of suffering and

vision which informs the play; he is allowed to become, like his own author, the bestower of suffering and vision. He is raised, in other words, to a position of godly art. This level of power and awareness, by far the most sophisticated achieved by any character in *King Lear*, is the organic consequence of Edgar's rise to strength and sympathy through the experience of suffering and baseness. The character who has been both man and beast is now seen briefly as god. The massive revolution of experience touches unerringly on the two extremes.

An equally sharp interaction of contraries operates on the play's political level. Here a classic element of change, announced and personified by Edmund, demolishes an obsolescent social order, but unwittingly provides the wherewithal for the development of a new and more vigorous order. To understand this dialectic at work, we should look again briefly at Edmund's early speeches, this time with emphasis on their philosophical and political significance.

Unlike Richard III, Claudius, or Iago, Edmund is not a villain who, by speaking much of right, wrong, good, or evil, acknowledges the moral significance of his actions. Rather he is an iconoclast who generally attacks the validity of social order ("curiosity of nations") in the name of what he considers to be a more dependable principle ("Thou, Nature, art my goddess"). He has no faith at all in political laws or moral abstractions. His criteria for active wisdom are sense perception (I.ii.6–9), animal energy (I.ii.12), imagination (I.ii.20), and the pragmatic rationality which condemns superstition and probes the weaknesses of fellow men (I.ii.118–123, 180–182). Implicit in his character throughout is the emphasis on individual will and the denial of common interests. Shakespeare is careful not to demean Edmund. To do so would be to repudiate the very considerable social and intellectual forces which this character represents. From the viewpoint of intellectual history, Edmund is a classic exponent of the mode of thought which W. R. Elton terms "relativistic skepticism" and Leo Strauss calls "vulgar conventionalism." This doctrine, whose earliest extant protagonists are Plato's Thrasymachus and Callicles, stipulates that all laws are conventional and unnatural, that there are no binding moral imperatives, and that life's chief *desiderata* are the power and pleasure of the individual.[11] Both as a philosophical thesis and as a general attitude towards experience, it exerted a significant influence on Renaissance thought and combined well with Machiavellian "realism" in supporting the cynicism and hedonism which lies at one end of the Renaissance moral spectrum.[12]

But Edmund's doctrine is not just a philosophical mode. It is an historically recurring frame of mind, whose manifestations are not limited to Greece and the Renaissance, and whose appearances in our own century are too numerous and obvious to require documentation. It is typical of stale cultures where values, no longer based on clear social necessity, have become hackneyed, formulaic, and abstract. Such cultures have lost touch with the urgent political experiences which are the bases of social order. They are characterized by governors whose only pressing goal is prolonged security; by ruling classes and educators who, taking stability for granted, busy themselves with pleasures, trifles, and fads; by parents whose childrearing consists of the inculcation of arbitrary moral constructs. Offering little or nothing that will excite or illuminate their young, these societies effectively spawn their own revilers. Edmund is an archetype of unenlightened change, an embodiment of the attitude which rejects society's unsupported assertions of value, and relies instead on what seems the only possible alternative, a norm of subjectivity and materialism. An activist who knows the abuses of order without ever having learned the roots of order, he is as much a product of his times as a reaction against them.

Shakespeare works out the causes and potential effects of Edmund's attitude in impressive detail. King Lear's initial actions—the mismanaged abdication, the patronization of Goneril and Regan, and the rejection of Cordelia and Kent—

all illuminate a society in which value has become so conventional as to be divorced from its sources in experience.
This factor alone gives credibility to the King's horrendous
errors. Lear persistently chooses by the appearance and not
the thing. He fondly believes that he can retain the honor
of kingship while giving up its power:

> Only we shall retain
> The name, and all th' addition to a king;
> The sway, revenue, execution of the rest,
> Beloved sons, be yours, . . .
> (I.i.135–138)

In dividing his realm, Lear denies the evidence of experience
(Cordelia has been his favorite daughter) and instead demands formalized assertions of his daughters' love for him.
Hearing these, he rejects Cordelia's indignant honesty and
chooses instead the stale formulations of rhetoric. His virtuous subjects, Cordelia and Kent, are unable to translate
their just claims into politically effective language. A parallel situation obtains in the second plot. In condemning Edgar, Gloucester relies on stylized expressions of good and evil
rather than on experience. Like Lear, Gloucester believes in
astrology; and in the context of *King Lear*, astrology is not
only a vulgar superstition ("an excellent foppery of the
world") but also an abdication from individual responsibility
(I.i.109–112, I.ii.103–133). To these manifold dismissals of
experience and responsibility may be added (on a symbolic
level) the King's abdication itself. In short, the world of
Act I shows all the symptoms of a "Problem Comedy" society.[13] It is a culture where conventions have drifted out
of touch with their real sources and where, analogously, language has inflated to the point where it is no longer able to
communicate emotion or describe experience effectively.

The clash which inevitably develops is one of 'fools and
knaves,' a conflict between the outworn and the unwashed.
The old order, so manifestly rat-eaten and devoid of moral
energy, cannot prolong itself. Conversely, the new order,
established with much gusto but without the slightest idea

of political cohesion, begins almost immediately to subside into chaos. Yet we watch with surprise as the disastrous interaction produces hopeful effects. The stormy heath becomes a school for damaged conservatives. Lear, Gloucester, Kent, and Edgar, deprived of the conventional props on which they have previously based their morality, weave new values out of their own misery and the coarseness of perceived phenomena. They regain touch with the few and awful certainties of life—with the sense of shared danger and suffering which lies at the root of the political impulse, with the weakness, loneliness, and depravity which haunt social order even during periods of supposed greatness and security. Psychologically, "the art of known and feeling sorrows" (as Edgar puts it) transforms both Lear and Gloucester:

> [Lear:]   Take physic, pomp,
> Expose thyself to feel what wretches feel,
> That thou mayst shake the superflux to them,
> And show the heavens more just.
>   (III.iv.33–36)
>
> [Gloucester:] Let the superfluous and lust-dieted man,
> That slaves your ordinance, that will not see
> Because he does not feel, feel your pow'r quickly;
> So distribution should undo excess,
> And each man have enough.
>   (IV.i.67–71)

Politically, the wounded party revives, now with a positive basis for unity. The surviving members, Edgar and Kent, become custodians of the new state. The clash between fools and knaves, between unheeding convention and unheeding subjectivity, has redeemed politics, uncovering the basis for renewed individual awareness and social strength. The dialectic implies a refutation of Edmund's bold attack on laws and values. Social order is shown to have a source in nature. The source is not available to most people at most times, but becomes apparent at moments of desperate stress. It is not divine ordinance or abstract value. It is shared suffering.

Suffering is, in a larger sense, the dominant psychological motive of *King Lear*. Not only does the play concern itself with suffering as a source of wisdom and fellowship; it looks beyond this to areas of suffering which afford neither vision nor hope: to madness, mute endurance, and untranslatable grief. The play's final lines touch upon these further reaches of emotion:

> The oldest hath borne most; we that are young
> Shall never see so much, nor live so long.[14]

Here the verbs, "to bear," "to see" and "to live," carry a message that has already been stated and repeated within the play:[15] that the experience of *King Lear* exposes a human reality so appalling as to make mere endurance into a heroic virtue. This reality, suggested at large by the play's structure, is unforgettably realized in the character of Lear himself. Like the victim stretched on the wheel of fire, Lear is the center of the play's dialectic, the point of friction amidst all its violent oppositions. As such he is the only figure who fully suffers and fully expresses the intensity of the revolution that is at work. Outside him rage the storm and the extreme moral and political conflicts which disjoint the state. Inside him rage equally destructive contrarieties: between his imagined dignity and his brutal treatment, between pledges of love and active hatred, between superfluous riches and houseless poverty, and between the gaudy trappings of civilization and the pathetic animals who wear them. These manifest and insistent paradoxes of form and matter, being and time, drive him insane. Like Othello's, his rage springs from and dwells upon the simultaneous assertion of polar contraries. But while Othello's rage is the fantasy of a deluded intelligence, Lear's madness is a disordered recognition of truth. His vision is insane, not because it is unrealistic, but because it touches on areas of truth so extreme as to have no apparent relationship to each other or to any unifying reality. Stunned by the paradoxes themselves, Lear is pathologically blind to the order which creates and comprehends them: the organic function of time as conflict and revolution whose existence is the chief philosophical motive of the play. Indeed, the awful fact of contrariety catches and holds him against the current of time, confining him within a single moment of prolonged and fruitless recognition.

This disastrous coincidence of awareness and blindness is perhaps the strongest experience of the play. It evokes and sustains in us a uniquely disquieting emotion: the shock we feel when we must reject our own beliefs, and in particular the dizzying realization that things we thought stable have basically and irrevocably changed. More generally, it reminds us that the problem of appearance and reality is inseparable from the phenomenon of time; and that one of the chief deterrents of man's historical effort to order his existence has been his recurrent inability to allow for the silent pulse of growth and decay. Lear's character is a passionate manifesto against time. From his first speeches, where he abdicates responsibility and clings to the tenets of an outworn order, to his dying assertion that Cordelia is still alive, he suggests man's terrified reluctance to weigh and measure by the fourth dimension.[16] Thus, Lear provides, in the overall experience, the necessary and tragic context for the elements of change and growth which are implicit in the characters of Edmund and Edgar. Lear's recalcitrance to change is as natural and universal as change itself; indeed, as we have seen, it is one of the major causes of change. Significantly, his outcry against change, and the destructive revolution which silences this outcry, end at the same moment.[17]

Macbeth

The extent to which *Macbeth* (1606) derives its power from the interaction of contraries has already been the subject of modern scholarship. In particular, two essays which appear in vol. 19 of *Shakespeare Survey* tell us something about the mechanics of this technique and suggest one of its intellectual backgrounds. In "Antithesis in *Macbeth*," G. I. Duthie shows how Shakespeare uses antithetical verbal structures to give the play its ominous resonance. In "Why Was Duncan's Blood Golden?" W. A. Murray relates important patterns of images in *Macbeth* to similar patterns in Paracelsian thought.[18] Read together, these essays provide an excellent starting-point for a more general examination of contrariety in *Macbeth*.

Duthie expands on Kenneth Muir's earlier remark that the style of *Macbeth* "consists of multitudinous antitheses."[19] These antitheses, Duthie shows, can be divided into two major forms: "expanded oxymoron," in which two contraries are seen as coexisting within a single experience, and "inversion," in which a thing is seen as turning into its contrary. As expanded oxymoron, he cites a number of the many paradoxical constructions which all but saturate key passages of the play:

> On his first appearance in the play (I.iii.38) Macbeth says, "So foul and fair a day I have not seen" . . . A few lines later Banquo, according to the Witches, is "Lesser than Macbeth, and greater," "Not so happy, yet much happier" . . . In II.iii, the Porter, having admitted Macduff and Lennox to the castle, speaks of drink and lechery. Drink both provokes and unprovokes lechery: "it makes him, and it mars him; it sets him on, and it takes him off . . . makes him stand to, and not stand to." Lady Macduff's little son is "Father'd . . . and yet he's fatherless" (IV.ii.27). Malcolm falsely blackens his own character, and then retracts: and Macduff says
>> Such welcome and unwelcome things at once
>> 'Tis hard to reconcile.
>> (IV.iii.138–139)

As inversion he cites a number of the many instances where paradoxical phenomena are seen as occurring in time:

> Lady Macbeth wants her milk to be changed into gall. By means of evil, meditated and executed, Macbeth puts rancours in the vessel of his peace . . . Confirmed in wickedness, Macbeth, who was originally sought out by the Witches, now seeks them out; and he declares that he will have personal satisfaction

Though palaces and pyramids do slope
Their heads to their foundations.
(IV.i.57–58)

In "this earthly world," where evil so often prevails, we find, according to Lady Macduff, that
to do harm
Is often laudable, to do good sometime
Accounted dangerous folly.
(IV.ii.74–76)

Duthie shows how Shakespeare uses specific rhetorical forms to build theme and establish an ethical context. Antitheses are seen as projecting "a state of affairs in which the normal order of things is disrupted." Applied (as they most often are) to the Macbeths, these antitheses suggest that extreme wickedness threatens to turn experience upside down, reversing contraries and attacking the roots of meaning itself. "Evil involves an abnormal relationship between opposites, good the normal one." Through the intervention of "divine assistance" (King Edward), this great inversion is itself upended. Macbeth is slain, social order regenerates, and value again becomes coherent.

Murray's essay, though focusing on a totally different aspect of the play, leads us into the same area of experience. Connecting passages in *Macbeth* with specific aspects of Paracelsian medicine, he maintains more generally that the key lines of imagery in the play form a "matrix of associations" which is essentially Paracelsian. The imagery of medicine, of sin as disease, of chaos, poison, blood, and sleep, of "spirits, witches, and ghosts," combines to establish "a structure in human memory, in time, a shared social experience" which is quite unmistakably the experience of Paracelsus' dynamic universe. Though now lost to us, this experience would have been immediately recognizable by Shakespeare's audience. With the whole dramatic and psychological fabric of *Macbeth* in mind, Murray aptly summarizes the Paracelsian view of health and disease:

... health was a rare neutrality between warring forces, in which everything was in movement either upwards in the scale of being towards perfect order, or downward towards complete disorder. There was no sharp distinction between matter and spirit, between living and non-living ... Man was a little universe, containing in himself the elements of the whole *Macrocosm*, the great cosmos, a word which Paracelsus himself invented for the needs of his theory.

From these summaries it should be clear that Murray and Duthie are, in effect, exploring two distinct stylistic aspects of a deeply unified intellectual structure. Oxymoron and inversion, as rhetorical figures, are uniquely congruent with the Paracelsian idea of nature. For Paracelsus, antithesis was part of the structure of nature, and paradox was the language nature spoke. Duthie's comment that Macbeth's wickedness involves the loss of the normal "relationships between opposites" would be a wholly proper conclusion of Paracelsian physic, where health is, as Murray puts it, "a rare neutrality between warring forces." Paracelsians would have applauded the organic and integrated world of the play *Macbeth*, in which moral disorder is equated with a confusion of contraries, moral evil and psychological disease are interrelated (as with Lady Macbeth), and cosmic order is linked with the health of man the microcosm.[20] Moreover, people familiar with Paracelsus' doctrine of free will[21] would not have seen *Macbeth*, with later critics, as a problem in causality. They would have understood that Macbeth, though potentially free, is driven along a fated course (as suggested by the Three Witches) by his increasing loss of inner balance. In short, audiences acquainted with Paracelsian doctrine would have found nothing at all strange or puzzling about Shakespeare's play. They would have seen it as a terrible but precise illumination of the workings of nature.

Besides the Paracelsian tonality, there are verbal and structural elements of contrariety which enhance the play's moral meaning and give it an architectural quality not unlike that of *King Lear*. Like the earlier play, *Macbeth* moves circularly in time, beginning and ending with bloody re-establishments of rightful political order; and, in each case, the violence of these changes is symbolized fearsomely by the severed head of the defeated usurper (I.ii.23, V.ix.20–21). Macbeth reaches the height of his power in the very middle of the play (III.v), and is projected on a downward course by the same act (the murder of Banquo) which removes his last imagined competitor. As it was with *King Lear*, more-over, this temporal motion is energized by the interaction of extreme moral polarities. Macbeth, the "hell-hound," murders the "gracious" Duncan, whose virtues are "like angels" (V.viii.3, III.i.65, I.vii.19). Conversely, Macbeth is ultimately defeated by forces supported by King Edward, himself a receptacle of divine attributes ("sanctity," "bene-diction," "blessings," "grace," etc., IV.iii.140–159). Look-ing ahead towards his coronation at Scone, Malcolm invokes "the grace of Grace" (V.ix.38); and this doubled appeal for benediction, in the play's moral context, reminds us that Macbeth's own desperate moral enterprise has been expressed in similarly doubled terms ("Things bad begun make strong themselves by ill," "blood will have blood," III.iii.55, III.v. 121). Macbeth's repeatedly expressed desire to purge him-self of moral scruples and become an unadulterated force of violent dominance is thus juxtaposed, at beginning and end, with expressions of moral purity which throw it into the sharpest relief.

There are relatively straightforward oppositions, but the reality they enclose is anything but simple. In *Macbeth*, as in *King Lear*, good and evil work together in paradoxical and sometimes alarming ways. Duncan's "meek" and trust-ing nature makes him vulnerable to his thane's attack. Con-versely, England's holy powers have as their agent the violent and vengeful Macduff who, according to his unlucky wife, "wants the natural touch," and who is indeed "of no wo-man born" (IV.ii.9, V.viii.31). Macbeth himself is a memor-able composite of opposites. Haunted and tyrannical, he is nonetheless vividly aware of his own deepening corruption, analyzing his villainy more piercingly and specifically than any of his enemies can. In the end his vigorous intellect cuts through all moral and religious abstractions, exposing ("To-morrow, and to-morrow, and to-morrow," V.v.19–28) the bare truth of evil: emptiness and absurdity. He faces this truth, and the terrible onslaught which directly follows it, with fear but without surrender. His final speech is among the most genuinely heroic in all drama. Macbeth is a villain, a "butcher" (V.ix.35), yet he is both epic in size and intimate in pathos. His character, together with other elements of language and structure, suggests that contraries in *Macbeth* do not operate the way they "should"—that their relationship is organic if not symbiotic.

The implications of moral ambiguity deepen when we reconsider some of the play's early action. In two ironic scenes, Shakespeare establishes Macbeth's social context, implying that this context itself may be partly responsible for his disordered energies. I.ii is devoted to the expository glorification of the "brave" and "noble" Macbeth. Wounded and bloody himself, a Sergeant describes the bold Scot in terms so hyperbolical, grisly, and allusive that they all but identify him as an archetypal letter of blood:

> For brave Macbeth (well he deserves that name),
> Disdaining fortune, with his brandish'd steel,
> Which smok'd with bloody execution,
> (Like Valor's minion) carv'd out his passage
> Till he fac'd the slave;
> Which ne'er shook hands, nor bade farewell to him,
> Till he unseam'd him from the nave to th' chops,
> And fix'd his head upon our battlements.
>   (I.ii.16–23)

He goes on to say that Macbeth and Banquo fought as though

> . . . they meant to bathe in reeking wounds,
> Or memorize another Golgotha, . . .
>   (I.ii.39–40)

Duncan responds to the wounded Sergeant in terms which again evoke the connection between virtue and blood:

> So well thy words become thee as thy wounds,
> They smack of honor both.
> (I.ii.43–44)

Dramatically, coming where they do, these lines may naturally evoke excited feelings of patriotism (Scottish or otherwise) and happy thoughts about the home team. Thematically and structurally, however, their ironic implications are hard to ignore. The wounded Sergeant can barely find words foul and loathsome enough to describe the carnage. The smoking blade which carves men like meat and unseams Macdonwald like a pig for roasting, the heroes who bathe in wounds and recreate the place of Crucifixion—these are images whose essential monstrosity is quickened by the fact that they are delivered with enthusiastic approval. The Sergeant is not just praising a hero; he is glorifying brutality; and Duncan's response, in which his own approval is expressed with a disgusting image of eating ("smack"), shows that he too is participating in this distortion of values. This inflated and unnatural language is thrown into ironic perspective by the action which precedes and follows it. The three Witches have just announced to us that "Fair is foul, and foul is fair" (I.i.11). The play will be filled with blood, and especially painful connections will be drawn between bloodshed and "washing" (II.ii.56–60, V.i.26–68). At the play's end, it will be the noble Macbeth, not the merciless Macdonwald, whose head is triumphantly brandished about; and the hero who is warmly described in terms of butchery at the outset will be dismissed as "this dead butcher" (V.ix.35).

These multiple ironies suggest a qualitative connection between Macbeth's villainy and the *ethos* of the kingdom he usurps. This is not to say that Duncan, Rosse, and the Sergeant are meant to be taken as forces of evil. Rather, these characters tellingly represent a strained and distorted social awareness which, espousing martial heroism without reference to its necessary political context, revels in and even glorifies permissible violence. For such an awareness, both the goals and the origins of warfare are forgotten; the means become ends. While such societies are not to be called evil in themselves, they are nonetheless the nurses of evil, especially in characters as violent and ambitious as Macbeth. Psychologically and politically, the glorification of violence as social virtue is but one step away from its acceptance as a means of individual enterprise.[22]

The disturbing proximity between these two states is made clear in an early scene where, in a kind of *reductio ad absurdum*, the two Macbeths twist the language of honor into the rhetoric of murder:

> [Lady M:]   Art thou afeard
> To be the same *in thine own act and valor*
> As thou art in desire? Wouldst thou have that
> Which thou esteem'st the ornament of life,
> And live a *coward* in thine own esteem,
> Letting "*I dare not*" wait upon "I would,"
> Like the poor cat i' th' adage?
>
> When you *durst* do it, then you were a man;
> And to be more than what you were, you would
> *Be so much more than man.*
> Macb.   Bring forth men-children only!
> For *thy undaunted mettle* should compose
> Nothing but males.
>   (I.vii.39–44, 49–51, 72–74. My italics.)

Here the degeneration of values into their opposites is figured blatantly and realistically. The Macbeths' language fulfills the Witches' crude generalization about good and evil: foul is indeed fair, and fair is foul. The moral ambiguity latent in the structure and psychology of *Macbeth* is thus enforced by the political implications and rhetorical dynamics of the early action.

These contrarieties unite with others in *Macbeth* to elaborate a tragic world where all things hold the seeds of good and evil, and where value must be judged not on quality but rather in terms of context and degree. This world finds a striking parallel, if not an ultimate source, in the natural philosophy of Paracelsus, as quoted and summarized in chapters above:

> In all things there is a poison, and there is nothing without a poison. It depends only on the dose whether a poison is poison or not.

> Every man is like a field, neither entirely good, nor entirely bad, but of uncertain kind.[23]

Also reminiscent of Paracelsus is the dense imagery of *Macbeth*, which develops profound and encompassing interrelationships between the individual and the cosmos. But while for Paracelsus the microcosm/macrocosm relationship is a simple truth of nature, Shakespeare uses it more specifically to show that Macbeth, like all men, creates his own cosmos by thought, choice, and action. Like Paracelsian man, Macbeth is basically free; in speech after speech, Shakespeare makes it clear that his hero's actions, from his interpretation of oracles to his nobility in defeat, are the products of his own choice. But while Paracelsus emphasizes the positive elements of freedom, Shakespeare dwells tragically and almost exclusively on its pitfalls: the press of circumstance, the passion and ignorance of men, and, above all, the manifold ambiguities of experience which, like sorceresses' prophecies, can pervert and baffle choice. These ambiguities are so pervasive and persistent that they can ruin freedom, luring characters like Macbeth into vortices of slavery. But ambiguity is also a strong testament to the existence of freedom. In a world without mystery or dilemma, freedom as we know it would not exist.

Given these considerations, true freedom may lie in a willing and knowledgeable acceptance of ambiguity, if not an active appropriation of its powers. A notion of this sort is suggested quite meaningfully by Shakespeare's characterization of the victorious prince, Malcolm. Like the speeches of other characters in *Macbeth*, Malcolm's words are full of contrariety; but while, for all the others, contrariety has ominous overtones, Malcolm uses it positively and effectively. We see this in his first substantial speech, which recounts the death of the rebellious Cawdor:

> . . . very frankly he confess'd his treasons,
> Implor'd your Highness' pardon, and set forth
> A deep repentance. Nothing in his life
> Became him like the leaving it. He died
> As one that had been studied in his death,
> To throw away the dearest thing he ow'd,
> As 'twere a careless trifle.
> (I.iv.5–11)

Malcolm's triple use of paradox (lines 7–8, 8–9, 10–11) suggests an appreciative awareness of the complexity of the tragic experience, where even villains may commit noble actions and where victors may pause to admire the virtue of the defeated. His elegant praise of a brave enemy cuts through the violence and partisanship which has characterized the early discourse, hinting at a political awareness which is not consumed by causes or the passion for revenge. Brief, later speeches enlarge on the implication that, unlike other characters, he is sensitive to the potentially positive effects of contrariety. Counselling his brother to flee Scotland after Duncan's death, he remarks,

> There's warrant in that theft
> Which steals itself, when there's no mercy left.
> (II.iii.145–146)

Later he tells the bereaved Macduff to make something good of his sorrow by turning it into effective anger:

> Be this the whetstone of your sword, let grief
> Convert to anger; blunt not the heart, enrage it.
> (IV.iii.228–229)

But Malcolm's positive attitude towards contrariety is most remarkably displayed in the lengthy conversation with Macduff which occurs just before the news of Macduff's family's death. Here, in a passage totally unnecessary to the plot,[24] the young prince tests his liegeman's integrity by painting himself as a villain compared to whom "black Macbeth/ Will seem as pure as snow" (IV.iii.52–53). He characterizes himself as boundlessly lecherous and avaricious, but fails to appall the tolerant Macduff until he extravagantly describes (in language reminiscent of the Macbeths themselves) the gross fruition of tyranny:

> The king-becoming graces,
> As justice, verity, temp'rance, stableness,
> Bounty, perseverance, mercy, lowliness,
> Devotion, patience, courage, fortitude,
> I have no relish of them, but abound
> In the division of each several crime,
> Acting it many ways. Nay, had I pow'r, I should
> Pour the sweet milk of concord into hell,
> Uproar the universal peace, confound
> All unity on earth.
>   (IV.iii.91–100)

This passage, the only long 'digression' in an otherwise taut dramatic sequence, takes on thematic meaning when seen in the context of the play's ambiguous moral structure, and in the light of Shakespeare's earlier characterizations of active virtue. Like Edgar in the heath-scenes of *King Lear*, Malcolm is able figuratively to 'become' his own opposite, taking on, briefly and harmlessly, Macbeth's character of desperate evil. This feat of imagination not only achieves an immediate political goal (the testing of a major ally) but also suggests a new level in the play's moral dialectic. Malcolm's ability to understand both good and evil—to take the extremes of human nature into himself—sets him apart from the otherwise destructive and inscrutable interaction of contraries which characterizes the moral experience of *Macbeth*. Unlike either the gracious Duncan, who ignores evil, or the black Macbeth, who espouses it, Malcolm sympathetically appropriates evil, transforming it into knowledge and making it the basis for wise action. Malcolm's behavior suggests that, even in a world as disordered and hazardous as the world of *Macbeth*, a coherent and productive attitude towards contrariety is indeed possible: that contrariety, like all forces of nature, must be obeyed in order to be controlled.[25]

Malcolm immediately disowns his frightening impersonation, leaving Macduff (as usual) dumbfounded. With Macduff as his lieutenant, he goes on to direct a successful, though characteristically deceptive and paradoxical, attack on the fortress at Dunsinane. His last speech, the final speech of the play *Macbeth*, refines and deepens his positive political role:

> We shall not spend a large expense of time
> Before we reckon with your several loves,
> And make us even with you. My thanes and kinsmen,
> Henceforth be earls, the first that ever Scotland
> In such an honor nam'd. What's more to do,
> Which would be newly planted with the time,
> As calling home our exil'd friends abroad
> That fled the snare of watchful tyranny,
> Producing forth the cruel ministers
> Of this dead butcher and his fiend-like queen,
> Who (as 'tis thought) by self and violent hands
> Took off her life; this, and what needful else
> That calls upon us, by the grace of Grace,
> We will perform in measure, time, and place.
> So thanks to all at once and to each one,
> Whom we invite to see us crown'd at Scone.
>   (V.ix.25–41)

The introduction of the English institution of the earldom implies the civilizing quality of the new order, and this implication is strengthened by Malcolm's language in general. Unlike the victory speeches in Act I, which were in fact celebrations of violence and honor, Malcolm's words make no reference to glory at arms. He does not reward his friends' courage but rather their "loves" (line 26). Not Malcolm but Macduff has been the bloody agent of justice, and Malcolm's humble appeal to "the grace of Grace" suggests that the new order, though partially dependent on such an agency, will not be defined by it. Neither Macduff's brutal virtue nor the pious heritage of Duncan and Edward is seen as valuable in itself. These opposites take on healthy and generative power only when they are combined within, and subjugated to, a broader vision of the commonwealth.

Antony and Cleopatra

Contrariety in Shakespeare's later Tragedies may be seen as the dominant element in a new metaphysics, a mimetic restructuring and restatement of the functions of being. Predicated on a rejection of the traditional modes of apprehending and communicating experience, it is nonetheless far from being a manifesto of chaos or absurdity. Rather it is an education in a special form of wisdom, a repeated counsel that intense experience is born of strife, and liable to change so dynamic that it appears to be utter reversal. Like a prism, powerful experience reorganizes and redirects the energy that is brought to it. To know is not to be learned in harmonious systems; it is rather to be aware of nature's wayward but not wholly unpredictable mobility. To teach this wisdom, Shakespeare contorts plot and language almost to the breaking-point. Plot cannot suggest reality unless it is founded upon massive oppositions. Language cannot suggest reality unless, with a frequency that approaches ritual, it rejects its own power of expression.

No play is truer to this mode of creation than *Antony and Cleopatra* (1606–1607). More than any other stylistic element, paradox gives the play its memorable tonality. Paradoxical structures of language occur more than one hundred times.[26] These devices cluster at climactic moments and concern vital aspects of social and psychological experience:

What our contempts doth often hurl from us,
We wish it ours again. The present pleasure,
By revolution low'ring, does become
The opposite of itself.
              (I.ii.122–136)

It hath been taught us from the primal state
That he which is was wish'd, until he were;
And the ebb'd man, ne'er lov'd till ne'er worth love,
Comes [dear'd] by being lack'd.
              (I.iv.41–44)

                    We, ignorant of ourselves,
Beg often our own harms, which the wise pow'rs
Deny us for our good; so find we profit
By losing of our prayers.
              (II.i.5–8)

Come then; for with a wound I must be cur'd.
              (IV.xiv.78)

                    And strange it is
That nature must compel us to lament
Our most persisted deeds.
              (V.i.28–30)

Dost thou not see my baby at my breast,
That sucks the nurse asleep?
              (V.ii.309–310)

These radical contradictions, striking enough in themselves, are multiplied to the extent that they saturate the dramatic experience, charging it with a strangeness akin to the shocking revelation of dreams. There is a persistent sense of the strain between reality and expression, of language that can touch but not enclose the vividness of things. Yet, as though the play itself were a massive and highly successful *recusatio*, the professed weakness is a source of strength. Through an unprecedented interaction of contraries, Shakespeare brings us closer than ever before to his version of the Gate of Horn, to an awareness of the remarkable truth.

Verbal paradox buttresses or parallels larger contradictions that are psychological, geographical, or structural. Every reader is aware that the two opposed worlds of Rome and Alexandria, as presented dramatically and as embodied respectively by Octavius and Cleopatra, are not just different places but different kinds of being. The maintenance of power (Rome) and the enjoyment of power (Alexandria) are portrayed with such remorseless polarity as to suggest that the two are mutually exclusive. Antony's uncanny ability to move within both spheres is also his downfall. Each of these two realms, moreover, is bifurcated by elements of opposition. Octavius' world of duty and honor is also characterized by ambition, dishonesty, and cynicism.[27] Antony's "dotage," on the other hand, seems to transcend its apparently limiting material context:

> His delights
> Were dolphin-like, they show'd his back above
> The element they liv'd in.
>   (V.ii.88–90)

The implied paradox is thematic. Antony and Cleopatra's delights, though profusely mundane, are understood to take the lovers quite beyond the realm of everyday experience we know as 'the world':

> *Cleo.* I'll set a bourn how far to be belov'd.
> *Ant.* Then must thou needs find out new heaven, new earth.
>   (I.i.16–17)

> [Enobarbus:]
> We cannot call her winds and water sighs and tears; they
> are greater storms and tempests than almanacs can report.
>   (I.ii.147–149)

> *Cleo.* His face was as the heav'ns, and therein stuck
> A sun and moon, which kept their course and lighted
> The little O, the earth.
>   (V.ii.79–81)

The structure of *Antony and Cleopatra* thus reiterates two major principles of contrariety: that experience, to the extent that it is strong or "real," is based on the interaction of conflicting forces; and that extreme courses lead to their own opposites. The lovers' final transcendence is causally dependent on their own material downfall. Octavius, whose rise to universal power is monomaniacal, becomes "paltry," a "knave," an "ass unpolicied," a "landlord" (V.ii.2, 3, 307–308; III.xiii.72). Cleopatra's wealth of pettiness, her cherishing of the voluminous present, leave her glorious and purified.

These intimations of a massive contrariety are substantiated in the character of Cleopatra, whom Maynard Mack has aptly termed "a kind of absolute oxymoron."[28] In her own speeches, the use of paradox reminds us of the oxymora of Petrarch and Bruno, suggesting the ambiguous quality of extreme emotion:

> I am quickly ill, and well,
> So Antony loves.
> >   (I.iii.72–73)

> Now I feed myself
> With most delicious poison.
> >   (I.v.26–27)

> There would he anchor his aspect, and die
> With looking on his life.
> >   (I.v.33–34)

> All strange and terrible events are welcome,
> But comforts we despise; . . .
> >   (IV.xv.3–4)

> The stroke of death is as a lover's pinch,
> Which hurts, and is desir'd.
> >   (V.ii.295–296)

Cleopatra not only sees life in terms of paradox; she effectively becomes a paradox for other characters. To vex and fascinate her lover Antony, she tells Alexas,

> See where he is, who's with him, what he does.
> I did not send you. If you find him sad,

Say I am dancing; if in mirth, report
That I am sudden sick.
(I.iii.2–5)

Enobarbus sees her analogously as a consummate enchant-
ress whose greatness resides in her ability to reverse the normal functions of experience:

I saw her once
Hop forty paces through the public street;
And having lost her breath, she spoke, and panted,
That she did make defect perfection,
And breathless, pow'r breath forth.
(II.ii.228–232)

By virtue of a more inclusive paradox, these massed contradictions do not result in psychological chaos, but rather in
a strange harmony described by both Antony and Enobarbus
as a phenomenon of "becoming":

Ant. Fie, wrangling queen!
Whom everything *becomes*—to chide, to laugh,
To weep; [whose] every passion fully strives
To make itself (in thee) fair and admir'd!
(I.i.48–51)

[*Eno.*]
Age cannot wither her, nor custom stale
Her infinite variety. Other women cloy
The appetites they feed, but she makes hungry
Where most she satisfies; for vildest things
Become themselves in her, that the holy priests
Bless her when she is riggish.
(II.ii.233–239. My italics.)

"Become," here, is used in its cosmetic sense; but Enobarbus' references to age, withering, and custom suggest the
word's temporal meaning as well. The mystery of Cleopatra's attractiveness, we suspect, has something to do with
the mystery of time.

"Become" is one of the most important single words in
the play. Its various forms occur seventeen times. In one
sense, as we have just seen, it is used to describe Cleopatra's

charm; in another, it is used to describe the shocking alter-
ations of time. Time reverses things. At the beginning, we
hear that Antony's "captain's heart"

> reneges all temper,
> And is *become* the bellows and the fan
> To cool a gipsy's lust.
> (I.i.8–10. My italics.)

Near Caesar, Antony's "angel/ *Becomes* a fear, as being
o'erpow'r'd" (II.iii.22–23). Antony himself sees time as
a wheel which forces pleasure to "*become*/ The opposite
of itself" (I.ii.125–126). Caesar describes the action of time
by comparing it implicitly to the tide, whose dominant
principle is that of reversal:

> And the *ebb'd* man, ne'er lov'd till ne'er worth love,
> *Comes* dear'd by being lack'd.
> (I.iv.41–44. My italics.)

This view of time may be seen operating in the play's larger
structures. The major figures, Cleopatra, Antony, and Caesar
himself, are constantly reversing their political courses. The
conclusion, with its apotheosis of the defeated lovers, implies
the grandest reversal of all. The very scene-structure, as the
action alternates between Egyptian and Roman worlds, gives
a sense of the ebb and flow between opposites. As in the
two preceding tragedies, the process of "becoming" is a
dynamic rhythm of contrareity. Extremes and oppositions
are exposed as the engines of time.

This is highly tragic material, suggesting intense experience
and perhaps the almost speechless awe of the conclusion of
King Lear. Yet for most interpreters, *Antony and Cleopatra*
is less tragic than elegiac, less a vehicle of awe than an evoca-
tion of wonderment. Shakespeare achieves this reversal of
tonality largely through his characterization of Cleopatra.
If the figure of Lear suggests those elements which give time
its terror and pathos, Cleopatra embodies those elements
which give time its charm, those fluid and incandescent
changes which tie us, moment by moment, to the process of

being. This unique effect is described, quite appropriately, in terms of "becoming": the one word which magically unites the properties of change and beauty. Like time itself, Cleopatra reverses the logical order of things. Seeing paradox in everything, she establishes herself, for Antony and others, as a paradox of the flesh. By flaunting reason and expectation, she incorporates the contrariety of time, and in so doing becomes the only fresh thing in a withering universe ("Age cannot wither her, nor custom stale / Her infinite variety"). In her provocations, her becomings, the incorporeal substance of time is momentarily vivid and immediate. Her final suicidal decision to do a deed which "shackles accidents and bolts up change" (V.ii.6) punctuates, but in no way qualifies, this unique period of being.

We cannot adequately appreciate the meaning of this phenomenon without seeing Cleopatra in terms of Shakespeare's artistic development or, moreover, without considering the relationship between her metaphysical implications and her unabashed female sexuality. If Cleopatra is the first Shakespearean character to suggest a positive reconciliation of being and time, she is also the first Shakespearean character in whom sexuality, unhampered by law or convention, appears in a generally positive light. If her tawny magnetism has any antecedent, it is not to be found in the plays at all, but rather in the poems: initially in the characterization of Venus in *Venus and Adonis*, and later more significantly in the darkly-favored Lady of the Sonnets. Both of these overtly sexual figures are counterpoised by opposed entities: in the early poem by the virginal Adonis, and in the Sonnets by the sublime but wayward young man. In both works the female's sexuality is linked with danger and destruction; while the male is abstracted or idealized, glorified in one case by metamorphosis, and in the other by poetic fame. In the Sonnets, moreover, the metaphysical and psychological implications of this dualism are made clearer. The *persona*'s love for the male is cognate with the desire for permanence and the principle of form. The *persona*'s love for the female

suggests the ravages of change and the principle of matter.
The superiority of the *persona*'s affection for the male is
linked to a relationship that is Platonic in both senses of the
word. The sexual relationship with the Dark Lady is seen as
something bad and shameful. The dilemma of the two loves
is encapsulated in Sonnet 144:

> Two loves I have of comfort and despair,
> Which like two spirits do suggest me still:
> The better angel is a man right fair,
> The worser spirit a woman color'd ill.
> To win me soon to hell, my female evil
> Tempteth my better angel from my [side],
> And would corrupt my saint to be a devil,
> Wooing his purity with her foul pride.
> And whether that my angel be turn'd fiend
> Suspect I may, yet not directly tell,
> But being both from me, both to each friend,
> I guess one angel in another's hell.
>   Yet this shall I ne'er know, but live in doubt,
>   Till my bad angel fire my good one out.

Beneath the biographical superstructure is an early attempt
to express the phenomenon of contrariety. Angel and evil
cohabit; and the sexual image may be seen to suggest the
simultaneous conflict and attraction of opposites in the
persona's mind. This union of contraries (to be understood
so positively in the later drama) is for the *persona* no more
than a complication of pain. He senses an irreducible division, an image that simultaneously beckons and rejects.[29]
In the Sonnets, sexuality is the focusing-point at which the
ambiguity of the traditional distinctions between good and
evil, form and matter, being and change achieves acute expression. The same dilemma is developed via the same medium in *Hamlet*, the Problem Comedies, and *Othello*.

With Cleopatra we sense a significant change in attitude.
Her character, as we have seen, embodies and strikingly
combines elements of sexuality, time, and the material
world. The exclusively negative value attached to these elements by the younger Shakespeare, however, is gone.

Though her pleasures and allurements are related to loss of measure, they nowhere imply sexual guilt; instead, her sexuality is suggestive of fancy and the generative principle. Her unusually positive relationship to time—her "becomings" and "infinite variety"—is treated verbally as a creative force. Her identification with material pleasures is not shown as something bestial, but rather is so complete that it seems to transcend the laws of matter ("for she makes hungry/Where most she satisfies"). Cleopatra is not a compromise or accommodation with worldly elements. Instead she represents a new and positive sense of the indivisibility of spirit and body, form and matter, and being and change.

Here as elsewhere, Shakespeare's treatment of contrariety has apparent ties with European philosophy. In this case, the parallels with Montaigne's comments on the same subject in "De l'Experience" (3.13) are strong enough to suggest that Shakespeare may have appropriated the ideas of his French contemporary as part of the intellectual substructure of his play. Both writers, first of all, have similarly paradoxical things to say about morality and truth:

[Montaigne (Florio):]
Vices were profitably brought in; to give esteem and make head unto vertue; . . .

[Shakespeare (Lepidus describing Antony):]
                    I must not think there are
Evils enow to darken all his goodness:
His faults in him seem as the spots of heaven,
More fiery by night's blackness; . . .

[Montaigne:]
It often cometh to passe, . . . that *truth* is whispered into Princes eares, not onely without fruit, but hurtfully and therewithal unjustly. And no man shall make me believe . . . that the interest of the *substance* should not sometimes yeeld to the interest of the *forme*. (My italics.)

[Shakespeare:]
Ant. [*to Eno.*] Thou art a soldier only, speak no more.

> *Eno.* That *truth* should be silent I had almost forgot.
> *Ant.* You wrong this presence, therefore speak no more.
> *Eno.* Go to then—your considerate stone.
> *Caes.* I do not much dislike the *matter,* but
> The *manner* of his speech;...[30]
> (My italics.)

When Montaigne describes an unnamed king,[31] he seems to anticipate Shakespeare's characterization of Antony:

> No state of mediocrity, being ever transported from one extreame to another, by indivinable occasions: no maner of course without crosse, and strange contrarieties: no faculty simple: so that the likeliest a man may one day conclude of him, shall be that he affected and laboured to make himselfe knowne by being not to be knowne.[32]

The most significant parallel, however, may be found in the way in which Montaigne integrates statements of this kind into a general view of experience. Shortly before the passage just quoted, Florio's Montaigne twice characterizes experience just the way Enobarbus will characterize Cleopatra—as an "infinit variety":

> [On self-knowledge:]
> My selfe, who professe nothing else, find therein so bottomlesse a depth, and infinite variety, . . .
>
> [On the actions of his contemporaries:]
> Not to marshall or range this infinit variety of so divers and so distracted actions . . .[33]

Later he argues that experience is a vast composition of contraries, and counsels that to live well is not to banish either side, but rather to accept the whole:

> Our life is composed, as is the harmony of the World, of contrary things; so of divers tunes, some pleasant, some harsh, some sharpe, some flat, some low and some high: What would that Musitian say, that should love but some one of them? He ought to know how to use them severally and how to intermingle them. So should we both of goods and evils, which are consubstantiall to our life. Our being cannot subsist without this commixture, whereto one side is no lesse necessary than the other.[34]

At the essay's conclusion, Montaigne brings this doctrine of experience most emphatically to bear on the traditional dichotomy between body and spirit. He condemns the philosophy which holds,

> that it is a barbarous aliance, to marry what is divine with that which is terrestrial: wedde reasonable with unreasonable; combine severe with indulgent, and couple honest with unhonest: that voluptuousnesse is a brutall quality, unworthy the taste of a wiseman.[35]

He quotes Seneca:

> *Who will not call it a property of folly to do slothfully and frowardly what is to be done, and one way to drive the body, and another way the minde, . . . ?*[36]

He broadly ridicules human pretentions to spiritual sanctity and earthly magnificence:

> Super-celestiall opinions and under-terrestrial manners, are things, that amongst us, I have ever seene to bee of singular accord.

> [On asceticism:]
> It is meere folly, insteade of transforming themselves into Angels, they transchange themselves into beastes: in lieu of advancing, they abase themselves.

> *And sit we upon the highest throne of the World, yet sit we upon our owne taile.*[37]

Here as elsewhere in his *Essais,* Montaigne sees the infinite variety of experience most specifically as a network of contrarieties. In this, his final essay, he urges his readers to accept and prosper from these oppositions, emphasizing conclusively that most galling of them, the dichotomy between mind and body.

Not only specific words and conceits, but larger elements of the intellectual tonality of *Antony and Cleopatra,* are in accord with the unconventional doctrine of "De l'Experience." Shakespeare's choice of paradox as the play's rhetorical foundation, his dynamic use of moral oppositions, and his unusually appreciative treatment of sensuality all suggest an attitude similar to Montaigne's. Cleopatra herself is like a goddess of contrariety, an image of that infinite variety of fascinating contradictions which Montaigne likens to "the harmony of the World."[38] But while Montaigne's essay predominantly develops the comic aspects of contrariety, Shakespeare's play realizes both the comic and the tragic implications. Individual speeches and the irresistible motion of the plot suggest repeatedly that, although the experience of contrariety may induce a sense of wonderment and a wise acceptance of life, this joy and wisdom are chronically alien to rational discourse and political reality. The destructive interaction of Egypt and Rome is the image of a world based on affirmation rather than acceptance, a world which misunderstands the tragic complexity of experience and thus is doomed to prolong it. Caught between the contradictory demands of her brother Caesar and her husband Antony, Octavia remarks thematically that she can find "no midway/ 'Twixt these extremes at all" (III.iv.19–20). The nature of this irreconcilable division is implied more fully in the choric figure of Enobarbus. The blunt soldier, initially a well of concise rationality, is ultimately destroyed by his recognition of the contrariety of experience and the concomitant disjunction of his own values. As he ponders whether or not to desert the grossly imprudent Antony, his words reflect a basic ambiguity in experience which makes individual integrity all but impossible:

> Mine honesty and I begin to square.
> The loyalty well held to fools does make
> Our faith mere folly; yet he that can endure
> To follow with allegiance a fall'n lord
> Does conquer him that did his master conquer,
> And earns a place i' the story.
>   (III.xiii.41–46)

Enobarbus' speech is a lesson in the language of contraries. Two sharply-drawn paradoxes (lines 42–43 and 45) set up a larger paradox: fidelity to Antony is at once bad and good. This paradox is constructed from two distinct but equally imperative frames of reference: the ethic of prudence, whose nemesis is folly, and the ethic of honesty, whose nemesis is broken allegiance.[39] These alternative frames of reference represent in little the two types of being symbolized respectively by Caesar and Antony. Enobarbus later deserts Antony, negating honesty; and the resultant shame, intensified by a new example of Antony's honesty (Antony sends Enobarbus the treasures he had left behind when he deserted) leads to one of the strangest deaths in Shakespeare: a suicide by thought alone (IV.vi.35, IV.ix). This unlikely end (Enobarbus and his manner of death are largely Shakespeare's invention[40]) underscores the complexity of the tragic dilemma, and implies the inability of a purely rational being to cope with it effectively.

The greatest victim of this pervasive ambiguity is Antony himself. Like Othello, Lear, and Macbeth, Antony's character derives much of its energy from the interaction of polarities—in this case, between the political exigencies of Rome and the encompassing ecstasies of Egypt. But while the earlier tragic heroes find only torment in contrariety, Antony accepts his paradoxical position with sanguinity, seeking to enclose both extremes of being within himself. Heroically, he stakes claims on both worlds: Caesar's "whole world" of global power and Cleopatra's "new heaven, new earth" of love and pleasure (V.i.40, I.i.17). The intensity and fullness of this effort make him godlike; in Cleopatra's great elegy he is a being of cosmic grandeur who "Crested the world" and shone upon "This little O, the earth" (V.ii.83, 81). Yet this planetary scope of experience is achieved at the expense of earthly folly and psychological entropy. Duped by both Caesar and Cleopatra, he chooses suicide, describing his own tragedy significantly not as an heroic downfall, but rather in terms which suggest a dissolution of personality:

Ant. Sometime we see a cloud that's dragonish,
A vapor sometime like a bear or lion,
A [tower'd] citadel, a pendant rock,
A fork'd mountain, or blue promontory
With trees upon't that nod unto the world,
And mock our eyes with air. Thou hast seen these signs,
They are black vesper's pageants.
Eros.   Ay, my lord.
Ant. That which is now a horse, even with a thought
The rack dislimns, and makes it indistinct
As water is in water.
Eros.   It does, my lord.
Ant. My good knave Eros, now thy captain is
Even such a body. Here I am Antony,
Yet cannot hold this visible shape, my knave.
                    (IV.xiv.2–14)

The image of the cloud as something at once gigantic and
momentary, magnificent and illusory, tells the story of tragic greatness and weakness better than any other speech in
the play. Antony's unique effort to possess and control the
warring extremes of experience has distended his personality, leaving it at once huge and insubstantial.

These paradoxes, ironies, extremes, and revolutions are
all typical of later Shakespearean tragedy. Yet, with the
characterization of Cleopatra in mind, we must remember
that Shakespeare has made this tragic frame a receptacle for
sustained evocations of wonder and delight. *Antony and
Cleopatra* is thus a kind of Problem Comedy in reverse—
a play in which tragic form and comic content unite unfa-
miliarly to effect a positive appreciation of life's evanescent
joys. Indeed, the generic transgression is such a happy one
as to make us wonder whether it is a transgression at all:
whether, on some deeper level of experience, the fusion of
comic and tragic may not be quite natural. As we have seen,
the characterization of Cleopatra is memorable and enchant-
ing precisely because it replicates in miniature the more
awesome process of becoming which dominates the tragic
scheme. A distillation of contrariety, Cleopatra suggests
that the gladness of comic art is, like tragedy, predicated

upon complex patterns of irony, conflict, and paradox; that the distinction between comedy and tragedy is less one of quality than one of scale.[41] By combining these two schemes of contraries, realizing the effects of each fully and hinting at their profound correlations, Shakespeare has made *Antony and Cleopatra* his most extensive drama, his closest approach to encompassing in art the dazzling miscellany of experience.

Notes to Chapter Five

1 When Hamlet and Claudius soliloquize separately in the praying-scene they speak similarly of the purifying effects of prayer (III.iii. 36–96). Hamlet's gibe to Ophelia about women's "paintings" (III.i. 142–144) comes directly after Claudius, in an aside, has alluded to "the harlot's cheek, beautied with plast'ring art" (III.i.50). And when Claudius cautions Laertes about the congenital defects of human resolve (IV.vii.110–126), he paraphrases lines which, under Hamlet's direction, the Player-King has already spoken (III.ii.186–215).

2 Sir Philip Sidney *Arcadia* (1590), 1.4; (1593), 1; *Works* 1:25–26; 4:5. And see above, pp. 20–22, 41–42.

3 John Milton, *Works*, 2:515.

4 Baldassare Castiglione *Il Libro del Cortegiano*, 3.38; *The Book of the Courtier*, trans. Charles Singleton (Garden City, N.Y.: Doubleday Anchor Books, 1959), pp. 240–41. The argument is advanced by Giuliano de' Medici. A number of things besides the discussion of the double standard connect *Othello* with Book 3 of *Il Cortegiano*, which is devoted to a lively and detailed controversy about female virtue. First, Giuliano makes emphatic reference to the need for defending virtuous women from slanders against their chastity. (Shakespeare's Emilia will become Desdemona's only active defender against Iago's slander.) Second, the only woman who figures importantly in the dialogue of *Il Cortegiano* is also named Emilia (Emilia Pia). Castiglione's Emilia is, with Giuliano, one of the primary defenders of the female sex in the debate of Book 3. Also she possesses, like Shakespeare's Emilia, a kind of worldly wisdom which delights in undercutting the abstract excesses of other characters. See *Il Cortegiano*, 3.17, 4.71; Singleton, pp. 218, 357.

5 Iago himself plagues us with a confusing assortment of motives

for his actions. He is annoyed at Cassio's promotion (I.i.8–33); he wishes preferment (II.i.308); he is in love with Desdemona (II.i.291–293); he is afraid that both Othello and Cassio have cuckolded him, and hence he wants revenge (I.iii.386–388, II.i.294–299, 307). His language also suggests less conscious motives at work: an attitude towards sexuality so negative that at one point it approaches perversion (I.i.86–117, and especially II.i.177, where he compares Desdemona's fingers to "clyster-pipes"—enema tubes), and perhaps even a frustrated idealism (II.i.148–160). In contrast with his many emotional responses is his avowed doctrine of radical free will and amoral self-aggrandizement (I.iii.311ff). None of these motives—not even the sum of them—would seem wholly to comprise Iago's *raison d'être;* they suggest rather the miscellaneous ramifications of an inner impulse which Iago neither understands nor controls.

6 IV.iii.65, II.iii.350, III.iii.90, V.ii.361, V.ii.347, V.ii.235.

7 The Gloucester story is derived from Sidney's *Arcadia* (1590), bk. 2, ch. 10.

8 I.i.82–85, 123–124.

9 Albany refers to Edmund's death as "but a trifle" (V.iii.296).

10 II.ii.165–166, III.ii.70–71, IV.i.19–21, IV.vi.221–223.

11 Plato *Republic* 343a–354c; *Gorgias* 481–523. W. R. Elton, *King Lear and the Gods* (San Marino: The Huntington Library, 1966), p. 126. Leo Strauss, *Natural Right and History* (Chicago: University of Chicago Press, 1953), pp. 114–15.

12 See Elton, *King Lear and the Gods,* pp. 125–28.

13 See above, pp. 93–95, 107–08.

14 These lines have been ascribed alternately to Albany (Q1, 2) and to Edgar (F1).

15 Twice Edgar is so moved by the suffering he sees that he is almost unable to continue his counterfeiting (III.vi.60–61, IV.i.52–54). Later he, Kent, and Albany compare Lear's tragedy to the Apocalypse (V.iii.264–265).

16 In this light, note particularly Lear's last dialogue with Cordelia, in which he describes their projected sojourn in prison as a fixed cycle of blessing and forgiveness, happily removed from political affairs which "ebb and flow" (V.iii.8–19).

17 Parallels between *King Lear* and Giordano Bruno's *De gli eroici furori* (London: John Charlewood, 1585) are numerous and specific enough to deserve some mention here. While these similarities do not necessarily suggest that Shakespeare is using Bruno's ideas as some of the structural and intellectual bases of his play, they nonetheless illustrate the extent to which both writers partake of a common fund of ideas, employing the same notions of contrariety to much the same effect.

Both Shakespeare and Bruno use madness and blindness as objective correlatives for spiritual torment and awakening. Bruno's general metaphor for the philosophical quest is *furore*, and the Fourth Dialogue of Part 2 of *De gli eroici furori* is devoted to nine blind men, whose physical disabilities represent various torments inherent in the ascent to truth. Lear and Gloucester's agonies, in like fashion, become sources of intense revelation. In Bruno, *furore* arises from a clear perception of the distinction between form and matter. King Lear's madness, as it dwells on the conflicts between past belief and present experience, between flattery and underlying malevolence, and, in general, between appearance and reality, seems to follow a similar course.

A second parallel can be found in the way both Bruno and Shakespeare treat the two contraries, beast and god. In his first soliloquy, Edmund associates himself with animal imagery and predicts that, though "base," he will rise:

> Edmund the base
> Shall top th' legitimate. I grow, I prosper:
> Now, gods, stand up for bastards!
> (I.ii.20–22)

Edgar, conversely, sinks to a level where he is, in his own words, "basest," "near to beast" (II.iii.7,9). As Tom o' Bedlam he figuratively lives out the implications of his degraded position, and later he rises paradoxically to a kind of godliness. At the end of the Third Dialogue of Part 2 of *De gli eroici furori* (less than two pages away from the First Blind Man), Bruno's Tansillo lays claim to a similar sort of ascent:

> From a more vile creature I become a god, I change into a deity from a base creature.

Tansillo's rise occurs because of his *furore*. In a similar way, as we have seen, Edgar's growth seems to find its origin in his feigned madness.

Both Bruno and Shakespeare emphasize the beneficial effects of adversity:

> [Lear:] The art of our necessities is strange
> And can make vild things precious.
> (III.iv.70–71)

> [Gloucester:] Our means secure us, and our mere defects
> Prove our commodities.
> (IV.i.20–21)

> [Tansillo:] Because for those who are favored by heaven, the greatest evils are converted into even greater good; for necessity nourishes labors

and studies, and these as a rule nourish the glory of immortal splendor.

> (Bruno, 1.1; *The Heroic Frenzies*, trans. Paul Eugene Memmo [Chapel Hill: University of North Carolina Press, 1964], pp. 84–85. The first of each of the following excerpts from Bruno cites the original edition. The second reference cites the Memmo translation.)

More specifically, both writers picture experience as a wheel in motion:

[Edgar:] The lamentable change is from the best,
The worst returns to laughter.
> (IV.i.4–5)

[Edmund:] The wheel is come full circle, I am here.
> (V.iii.175)

[Tansillo:] There is in nature a revolution and a circle in virtue of which, for the perfection and aid of others, superior things incline toward the inferior, and for their own excellence and felicity inferior things are raised to the superior.
> (1.3; p. 120)

Bruno's wheel traps beasts, men, and gods in a permanent cycle of development and degeneration. A similar circularity of growth and decay, prosperity and disaster, accompanied by spiritual frenzies not unlike those described by Bruno, governs the experience of Lear, Edgar, and Gloucester. Bruno's Tansillo and Shakespeare's Lear use the same metaphor—a hero bound upon a burning wheel—to describe their agonies:

[Tansillo:] . . . like Ixion, I must pursue and escape myself . . .
> (1.2; p. 102)

[Lear:]   . . . but I am bound
Upon a wheel of fire, . . .
> (IV.vii.45–46)

In both cases, this fiery torment is connected with the perception of contrariety. I have shown at length how Shakespeare makes contrariety both the theme and the structure of *King Lear*. Bruno maintains that contrariety is the dominant motive of nature:

> . . . nothing results from an absolutely uncontested principle, but everything results from contrary principles . . .
> (2.1; p. 187)

> . . . all things are made of contraries . . .
> (1.2; p. 98)

Bruno defines wisdom as the awareness and acceptance of contrariety, both in external phenomena and in the philosopher's own spirit. As his modern editor, Paul Eugene Memmo, notes,

> Only when the individual reconciles eventually the opposites of form and matter in his soul will the deity favor him.
> (p. 235, n. 10)

Edgar's implied ability to remain virtuous while accepting within himself the potentialities of the villain and the beast is analogous to this inner reconciliation. In a larger sense, the experience of *King Lear* may be seen on one level as imparting intellectual virtue of this sort to its audience and readers.

These similarities aside, however, there are unequivocal differences between Bruno's avowed philosophical goal and the idea of wisdom implied by Shakespeare in *King Lear*. Bruno's philosophy is aristocratic. His Frenzied One is an intellectual titan whose quest takes him far above the common level of humanity. Conversely, Shakespeare's vision focuses on the indivisible communality of mankind. Edgar's hardwon wisdom, far from elevating him to pinnacles of superiority, makes him "pregnant to good pity"; and this wisdom is cognate with the image of shared suffering which dazzles Lear himself, and serves as fulcrum for the whole dramatic experience. Here, as he will in *The Tempest*, Shakespeare implies that wisdom is inseparable from humility; and this avowal of weakness is made gracious and memorable by the fact that it grows from a rarely equalled intensity of vision (see below, pp. 204–08).

18 *Shakespeare Survey* 19 (1966): 25–33 and 34–44, respectively.

19 In the Arden *Macbeth* (1951), pp. xxxiii–xxxiv.

20 See above, pp. 22–27.

21 See above, pp. 27–28, 39–40, 87.

22 Relevant to this point, and to Shakespeare's development of Macbeth in general, is Socrates' discussion of "guardians" in the *Republic* of Plato: 375a–376c, 416a, 440d, 466d.

23 Jacobi, p. 169; Sudhoff and Matthiessen, 11:138. Jacobi, p. 103, Sudhoff and Matthiessen, pt. 2 (Munich: O. W. Barth, 1923), 1:69. These passages are quoted above on pp. 26 and 37. Also see Bostocke, ch. 2.

24 This passage is in Shakespeare's source, Holinshed's *Chronicles* (1587); but it is nonetheless significant that Shakespeare should interrupt the pace of his drama to include it here.

25 This is a Baconian paradox. See the *New Organon* 1.3.

26 Note for example the clusters of paradoxes in V.ii: lines 2, 8, 15–16, 26–28, 236–237, 243, 244, 252, 253, 260, 279, 286–287, 295, 296, 307–308, 309–310, 344, 348, 360–363; or in II.ii: lines 24, 100–101, 131, 133, 134, 177, 178, 204, 205, 231, 232, 235–236, 236–237, 238–239.

27 Note particularly Caesar's characterization in III.iv.1–10, III.v, III.xii.26–33, IV.vi.10–19, and V.ii.179–189. Frank Kermode's remark

that Caesar is "chilly" and "cunning" and his claim that Caesar possesses "Machiavellian *virtù*" (*The Riverside Shakespeare*, p. 1345) are
understatements.

28 Maynard Mack, Introduction to *Antony and Cleopatra* in *The
Pelican Shakespeare*, Alfred Harbage, ed. (Baltimore: Penguin, 1970),
p. 1170.

29 This dilemma is emphasized throughout the "Dark Lady" sonnets and particularly in the famous Sonnet 129.

30 *The Essayes of Montaigne*, trans. John Florio (1603; reprint
ed., New York: Modern Library, n.d.), pp. 990, 975; *Antony and
Cleopatra*, I.iv.10–13, II.ii.107–112.

31 Donald Frame identifies this monarch tentatively as Henry IV
of France in *The Complete Essays of Montaigne* (Stanford: Stanford
University Press, 1948; reprint ed., 1965), p. 825, n. 3.

32 Florio, p. 974.

33 Ibid., pp. 972, 974; see also p. 974, "infinit diversity," and
p. 963 (the first page of the essay): "No quality is so universall on
this surface of things, as variety and diversity." Montaigne himself
uses the appropriate Romance cognates.

34 Ibid., p. 987.

35 Ibid., p. 1010. Florio mistranslates the beginning of this
sentence, which should read, "She makes quite a baby of herself . . . ";
or see Frame, p. 855.

36 Ibid., p. 1012.

37 Ibid., pp. 1012–13.

38 Ibid., p. 987.

39 On the distinction between these two ethics, see Cicero *De
Officiis* passim; Machiavelli, *Il Principe*, ch. 15; Montaigne "De l'Utile
et de l'Honneste" 3.1, and Bacon "Of Fortune."

40 In his *Life of Antony*, Plutarch speaks briefly of a Domitius
who deserted Antony, repented, and died shortly thereafter; but this
Domitius was "sicke of an agewe." See Geoffrey Bullough, *Narrative
and Dramatic Sources of Shakespeare* (New York: Columbia University Press, 1957–1975), 5:298.

41 On this subject see the conclusion of Plato's *Symposium*,
where Socrates remarks that comedy and tragedy spring from the
same genius, and Castiglione *Il Libro del Cortegiano* 2.46; Singleton,
pp. 145–46.

CHAPTER 6

The Tempest: Prospero as Hero
of Contraries

It has been said that great classical art has the look of the familiar. The implication of this statement is that forms of truth are innate and universal; that great art so totally embodies these inner forms that, even when seen for the first time, it gives the impression of something intimately and anciently known. Under such circumstances, art becomes something more than a sophisticated means of creating or imitating specific experiences. It becomes a vehicle—perhaps the only one—for realizing and conveying a deeply-felt unanimity. The profound message of great classical art—of the *Laocoön,* for example—is not that all is good or beautiful or orderly. It is not that all is tragic or mean or chaotic. It is, more accurately, that all is shared.[1]

If praise of this sort may be accorded to Shakespeare, it is not only because of his verbal expressiveness, but also because of the remarkable way in which he organizes character, action, and time. From this structural viewpoint, none of his dramas, not even the Tragedies, rewards study more than *The Tempest* (1611). Here, themes and images, parallels and oppositions are woven into a broader temporal fabric whose reiterative structure is so orderly and consistent that it resembles those musical forms which are canonic or built upon a ground base.[2] Here also, as in some of his earlier plays, the clash of character and action is echoed by the dia-

lectical use of conflicting ideologies. This dramatic architecture is further strengthened by a highly effective appropriation of the classical unities. The result is an experience
which, for all its profound intention and spacious allusive-
ness, is magically familiar and immediate.[3] Paradoxically,
this balanced and intricate structure opens avenues not just
to our rational selves, but to the mute energies that lie beneath. Indeed, the pervasive correlatives and reiterations of
The Tempest resemble the symbolic and reiterative structure
of dreams.

The Fictive Structure

The Tempest has three plot-lines, all revolving around
Prospero and Ariel. These are figured in action at least four
times each and are kept separate from each other until the
final scene. Plot A concerns Alonso, Gonzalo, and the other
Italian courtiers; it begins in I.i, and its chief events are Antonio's attempted *coup* (II.i) and Ariel's arraignment of
Alonso, Antonio, and Sebastian (III.iii).[4] Plot B stars Caliban, who is introduced in I.ii; it concerns his meeting with
Stephano and Trinculo (II.ii) and their conspiracy against
Prospero. Plot C is about the love of Ferdinand and Miranda,
who meet in I.ii and whose engagement is solemnized by the
great masque of IV.i. These plot-lines alternate as follows:

I		II		III			IV	V
i	ii	i	ii	i	ii	iii	i	i
A	BC	A	B	C	B	A	CB	ACB

Mark Rose has drawn our attention to the remarkable balance and order of this design.[5] The central scenes (I.ii–IV.i)
form a bilateral symmetry or palindrome of action (BCABC
BACB). This and the use of repetitive sequence (ABC, ABC,
BAC, BACB) establish a subliminally evocative rhythm of
action, suggesting underlying principles of order and matur-
ing revolutions of time. Like circling revelers the three
stories parade themselves around the center, developing in
measured steps towards the encompassing conclusion of V.i.

The symmetry carries beyond chronological organization and into repeated action and unified theme. Plots A, B, and C all reach their crises on the penultimate revolution (III.iii, IV.i), and each time the crisis is achieved through a masque or vision created by Prospero and managed by Ariel. While the three lines contain a number of common thematic elements, that one which unifies them most fully, and in each case precipitates the crisis, is the theme of rebellion. Caliban and Antonio not only attempt usurpation onstage, but are shown to have rebelled in the past as well (I.ii.345–348, 75–132). Prospero arrests Ferdinand, accusing him, with conscious injustice, of treasonous intentions:

> Thou dost here usurp
> The name thou ow'st not, and hast put thyself
> Upon this island as a spy, to win it
> From me, the lord on't.

> Speak not you [Miranda] for him; he's a traitor.
>   (I.ii.454–457, 461)

Ferdinand, we know, is neither imposter nor usurper. Prospero's rough treatment of him is (aside from its obvious dramatic purpose) preventive rather than punitive:

> They are both in either's pow'rs; but this swift business
> I must uneasy make, lest too light winning
> Make the prize light.
>   (I.ii.451–453)

Yet the emphasis on rebellion is significant and looks ahead towards a scene in which the theme will be expanded strikingly. We will see in the crucial masque that Ferdinand's potential rebellion is psychological rather than political; it will be metaphorically connected with the excesses of the mythical lawbreaker, Venus; with Caliban, the half-human rebel whose treasons are both social and sexual; and with the character who is, in a heroic sense, the greatest rebel of all, Prospero himself. The concentration on rebellion is tireless, dealing with not only the political but also the psychological aspects of the subject, and culminating with Prospero's effort, in three successive scenes, to purge offending nature with visions.[6] As with musical forms based on reiteration—fugue, canon, passacaglia—differing textures of ideas are set up against a persistent tonal echo; individual experience moves within a responsive structure of statements, memories, and returns.

The Ethical Structure

The dynamics of plot and theme are reinforced by an elegantly patterned dialectic of conflicting ideologies. Here, as in earlier plays, characters become the spokesmen for various current philosophies, sophisticated or vulgar. But seldom is the range of ideas as broad, or the treatment as explicit, as in *The Tempest*. Prospero's island becomes at times a fabulous academy where the dominant or sensational ideas of Shakespeare's day are debated, sometimes in individual discourse, sometimes in dialogue, and sometimes in the language of dramatic action. We cannot fully understand Prospero or the design of his creator without a detailed analysis of this pattern of ideas.

Shakespeare's debt to Montaigne in Gonzalo's "commonwealth" speech of II.i has been acknowledged for over two hundred years.[7] Moreover, it is clear to most modern readers that Gonzalo's genial commonwealth, where the abundance of nature and the lack of civilized uses makes people "innocent and pure," must be of ponderable significance in a play that is itself utopian in theme and moral in discourse. Scholarship has remained unaware, however, that in Gonzalo's version the sense of Montaigne's original has been twisted, if not totally subverted. Shakespeare is guilty not only of theft but of willful assault, and the nature of this violence is directly pertinent to the meaning of the play.

Gonzalo brings up his commonwealth in an effort to take

Alonso's mind off the shipwreck and the supposed death
of his son Ferdinand. As diversion the speech is a failure;
Alonso is not listening at all. The speech is not referred to
explicitly again, and it plays no role in the development of
the plot. Had it no thematic significance, it would be nothing but a digression, a charming Renaissance set-piece on
the subject of idealized politics:

> I' th' commonwealth I would, by contraries,
> Execute all things; for no kind of traffic
> Would I admit; no name of magistrate;
> Letters should not be known; riches, poverty,
> And use of service, none; contract, succession,
> Bourn, bound of land, tilth, vineyard, none;
> No use of metal, corn, or wine, or oil;
> No occupation, all men idle, all;
> And women too, but innocent and pure;
> No sovereignty—
> *Seb.*   Yet he would be king on't.
> *Ant.* The latter end of his commonwealth forgets
> the beginning.
> *Gon.* All things in common nature should produce
> Without sweat or endeavor: treason, felony,
> Sword, pike, knife, gun, or need of any engine,
> Would I not have; but nature should bring forth,
> Of it own kind, all foison, all abundance,
> To feed my innocent people.
> (II.i.148–165)

Shakespeare's source reads as follows:

> It is a nation, would I answer Plato, that hath no kind of traf-
> fike, no knowledge of letters, no intelligence of numbers, no
> name of magistrate, nor of politike superioritie; no use of service,
> of riches or of povertie; no contracts, no successions, no parti-
> tions, no occupation but idle; no respect of kinred, but common,
> no apparell but naturall, no manuring of lands, no use of wine,
> corne, or mettle. The very words that import lying, falshood,
> treason, dissimuluations, covetousnes, envie, detraction, and par-
> don, were never heard of amongst them. How dissonant would
> hee find his imaginarie commonwealth from this perfection![8]
> *Hos natura modos primum dedit.*

> Nature at first uprise,
> These manners did devise.

> . . . for to this day they yet enjoy that naturall ubertie and fruit-
> fulnesse, which without labouring toyle, doth in such plenteous
> abundance furnish them with all necessary things, that they need
> not enlarge their limits.

> These [brethren] leave this full possession of goods in common,
> and without division to their heires, . . .[9]

Shakespeare's fidelity to specific points and even specific phrases in Florio's *The Essayes of Montaigne* is unquestionable. Equally remarkable, however, is his lack of fidelity to Montaigne's general meaning. By a subtle change in emphasis, a few added words and, above all, a complete disregard for context, Shakespeare has all but reversed the doctrine inherent in Montaigne's exposition. In so doing he has changed virtuous cannibals into innocent pacifists.

Montaigne's natives are warriors. They use wooden swords, sharpened at the end; with these they will fight to the death. If victorious they return home with their enemies' heads.[10] If they take captives, they treat them courteously for a while and then eat them, as "an extreme, and inexpiable revenge."[11] They go to war gladly, neither for material nor for territorial gain, but for pure "jelousie of virtue."[12] Virtue, in its classical, warlike sense, is the idea that dominates their lives. As the warriors sit at long tables drinking beer, priests pass among them singing of two paramount obligations: "*First, valour against their enemies, then lovingness unto their wives.*"[13]

The cannibals' violent side is one of the chief subjects of Montaigne's essay. But Shakespeare omits this element, filling the resultant void with an opposed idea that is wholly his own making:

> Sword, pike, knife, gun, or need of any engine
> Would I not have.

He rounds out this new idea by making the dominant moral principle of the commonwealth not virtue but innocence:

> ... but innocent and pure; ...

> To feed my innocent people.

These quantitatively small changes have a radical effect. With the end of Gonzalo's speech, Montaigne's robust barbarians have vanished, and we see instead a nation of lambs. Two philosophies could hardly be more opposed than those which, respectively, connect 'untouched' nature with violent aggression and with innocuous innocence. Indeed, Gonzalo's doctrine is less like Montaigne's probably ironic militarism than like the implied behaviorism of Thomas More, who has Raphael Hythloday describe Utopians who avoid violence because it is dangerous and corrupting:

> The citizens are not allowed to do the slaughtering [of animals]. The Utopians think that slaughtering destroys the sense of compassion, the most distinctively human feeling of our nature.[14]

Similarly, the Utopians have rejected the use of money because they believe it to be conducive to avarice; and they prefer hiring mercenaries to going to war themselves.[15] Like Gonzalo's innocent people, More's Utopians are examples of the doctrine which holds that aggressive and rebellious passions are not instinctive, but are rather the result of social practices.

What function in the philosophical structure of *The Tempest* is better served by Gonzalo's doctrine than by Montaigne? Answering this question forces us back into the text of the play, and through this to broader areas of Renaissance ethical inquiry. The thematic importance of Gonzalo's speech is underlined in an essay by Hans Speier:

> All the aptitudes of man and the dangers of nature which render sovereignty both necessary and precarious are disregarded in Gonzalo's dream ...

Shakespeare's answer to Gonzalo's dream is *The Tempest* as a whole.[16]

Speier sees Gonzalo's speech as a foil for experience, an intellectual thesis ironically qualified by the "reality" of its dramatic context.[17] We may see how this dialectic operates by comparing Gonzalo's doctrine with three other important elements: the character of Caliban, Prospero's remarks about nature, good, and evil in I.ii, and the action of II.i.

Listening to Gonzalo's speech, Antonio remarks shrewdly that "the end of his commonwealth forgets the beginning." This comment (especially in terms of its speaker) is so evocative that we may feel justified in taking it out of context. Certainly, if anything in *The Tempest* may be said to represent the "beginning" of politics—the primitive human raw material—it is Caliban. This character is traditionally seen as a figuration of chaotic natural energy—gross and dangerous yet inalienable from the human condition. To Frank Kermode, Caliban is "the natural man," "an extraordinarily powerful and comprehensive type of Nature"; to Northrop Frye, he is "nature without nurture."[18] We need go no further than Caliban to understand exactly what Gonzalo "forgets"; Caliban is a walking rebuttal to Gonzalo's utopian theory that civilization is the corrupter of innocent nature. Instead, Caliban represents a much more venerable theory of human nature, involving the irresolvable duality between man's orderly and anarchic instincts. This theory's chief source is Plato, and its countless Renaissance spokesmen include Francis Bacon:

[Plato on the soul as a charioteer and two horses:] The well-conditioned horse is erect and well-formed; he has a lofty neck and an aquiline nose, and his color is white, and he has dark eyes and is a lover of honor and modesty and temperance, and the follower of true glory; he needs not the touch of the whip, but is guided by word and admonition only. Whereas the other is a large misshapen animal, put together anyhow; he has a strong short neck; he is flat-faced and of a dark color, grey-eyed and bloodshot, the mate of insolence and pride, shag-eared, deaf, hardly yielding to blow or spur.[19]

[Bacon:]
. . . for certainly man is of kin to the beasts by his body, and if he be not of kin to God by his spirit, he is a base and ignoble creature.[20]

Caliban is not so much "nature" or "natural man" as the natural beast in man. As such, he is the ideal correlative of the unruly instincts which operate on other levels of *The Tempest*.

Gonzalo's remarks also reflect dialectically on that section of Prospero's expository speech to Miranda (I.ii) in which Prospero describes Antonio's usurpation of Milanese rule:

> I, thus neglecting worldly ends, all dedicated
> To closeness and the bettering of my mind
> With that which, but by being so retir'd,
> O'er-priz'd all popular rate, in my false brother
> Awak'd an *evil nature*, and my trust,
> Like a good parent, did *beget* of him
> A falsehood in its *contrary*, as great
> As my trust was; . . .
> (I.ii.89–96. My italics.)

The thematic significance of these lines is emphasized by the use of the word "contrary." Gonzalo uses the same word in the same ethical context ("I would by contraries/ Execute all things"), and the double use of this weighted word makes it all the clearer that the two implied views of human nature are totally opposed to each other. In Gonzalo's commonwealth, nature's innocence is fostered by the remission of law and constraint; for Prospero, on the other hand, it is this very remission ("trust," "confidence," and the "remov'd" position of the governor) that "awakes" and "begets" "an evil nature" in the governed. Prospero's analysis of experience is even more devastating to Gonzalo's doctrine than is the figure of Caliban. If Caliban's presence

argues that Gonzalo's gentle government is unrealistic because bestial instincts are native to man, Prospero's story
implies that bestial behavior may indeed be the result of
gentle government. Evil not only exists in nature but, paradoxically, can be engendered by goodness.

This violent interplay of doctrines is further complicated
by the action which shortly follows Gonzalo's "commonwealth" speech. Directly, Ariel puts everyone but Antonio
and Sebastian to sleep. The purpose of this stratagem of
Prospero's is unexplained; presumably it is to let Antonio
renew his old guilt by attempting to murder Alonso and
Gonzalo. Antonio wins Sebastian to this project in speeches
of sustained and lively rhetoric. The dominant image of his
dialogue is that of sleeping versus waking. Alonso's sleep is
used as a circumstance propitious for easy murder and also,
metaphorically, as a means of distinguishing slothful, "ebbing" men from men who are alert and able to capitalize on
their opportunities:

> Noble Sebastian,
> Thou let'st thy fortune sleep—die, rather; wink'st
> Whiles thou art waking.
>
> Th' occasion speaks thee, . . .
> (II.i.215–217, 207)

Conscience is dismissed as something immaterial and therefore negligible (lines 276–280). And Sebastian need fear no
retribution from Alonso's courtiers: "They'll take sugges-
tion as a cat laps milk" (line 288).

Antonio's philosophy suggests another opposed alternative to Gonzalo's view of nature. Here, destructive aggression is not only asserted but endorsed in a speech heavy
with positive, natural metaphors. The implied morality is as
follows: good men tend to trust, and trusting makes them
weak against attack; weakness is seen as a negative thing,
like ebbing and sleeping; enterprising, acquisitive men, more
energetic and alert, are therefore to be preferred. Good and

evil insidiously interchange roles. Goodness "sleeps" and "ebbs." Evil is seen as something that "flows," a positive, natural force. Moreover, true to Prospero's contention, evil actions are seen as emanating from their contrary—Alonso and Gonzalo's unsuspecting sleep.

Here again Shakespeare is using character and action to bring up a Renaissance philosophical vogue. Antonio's speech is accurate shorthand for Machiavelli—not the butchered Machiavelli of Gentillet but the careful literary strategist of *The Prince* and *The Discourses*. The chief points in Antonio's reasoning—the description of murder as courageous, the emphasis on profiting from occasion, the negative attitude towards conscience, and the cynicism about possible consequences—all occur, for example, in a single chapter of *The Discourses*, "Showing that Men are Very Rarely either Entirely Good or Entirely Bad" (1.27).[21] And when Antonio urges Sebastian to commit a deed "Whereof what's past is prologue" (line 254), he not only refers back to his own rise to power in Milan, but also asserts a primary tenet of Machiavellian philosophy: that men may structure future action according to rules derived from history.[22] Antonio's unabashed villainy in action becomes the dramatic medium for the most cynical of Renaissance political theories.

We see then that on one level *The Tempest* is a playing-field of philosophies, where traditional or modish doctrines are codified and set against each other or against structures of experience. It is like a Platonic dialogue in which characters not only endorse doctrines but act out their ethical consequences. In this lively confrontation there seem to be no winners. Caliban's vulgar anarchism, as refined by Stephano into an equally vulgar tyranny (III.ii), is easily thwarted. Gonzalo's optimistic behaviorism, though buttressed by his attractive and "holy" character, is clearly against the grain of the dramatic reality. Antonio's Machiavellianism, dynamic and alert, is foiled by the more disinterested alertness of Prospero and Ariel. Vivid as these theories may be, it is not they themselves, but rather their whole context, dialectical and encompassing, that would appear to hold the true doctrine or wisdom of *The Tempest*. And if that wisdom is offered up at all, it is through the figure who uniquely manipulates the context, Prospero himself.

Modern criticism has given much attention to the negative or 'tyrannical' side of Prospero's character—a roughness of manner established in the exposition scene and sustained through the first four acts. Why, in particular, does Prospero put Ferdinand and Miranda through clearly undeserved torments before giving them his blessing? Prospero's own explanation, that he does this to teach them the true value of their love (I.ii.451–453), is helpful but not completely satisfying. Prospero's 'intentions' have been variously interpreted. Dover Wilson's contention that Prospero is a "terrible old man," bent on revenge against the Italian party until he is taught mercy by Ariel, is opposed by F. D. Hoeniger, who explains Prospero's roughness as salutary, and part of a coherent attitude towards education and government.[23] Hoeniger argues sensibly that Prospero cannot possibly wish to take revenge on Alonso if he expects Miranda to marry Alonso's son. In enlarging on Hoeniger's theory I would like to show that Prospero's method is not only justified by the play's dialectic but also, as much as any other element in *The Tempest*, allied with the philosophical concerns of the sixteenth century.

Prospero's government of his island is obviously in sharp contrast with his previous government of Milan. The change may be seen as one from contemplative virtue ("thus neglecting wordly ends, all dedicated / To closeness and the bettering of my mind," I.ii.89–90) to an active virtue of vigilance, assertiveness, and control. This implied endorsement of active virtue is reminiscent of Castiglione, the English poet-humanists, and Shakespeare's own earlier drama; indeed, the idea is one of the foundations of Renaissance moral philosophy.[24] In *The Tempest*, however, Shakespeare makes this doctrine at once more specific and more complex. According to Prospero, it was not his general disengagement from political affairs that caused the real trouble in Milan so much as his particular trust of Antonio. His trust did not merely allow scope for Antonio's wickedness; rather, it "begot" Antonio's wickedness. Goodness, by one of the simplest of its expressions, engendered its contrary. Active virtue is thus obliged to fight an evil that grew from goodness.

Prospero's description of his fall from power is a political myth which justifies his present government. In the light of the past his gruffness, his chronic severity, and his "rough magic" take on meaning and coherence. In place of the confidence sans bound, is an active sternness which not only punishes evil deeds but also discourages the potential eruption of evil by a constant challenge to the virtue and awareness of the governed. When Prospero bullies and threatens his servants, when he makes arduous the courtship of Ferdinand and Miranda, his words and actions reflect a hard-won knowledge of the waywardness of nature, suggesting that even the two young lovers, as sharers in the human condition, must be protected from their own baser instincts. For the Italian princes, his roughness is a purgative, awakening them to their guilt and seeking to prepare them for "a clear life ensuing" (Ariel's words in III.iii.82). If his method is paradoxical, it is because, as the whole design of *The Tempest* amply shows, the relationship itself between good and evil is paradoxical and dynamic. Prospero has learned that experience can reverse the normal functions of value. He has learned that contraries can provoke evil. Now he knowledgeably tests their power to provoke good.

In the substance of Prospero's method, even in the language attached to it, are echoes of Shakespeare's earlier concern with the moral implications of Paracelsian thought. The Galenists, we remember, argued that *contraria contrariis curantur* ("contraries are cured by contraries"); the Paracelsians, that *similia similibus curantur* ("likes are cured by likes"). In *Romeo and Juliet* and in the Problem Comedies, Shakespeare seems to be transposing the Paracelsian view into a moral context.[25] Major figures in these plays distinguish themselves from their fellow characters by using craft against craft, evil against evil. In *The Tempest*, the moral implications of the medical dispute are revived again. Gonzalo's remark that he would govern "by contraries" means not only that his rule would be "contrary to traditional usages" (the normal explanatory note) but also that he expects the basic civil diseases—treason, felony, aggression—to succumb to their contraries—benignity of nature, gentleness of government. Prospero's analysis of his earlier fall and, as Speier puts it, "the whole of *The Tempest*," refute this theory. Prospero asserts that contrary begets contrary and returns to the homeopathic ethic of the Problem Comedies.

The Allegorical Structure

Elements of *The Tempest* persistently invite allegorical interpretation. Prospero is a magician whose powers resemble a god's. Like a god he controls the elements, foresees the future, orchestrates events, punishes, and pardons. There are also strong links between Prospero and the character of the artist. Prospero creates visions in which spirits take parts and recite lines. He personally organizes much of the action, as an artist would his own work. He calls his magic his "art."[26] Some of his later speeches suggest an artist's view of his own coming retirement.

Equally suggestive is the context in which Prospero appears. The two servants, Ariel and Caliban, correspond to the two antithetical elements of a traditional duality: Ariel, to those aspects of human nature which are abstract and intellectual; Caliban, to those which are concrete and physiological. Prospero asserts mastery over both extremes. Yet, if only because they are the necessary adjuncts of his power,

his character is not wholly distinct from them.[27] This relationship is complicated by the fact that both servants wish
to escape from Prospero, that he treats both harshly, and
that, in the end, he releases Ariel and keeps Caliban.

Finally, there is Prospero's creation, the great masque
(Act IV). Its characters, the goddesses Ceres, Iris, and Juno,
are described in language that is heavy with natural sym-
bolism. They make reference to mythic events which have
a clear relationship to the moral concerns of the play as
a whole. This connection is reinforced structurally when
the masque is interrupted by Caliban's conspiracy. The interruption produces a marked change in Prospero's mood
and behavior. It is dramatically the only unexpected event
in the play and may be seen as a sort of thematic crisis.

Our study of Shakespearean contrariety up to now provides material for an interpretation of some of these elements. Prospero's rough magic, as we have seen, is cognate
with his other varied and continuous bullyings of nature;
it is a logical, though fabulous, metaphorical extension of
his human insight and power. Something similar may be
said about Ariel and Caliban. Prospero's ethereal minister
and his bestial servant may be seen as metaphorical exten-
sions of the two aspects which preeminently characterize his
moral awareness: his unusually keen understanding, and the
syndrome of passion and disorder upon which this understanding is repeatedly focused. With the politics and ethics
of *The Tempest* in mind, we may conclude moreover that,
as psychological attributes, Ariel and Caliban are necessary
not only to Prospero but also to each other. Prospero's vision is distinguished and effective because it is predicated on
an understanding of disorder; his intellect is refined and
magical to the extent that it takes its own opposite into account. This contrary yet interdependent relationship is
generally analogous to the notions of psychological duality
formulated by Paracelsus and Bruno and analyzed in chapters above. These earlier writers (who incidentally both as-

sociate themselves with the idea of the Magus) see the philosopher's relationship to the astral and earthly principles as being troubled and perilous; yet both imply that the validity of the higher principle somehow depends upon the philosopher's recognition and acceptance of the lower one.[28] Throughout his middle and later career, Shakespeare has labored repeatedly to wrestle this duality into coherence. As early as *Romeo and Juliet*, he has suggested that the two contrary realms of experience are, in fact, profoundly interrelated; and in later plays he has explored these relationships psychologically and in structures of characters and time. Now, at the end of his career, he revives the question, posing it with mythic force and compressing its ramifications into the scope of a single character. Prospero may be seen as Shakespeare's hero of contraries. *The Tempest* may be seen as a mature and conclusive reevaluation of Shakespeare's dominant intellectual concerns.

It is only natural that a literary hero of such proportions should test the ultimate limits of his power. In creating his great masque, Prospero seems to be making an attempt of this kind. To understand what is happening at this point in the drama, we must take the masque's context, its mythological associations and its natural imagery very seriously. The masque is, first of all, a moral allegory created expressly for the edification of Ferdinand and Miranda. Prospero has just (IV.i.53) enjoined Ferdinand to refrain from premarital sexual intercourse, and the masque illustrates this counsel by banishing the goddess Venus and her son Cupid. Iris makes this connection explicit as she comforts the fearful Ceres:

> Of her [Venus'] society
> Be not afraid. I met her Deity
> Cutting the clouds towards Paphos; and her son
> Dove-drawn with her. Here thought they to have done
> Some wanton charm upon this man and maid
> [Ferdinand and Miranda],
> Whose vows are, that no bed-rite shall be paid

Till Hymen's torch be lighted; but in vain,
Mars's hot minion is return'd again; . . .
                    (IV.i.91–98)

Prospero's earlier maxim, that "too light winning / Make[s] the prize light," here reappears dramatically, almost emblematically. The concord and bounty of the goddesses—honor, riches, earth's increase, etc.—are made dependent on the absence of Venus or inordinate lust.

The second level of meaning involves the four elements. It was noted by Hartley Coleridge and later by G. Wilson Knight that the goddesses of the masque suggest elemental powers.[29] Iris, the "watery arch" with "honey-drops" and "refreshing showers," suggests water; Ceres, with her "turfy mountains," "meads," and "banks," earth; Juno, "Queen o' the sky," air. Thus a natural texture enriches the effect of the ceremony. It is not merely heavenly powers but elemental nature, apparently in harmony with itself and with the human institution of marriage, that blesses the betrothal of Ferdinand and Miranda.

But Prospero's art and the cosmology of *The Tempest* are emphatically related to four elements, not three.[30] With the four elements in mind, moreover, the forced absence of Venus must be seen as important. Just as the goddess Venus is missing, so is the element, fire; and within a brief space, Shakespeare four times evokes the traditional connection between venereal longings and fire. Prospero has told Ferdinand to beware of lust as "the fire i' th' blood"; Ferdinand promises to restrain "the ardor of my liver"; Iris mentions "Hymen's torch" and refers to Venus as "Mars's hot minion" (IV.i.53, 56, 97, 98). Elizabethan science connected the liver with choler and the element fire in the human body and also connected Mars (via choler) with fire.[31] Moreover, just as Iris, Juno's messenger, mediates between Ceres and Venus in the masque, water and air mediate between earth and fire in a popular Renaissance theory of the elements. As Joshua Sylvester puts it in his widely-read translation of Du Bartas,

> But least the Fire, which all the rest embraces,
> Being too-neere, should burne the Earthe to ashes:
> As chosen Umpires, the great All-Creator
> Betweene these Foes placed the Aire and Water: . . .[32]

Du Bartas is presenting the traditional doctrine which puts earth at the center of things, enclosed by spheres of water, air, and fire, respectively. Earth and fire are "foes," as are Ceres and Venus in the masque. Earth, like Ceres, is peaceable; fire, like Venus, is the aggressor. Only the interposition of water and air prevents a conflict that would destroy the universe.[33]

The connection between the goddesses and the elements is important because it suggests a forcible reorganization of the basic qualities of nature. Among both goddesses and elements a vital component is suppressed; and the implication is that, if this element were included, it would disrupt the whole and ruin the effect of the ceremony. Shakespeare's audience, who were taught that both goddesses and elements lived in strife, would sympathize with Prospero's apparent desire to exile the most unruly of them, at least temporarily, in the interests of harmony. Ferdinand's admiring remarks on the masque further enrich the sense of concord:

> This is a most majestic vision, and
> Harmonious charmingly.

> Let me live here ever;
> So rare a wond'red father and a wise
> Makes this place Paradise.
>   (IV.i.118–119, 122–124)

Ferdinand briefly evokes a third figurative realm of concord and unity—the Garden of Eden.

The goddesses' blessings and Ferdinand's remarks are followed by a "graceful dance" of spirits as sicklemen and nymphs which, by its music and its elemental associations, prolongs the desired impression of natural concord. But this impression and the masque itself are cut off when Prospero remembers Caliban's conspiracy. Ferdinand and Miranda notice that Prospero is "in some passion." He responds to their concern with a famous but enigmatical speech:

> Our revels now are ended. These our actors
> (As I foretold you) were all spirits, and
> Are melted into air, into thin air,
> And like the baseless fabric of this vision,
> The cloud-capp'd towers, the gorgeous palaces,
> The solemn temples, the great globe itself,
> Yea, all which it inherit, shall dissolve,
> And like this insubstantial pageant faded
> Leave not a rack behind. We are such stuff
> As dreams are made on; and our little life
> Is rounded with a sleep. Sir, I am vex'd;
> Bear with my weakness, my old brain is troubled.
>   (IV.i.148–159)

To understand the intensity of Prospero's reaction, we must realize that the masque is more than an ethical allegory concocted for young lovers. The symbolic attempt to tame and civilize nature by banishing disruptive forces is a radical extension of Prospero's method of operation on all three plot levels. The rebellious and lecherous Caliban was isolated and suppressed, penned up in a "rock." Ferdinand and Miranda have been guided through an erotic relationship devoid of light winning and lust in action. The plotters and usurpers, Antonio, Alonso, and Sebastian, have been subjected to a purgation of terror and madness. The masque suggests an analogous but even more ambitious social goal: an elemental reorganization of nature in which disorder is not merely controlled but effectively banished. The masque is a daring image of man-made redemption, an image of nature purified by knowledge and art.

As both G. Wilson Knight and E. M. W. Tillyard have briefly suggested, the interruption of the masque radically modifies this image by calling to mind, in the figure of Caliban, a quality of nature that seems essentially irredeemable.[34] Prospero's own words, spoken shortly after the interruption, support this interpretation:

> A devil, a born devil, on whose nature
> Nurture can never stick; on whom my pains;
> Humanely taken, all, all lost, quite lost;
> And as with age his body uglier grows,
> So his mind cankers.
> (IV.i.188–192)

Caliban, whose baseness eludes both the promise of nature and the scope of art, represents an ultimate limitation to the human improvement of humanity. His lechery and destructiveness call up the syndrome of Venus, Cupid, and Mars and the insistent presence of exactly those elements which Prospero would have banished from his masque and his world. If Prospero's majestic vision is the expression of a philosophical attitude, the reminder of Caliban's permanence is proof that this attitude is faulty. Prospero is vexed, not because he must make a minor tactical adjustment, but rather because his power, both political and aesthetic, has been conclusively limited.

Prospero's response to this setback, the speech, "Our revels now are ended," is, like the masque, partially understandable in terms of Renaissance science. Its statement of the impermanence of earthly things arises thematically from the experience of the masque, where natural elements are seen in a state of strife. Shakespeare's audience would have been acquainted with the theory, presented also by Du Bartas, that the impermanence of things derives from the conflict of the four elements. Du Bartas thus explains the "change of Formes":

> Now the chief motive of these Accidents
> Is the dire discord of our Elements:
> Truce hating Twinnes, . . .

and later,

> Things that consist of th' elements uniting,
> Are ever tost with an intestine fighting;

Whence springs (in time) their life and their deceasing,
Their divers change, their waxing and decreasing:
So that, of all there is, or may be seene
With mortall eyes, under nights horned Queene,
Nothing retaineth the same form or face,
Hardly the halfe of halfe an howers space.[35]

In Du Bartas' universe, cosmic battle necessitates cosmic change and thus the impermanence of forms and institutions. The same idea applies to Prospero's moral world. If the destructive influences of Venus and Caliban are recognized as unalterable components of human nature, then Prospero's quest for a harmonious social order, as well as its mimetic figuration in art, must be seen as baseless and impossible. The dignified resignation of Prospero's speech suggests that finally he is in accord with this reality.

After the masque, the cycle of ambition, enterprise, and failure is immediately reiterated in the subplot. The plebeian rebels enter, *"all wet."* Ariel has hung out *"glistering apparel."* Stephano and Trinculo don monarchic garments and begin kinging it. Caliban's sensible warning that the apparels are "trash" and "luggage," unsuitable to the current state of political affairs, is ignored. Stephano and Trinculo shun reality and exult in illusion until they are routed and hounded from the stage by Ariel and his spirits. A similar experience has already occurred in the so-called "antemasque," when Ariel, posing as a harpy, disrupts a lavish but illusory banquet, thwarting Antonio's renewed efforts at regicide, accusing him, Sebastian, and Alonso of high offences, and subjecting the three of them to an "ecstasy" of desperation (III.iii). The use of masque elements to elaborate a formula of aspiration and disillusionment is thus critical to all three plot-levels. With dreamlike repetition and dreamlike variation, Shakespeare establishes a profound pattern of rebellion and defeat.[36]

This pattern is only part of a grander design. Every major character desires in some sense to transcend laws and limits. Each sees these laws and limits differently—erects his own prison according to his own lights. Caliban rebels in order to exchange involuntary slavery for voluntary slavery; he would be "for aye" Stephano's foot-licker. Ariel, that harnessed abstraction, wishes to return to his abstract element, the air; a fitting contrary to Caliban's lust for slavery, he wishes what we might infer to be a total and absurd freedom, a freedom *from* choice. Stephano rebels for possessions and pleasure; Antonio, more nobly corrupt, reveres active power. The lovers, Ferdinand and Miranda, chafe against the benign delays of social order. Gonzalo, an archetypal liberal, would subvert social order in a unilateral assertion of trust. An overcivilized man, he is ignorant of the myth of Caliban and the basis of civilization. Prospero establishes and controls the context which limits these aims and these visions. In a highly positive sense, he embodies the limiting and coercing propensities of civilization. Yet, as we have seen, Prospero is a rebel, too. A champion of civilization, he rebels in its name against the restrictions of a broader natural context. His pains in reshaping nature are infinite and varied. He shuts Caliban up in a rock and threatens to do something similar with Ariel. He purges the courtiers with a vision. He shatters trees, shakes promontories, dims the sun, and makes storms. In the same way that a natural scientist would use abstract logic in an effort to change nature, he employs Ariel on earthly errands of repair. He seeks to civilize Ferdinand and Miranda with a masque which mythologically suggests his own vision of a subdued nature. In the *New Atlantis*, Francis Bacon would create a vision rather like Prospero's: an island dedicated to the knowledge that would reorganize nature and tame its massive energies. But unlike Bacon's scientists, Prospero fails. Like his own Caliban, he realizes and accepts his failure.

In Prospero's case the mythic formula so elaborately set up, the cycle of rebellion and failure, takes on another meaning. Civilization may legislate against rebellion; but in a larger sense (reminiscent of *Genesis* and *Prometheus Bound*), civilization is itself a form of rebellion, a comprehensive reordering of huge and unspecified forces. These forces, however stifled or redirected, are never permanently remade. They unite in a wildness which infringes on civilization from without, which threatens to erupt within. Yet, bearing in mind the reiterated implications of the mature Tragedies, we must see these forces as also providing the energy through which civilization endures and is reborn. Abstractions, which mount to the skies, have no meaning when divorced from these primeval and immanent realities. Like Caliban they were here at the beginning and remain throughout; like Caliban they crave recognition and deny explanation. They are abused by philosophers, but apparently are less objectionable to wise men:

> This thing of darkness I
> Acknowledge mine.
> (V.i.275–276)

The Apologetic Structure

Projecting these considerations further, we see the outlines of what might be called an aesthetic autobiography. Caliban and his rebellion suggest very vividly the issue which, over many years, has been Shakespeare's chief philosophical concern—the revolt of untamable inner forces against restrictive social constructs. Caliban is related genealogically to earlier Shakespearean characters who, like him, personify the assault on law and stable value: Venus, Tarquin, the Dark Lady, and even Falstaff. He is a mythic archetype of the "rude will" which Friar Lawrence alludes to in *Romeo and Juliet* and the "basest weed" in Sonnet 94; he symbolizes the outrageous forces which, in *The Merchant of Venice* and the three Problem Comedies, mount attacks on justice, order, language, and sexual morality. In the Problem Comedies, these eruptive forces appear predominantly as a disease which revolutionary moralists set out to cure. In the mature Tragedies, however, Shakespeare's attitude towards these rebellious instincts changes profoundly. Man's discordant energies lose their inferior status of disease and appear emphatically as part of the natural structure. They are seen as producing good as well as evil, and the rough conflict they create is accepted as one of the innate characteristics of experience. A development of the same sort occurs in *The Tempest*. Prospero uses his "art" systematically to rid his unwilling subjects of their rebellious impulses. He would banish Venus from the heavens and, by implication, fire from the elements. His vision of a purified Nature fails because of Caliban; the masque dissolves, "an insubstantial pageant." He accepts Caliban and acknowledges the bestial rebel to be his own. This failure of reforming zeal, and this willing appropriation of darkness, are the critical actions of *The Tempest*. They may also point autobiographically to a critical development in Shakespeare's writing career: the acceptance of contrariety and the experience of the great Tragedies.

Notes to Chapter Six

1   The notion of Greek Art as expressive of ideal and universal forms derives from German classicism of the eighteenth and nineteenth centuries. In *Naive and Sentimental Poetry* (1795–96), Schiller praises the Greeks for their closeness to nature and remarks that natural scenes (including "monuments of ancient times") are delightful because, *"They are what we were*; they are what *we should once again* become. . . . they are also representations of our highest fulfillment in the ideal, thus evoking in us a sublime tenderness." Trans. Julius A. Elias (New York: Ungar, 1966), pp. 83–85.

2   Music of this sort (for example, the "catch") was cultivated during Shakespeare's time. See *The Tempest*, III.ii.116–127.

3   Erwin Panofsky makes a similar point about classical architecture in contrasting the interior of St. Peter's with that of a typical Gothic cathedral: "In a classic temple—and, consequently, in a Renaissance church—the bases, the shafts, and the capitals of the columns

are proportioned, more or less, according to the relation between the foot, the body, and the head of a normal human being. And it is precisely the absence of such an analogy between architectural and human proportions that caused the Renaissance theorists to accuse medieval architecture of having "no proportion at all." The doors of St. Peter's rise to about twelve meters and the cherubs supporting the holy-water basins to nearly four. As a result, the visitor is permitted, as it were, to expand his own ideal stature in accordance with the actual size of the building and for this very reason often fails to be impressed by its objective dimensions, however gigantic they may be (St. Peter's has been described, only half facetiously, as "small but neat"); whereas a Gothic cathedral of much lesser dimensions forces us to remain conscious of our actual stature in contrast with the size of the building." *Renaissance and Renascences in Western Art* (New York and Evanston: Harper and Row, 1960), p. 29.

4   These act-scene divisions are from our earliest text of *The Tempest*, the First Folio. I cite them merely as a convenience, for my analysis in no way depends on them.

5   Mark Rose, *Shakespearean Design* (Cambridge, Mass.: Harvard University Press, Belknap Press), pp. 173–74.

6   Ariel frights the courtiers in III.iii. Prospero creates his masque for the young lovers in IV.i; immediately afterwards he thwarts the Caliban uprising with *divers spirits in shape of dogs and hounds, hunting them about* (stage direction after IV.i.254).

7   See Shakespeare's *Works*, ed. Edward Capell (1768), p. 63b, or *The Tempest*, *New Variorum Edition*, ed. H. H. Furness (New York: Lippincott, 1892; reprint ed., New York: Dover, 1964), p. 104.

8   Plato himself seems to answer this objection in *The Republic* bk. 2, 368–72.

9   *The Essayes of Montaigne*, trans. John Florio (1603; reprint ed., New York: Modern Library, n.d.), first quotation, p. 164; two following, p. 167.

10   Ibid., p. 166.

11   Ibid.

12   Ibid., p. 167.

13   Ibid., p. 165.

14   Thomas More, *Utopia*, ed. H. V. S. Ogden (New York: Appleton-Century-Crofts, 1949), p. 39.

15   Ibid., pp. 43–45, 66.

16   Hans Speier, "Shakespeare's *The Tempest*," in *Social Order and the Risks of War* (1952; reprint ed., Cambridge, Mass., and London: M. I. T. Press, 1969), pp. 138, 135.

17   W. R. Elton calls this method (as employed in *King Lear*) "Irony as Structure." *King Lear and the Gods* (San Marino: The Huntington Library, 1966), pp. 329–34.

18   *The Tempest*, ed. Frank Kermode (New York: Random House, 1964), intro., pp. xxxviii, xliii; *The Tempest*, ed. Northrop Frye (New York: Penguin, 1970), intro., p. 16.

19   *Phaedrus*, in *The Works of Plato*, trans. B. Jowett (New York: Dial Press, n.d.), 3:413 (253d-e).

20   Francis Bacon, "Of Atheism," *Essays* (1624).

21   This chapter tells of Giovanpaolo Baglioni, who had an opportunity to murder Pope Julius II but did not avail himself of it.   The deed is described as demanding "magnanimity" and "courage"; Giovanpaolo is offered "opportunity"; Machiavelli discounts the influence of any "conscientious scruples" and concludes that, compared with the grandeur of the deed, the resultant dangers would not be great.

22   As Machiavelli suggests in the dedicatory letters of both *The Prince* and *The Discourses*.

23   Dover Wilson, *The Meaning of The Tempest* (Newcastle upon Tyne: The Literary and Philosophical Society of Newcastle upon Tyne, 1936), p. 14; F. D. Hoeniger, "Prospero's Storm and Miracle," *Shakespeare Quarterly* 7 (1956):35.

24   See pp. 19–22, 41–44, 101 above.

25   See pp. 35–43 and Chapter 4 above.

26   Doffing his magic mantle, Prospero says, "Lie there, my art" (I.ii.25).   On this metonymy, see the *Aeneid* 5.484: *hic victor caestus artemque repono.*

27   Ariel is of course indispensable and cannot be released until Prospero's mission is complete. Early on, Prospero also admits that Caliban performs indispensable functions: "But as 'tis,/We cannot miss him" (I.ii.310–311).

28   On Paracelsus and magic, see Walter Pagel, *Paracelsus: An Introduction*, pp. 38, 62–65, 111–12, 149, 218–26, 284–301, 315–35; on Bruno and magic, see Frances Yates, *Giordano Bruno and the Hermetic Tradition* (Chicago: University of Chicago Press, 1964). Bruno speaks of contrariety as magic in *De la causa, principio et Uno* (Fifth Dialogue); see Sidney Greenberg, *The Infinite in Giordano Bruno* (New York: King's Crown Press, 1950), p. 172.   On contrariety and psychology, see above, pp. 25–35.

29   Hartley Coleridge, *Essays and Marginalia* (London, 1851), 2:132–133.   G. Wilson Knight, *The Crown of Life* (London, Methuen: 1947), p. 245.

30   In two important speeches, Prospero's art is related to all four elements. Miranda at the beginning of I.ii:

> If by your art, my dearest father, you have
> Put the wild *waters* in this roar, allay them.
> The *sky* it seems would pour down stinking *pitch*,
> But that the *sea*, mounting to th' *welkin's* cheek,
> Dashes the *fire* out.
>   (I.ii.1–5. My italics.)

Prospero in the final scene:

>   I have bedimm'd
> The noontide *sun*, call'd forth the mutinous *winds*,
> And 'twixt the green *sea* and the azur'd *vault*
> Set roaring war; to the dread rattling thunder
> Have I given *fire*, and rifted Jove's stout oak
> With his own *bolt*; the strong-bas'd *promontory*
> Have I made shake, and by the spurs pluck'd up
> The pine and cedar.
>   (V.i.41–48. My italics.)

31   See Sir Thomas Elyot, *Castel of Helth* (1541), p. ix; John W. Draper, *The Humors and Shakespeare's Characters* (Durham, N. C.: Duke University Press, 1945), pp. 46–48; and R. Klibansky, E. Panofsky, and F. Saxl, *Saturn and Melancholy* (London: Nelson, 1964), pp. 127, 128 (n.5), 187, 397.

32   *Bartas: His Devine Weekes and Works*, trans. Joshua Sylvester (1605; reprint ed., Gainsville, Fla.: Scholars' Facsimiles and Reprints, 1965), p. 41.   This was undoubtedly one of the most popular pieces of literature on science and religion in Shakespeare's time.   It was much praised by Shakespeare's contemporaries and, complete or in excerpts, went through eighteen English editions between 1590 and 1611.   See H. Ashton, *Du Bartas en Angleterre* (Paris, 1908), pp. 366–70.

33   But both [water and air], uniting their devided zeales,
      Tooke-up the Matter, and appeas'd the brall
      Which doubt-lesse else had dis-Created All.
                    (Sylvester, *Bartas*, pp. 41–42)

34   Knight, *The Crown of Life,* (London: Methuen, 1948), p. 246; E. M. W. Tillyard, *Shakespeare's Last Plays* (London: Chatto and Windus, 1962), p. 80.

35   Sylvester, *Bartas*, pp. 39, 65–66.

36   This interpretation of Prospero's masque was originally published in the *South Atlantic Quarterly* 71 (1972): 401–409.

INDEX

Achilles: 83–86, 117n
Active virtue: 21–22, 42–43, 64, 71–72, 127–28, 146–48, 163–64, 196–98
Aeneid: 210n
Agamemnon: 77–78, 81, 83, 115n
Agrippa, Heinrich Cornelius: 15, 17, 44n, 46n, 106, 116n
Ajax: 83–84
Albany, Duke of: 139, 141–43, 180n
Alcibiades: 16
Allegory: 198–207
All's Well that Ends Well: 9, 48n, 70, 75, 82, 87–98, 104, 115n, 117n, 120
Alonso: 186, 189, 194–95, 196, 203
Amerio, Romano: 48n
Angelo: 72n, 99–106, 110, 113, 117n, 134, 139
Antithesis: 3, 154–56
Antonio (*Merchant of Venice*): 54, 56, 60–66
Antonio (*Tempest*): 186–87, 192–97, 203–06
Antony: 4, 121–23, 167–79
Antony and Cleopatra: 8–10, 121–23, 137, 165–79, 184n
Apemantus: 5
Aquinas, St. Thomas: 22, 72n
Ariel: 139, 187, 194–99, 205–06, 209n, 210n
Ariosto, Alfonso: 19
Aristotle: 15, 16, 19, 35, 45n, 46n, 53–54, 72n
Arragon, Prince of: 56–58, 61
Ashley, Robert: 46n

Ashton, H.: 211n
As You Like It: 6

Bacon, Francis: 17, 46n, 89, 116n, 183n, 184n, 192–93, 206, 210n
Baglioni, Giovanpaolo: 210n
Bald, R. C.: 48n
Banquo: 154, 157, 158
Barb, A. A.: 49n
Bassanio: 51, 52, 56–58, 60, 61, 64–66
'Becoming': 169–71
Bembo, Pietro: 19, 21
Bertram: 87–95, 98, 117n, 120
Bohr, Niels: 13
Borgia, Cesare: 103
Born, Lester K.: 116n
Bostocke, R. ("R. B."): 29–30, 36–37, 49n, 88, 115n, 183n
Bradbrook, Muriel: 72n
Bradley, A. C.: 8, 11n
Britomart: 128
Brown, John Russell: 72
Bruno, Giordano: 3, 16, 17, 18, 23, 30–35, 45n, 48n, 49n, 114, 168, 180–83n, 199–200, 210n
Bullough, Geoffrey: 184n
Burckhardt, S.: 72n
Burgundy, Duke of: 139, 142
Burnet, John: 45n
Burton, Robert: 28, 48n
Bury, R. G.: 46n

Caesar, Octavius: 8, 121, 167, 170, 176, 177, 183–84n
Caliban: 8, 139, 186–87, 192–95, 198–99, 203–08, 209n, 210n

213

Callicles: 149
Calvin, John: 17, 27, 30, 145*n*
Capell, Edward: 209*n*
Cassio: 130, 180*n*
Castiglione, Baldassare: 3, 15, 17,
    18-22, 30, 31, 35, 43-44, 45*n*,
    47*n*, 49*n*, 73*n*, 112, 114, 127,
    129, 179*n*, 184*n*, 196
Ceres: 199-202
Chaucer, Geoffrey: 127
Christianity: 18, 21, 22, 30, 41, 43,
    51, 56, 63, 108-09, 112-13, 123,
    124, 126-27
Cicero: 101, 116*n*, 184*n*
Coincidentia oppositorum: 15
Claudio: 103-07, 110, 113
Claudius: 119-20, 148, 179*n*
Cleopatra: 8, 121, 122, 167-79
Coleridge, Hartley: 201, 210*n*
Colie, Rosalie: 13, 17, 44*n*, 45*n*
Commutative justice: 53-55, 58,
    61, 69
Complementarity: 2, 13
Condell, Henry: 115*n*
Constance: 127
Contraria contrariis: 27, 29, 197-98
Copernicus, Nicholas: 30
Cordelia: 8, 121, 138, 141-43,
    149-51, 153
Cornwall, Duke of: 139, 142-43
Cressida: 86, 117*n*
Cupid: 200, 204
Cusa, Nicholas of: 15, 31, 44*n*
Cymbeline: 6

Dark Lady: 171-72, 184*n*, 207
Debus, Allen G.: 48*n*
Dee, John: 28, 46*n*, 48*n*
Dell, Floyd: 48*n*
Desdemona: 1-2, 8, 121, 123,
    124-37, 139, 179*n*, 180*n*
Dialectic: 9, 14, 16, 34, 103, 108,
    152, 163, 185-86, 188-96
Diana (*All's Well*): 90; Bruno's myth
    of, 34
Distributive justice: 53-55, 58,
    61, 69
Domitius: 184*n*
Donne, John: 28-29, 48*n*, 88
Draper, John W.: 211*n*
Du Bartas, Gillaume Salluste: 201-02
    204-05, 211*n*
Duke (*Measure for Measure*): 75-76,
    99-114, 117*n*, 134, 139, 146

Duke (*Merchant of Venice*): 59-60
Duncan: 123, 157, 159, 162-65
Duns Scotus: 22
Duthie, G. I.: 154-55, 156
Dyer, Sir Edward: 28

Edgar: 121-23, 138, 141-48,
    150-53, 163, 180-83*n*
Edmund: 121-23, 138, 140-53,
    180-82*n*
Edward, King: 155, 157, 165
Elbow: 108-10
Elias, Julius A.: 208*n*
Eliot, T. S.: 24
Elton, W. R.: 11*n*, 12, 44*n*, 148,
    180*n*, 209*n*, 210*n*
Elyot, Sir Thomas: 53-54, 59, 72*n*,
    73*n*, 80, 211*n*
Emilia: 122, 126, 129, 130, 179*n*
Enobarbus: 121, 167, 169, 173-77,
    184*n*
Ens: 23-24, 37
Epictetus: 45*n*
Erasmus, Desiderius: 17, 46*n*, 106,
    112, 116*n*, 117*n*
Escalus: 110-11

Fall of Man: 76, 146, 147
Falstaff: 9, 207
Fell-Smith, Charlotte: 48*n*
Ferdinand: 186-89, 196, 197, 206
Feuillerat, Albert: 45*n*
Ficino, Marsilio: 27, 46*n*
Fish, Stanley: 14, 44
Florimell: 128
Florio, John: 116*n*, 117*n*, 173-75,
    184*n*, 190, 209*n*
Fool (*King Lear*): 140-42
Fortinbras: 120, 139
Frame, Donald M.: 47*n*, 184*n*
France, King of: 138, 139, 142
Free will: 27-28, 38-40, 87, 156,
    161
Fregoso, Ottaviano: 19, 21
French, Peter: 46*n*, 48*n*
Freud, Sigmund: 130
Frye, Northrop: 8, 11*n*, 192, 210*n*
Furness, H. H.: 209*n*

Galenism: 23, 27, 29, 36, 76, 89,
    115*n*, 197
Genesis: 206
Gentillet, Innocent: 195
Gertrude: 119

Gloucester, Earl of: 138–42, 145–47, 150–51, 180*n*, 181–82*n*
Goddard, Harold: 116*n*
Golding, Arthur: 45*n*
Goneril: 138–43, 149
Gonzaga, Cesare: 19
Gonzalo: 188–98, 206
Gratiano: 51, 52, 61–65
Greenberg, Sidney: 48*n*, 210*n*
Grimald, Nicholas: 101, 116*n*
Griselda: 127
Guterman, Norbert: 47*n*
Guzzo, Augusto: 48*n*

Hamlet: 4, 83, 110, 119–23, 137, 139, 172, 179*n*
Hamlet: 4, 110, 119–20, 134, 139, 179*n*
Hapgood, R.: 72*n*
Harbage, Alfred: 184*n*
Hawkins, Harriet: 14, 44*n*
Hayward, John: 48*n*
Hector: 84, 85, 115*n*, 117*n*
Helen: 117*n*
Helena: 75–76, 87–99, 104, 109, 114, 116*n*, 117*n*, 120
Heminge, John: 115*n*
Heninger, S. K.: 14, 44*n*, 45*n*, 72*n*
Henry IV (2): 7
Henry IV: 9
Henry IV of France: 184*n*
Henry V: 7, 13
Henry V (Hal): 9, 134
Henry VIII: 8
Heraclitus: 16, 17, 45*n*
Hermeticism: 17, 31, 46*n*, 49*n*
Hester, John: 28
Hobbes, Thomas: 82
Hoeniger, F. D.: 196, 210*n*
Holinshed, Raphael: 183*n*
Holland, N. N.: 102–03, 116*n*
Holland, Philemon: 45*n*
Homeopathy: 26–29, 88–93, 104–05, 198
Homer: 10
Hooker, Richard: 80
Humoralism: 23–24, 30
Hythloday, Raphael: 191

Iago: 1–2, 8, 121–39, 148, 179–80*n*
Inversion: 154–56
Iris: 199–202
Isabella: 75, 103–07, 110, 113

Jacobi, Jolande: 47–50*n*, 115*n*, 183*n*
James I: 89, 116*n*
Jessica: 51, 56, 61, 66–68
Jonson, Ben: 28, 48*n*
Jordan-Smith, Paul: 48*n*
Joseph, Sister Miriam: 11*n*
Jowett, Benjamin: 210*n*
Juliet: 40
Julius II, Pope: 210*n*
Julius Caesar: 121–22
Juno: 199–202

Kaufmann, Walter: 73*n*
Kent, Earl of: 138–43, 149–51, 180*n*
Kermode, Frank: 183–84*n*, 192, 201*n*
King (*All's Well*): 87–89, 92–96, 99
King John: 7
King Lear: 8, 9, 10, 11*n*, 76, 121, 122, 137–53, 156, 157, 163, 170, 180–83*n*
King Lear: 121, 138–43, 149–53, 170, 177, 180*n*, 181–82*n*
Klibansky, R.: 211*n*
Knight, G. Wilson: 8, 11*n*, 115*n*, 201, 203–04, 210*n*, 211*n*
Kristeller, Paul Oskar: 48*n*

Lady Macbeth: 121, 154–56, 160
Laertes: 110, 120, 139
Lafew: 90, 91
Lancastrian Tetralogy: 9, 76
Language, satire of: 39, 91–96, 116*n*
Laocoön: 185
Launcelot Gobbo: 53, 61
Lavatch: 93–94
Lawrence, Friar: 36–40, 43–44, 57, 64, 71, 85, 114, 207
LeRoy, Louis: 46*n*
Lorenzetti, Ambrogio: 72*n*
Lorenzo: 66–69
Love's Labour's Lost: 133–34
Lucio: 99, 103, 105–08
Luther, Martin: 27, 30

Macbeth: 10, 28, 121, 137, 153–65
Macbeth: 4, 121, 123, 154–65, 177, 183*n*
McCanles, Michael: 44*n*
Macdonwald: 159
Macduff: 154, 157, 162–65
Machiavelli, Niccolò: 27, 31, 49*n*, 97–98, 102–06, 112, 116*n*, 149, 184*n*, 195, 210*n*

Mack, Maynard: 168, 184n
Magus, idea of the: 200
Malcolm: 123, 157, 162-65
Mars: 201, 204
Matrix, notion of the earth as: 36, 49n
Matthiessen, Wilhelm: 47-50n, 115n, 183n
Mayerne, Theodore Turquet de: 48n
Measure for Measure: 6-9, 70, 75, 98-114, 116n, 120-24, 134, 137, 146
Medical metaphor: 75-76, 86-89, 104-05, 113, 207-08
Medici, Giuliano de': 179n
Memmo, Paul E.: 33, 49n, 182-83n
The Merchant of Venice: 9, 51-73, 82, 207
Mercutio: 38
Middleton, Thomas: 28, 48n
Miller, Perry: 45n
Milton, John: 15, 19, 43-44 and n, 47n, 128, 179n
Miranda: 8, 186, 193, 196, 197, 200-03, 206, 210-11n
Montaigne, Michel de: 3, 17, 24, 46n, 47n, 100-04. 106, 116n, 117n, 173-76, 184n, 188-91, 209n
Montefeltro, Guidobaldo da: 18
More, Sir Thomas: 17, 46n, 112, 117n, 191, 209n
Morocco, Prince of: 56-58
Muir, Kenneth: 11n, 154
Murray, W. A.: 48n, 116n, 154-56

Neoplatonism: 15, 16, 19, 33-35, 46n
Nerissa: 62-65, 68-69
Nestor: 77-78, 83-84

Ogden, H. V. S.: 209n
Ophelia: 119, 179n
Orco, Remirro de: 103
Oswald: 139, 142
Othello: 1-2, 10, 121, 122-37, 139, 172, 179-80n
Othello: 1, 4, 121, 124-37, 152, 177, 180n
Oxymoron: 3, 32-33, 154, 168

Pagel, Walter: 23, 47n, 49n, 50n, 210n
Pandarus: 5, 85

Panofsky, Erwin: 208n, 211n
Paracelsus: 3, 9, 15-18, 22-31, 34, 40, 43, 45n, 47n, 48n, 76, 84, 87-90, 105, 114, 115n, 155-56, 161, 197-200, 210n
Paradox: 1-8, 40-43, 57-58, 90, 95, 104, 112, 136, 156, 165-69, 171, 176-77, 197
Parolles: 48n, 90-95, 98, 109, 117n, 120
Partridge, Eric: 73n
Patroclus: 85
Patterson, Frank Allen: 44n
Petrarch: 17, 32-33, 38-39, 49n, 168
Philanax: 127
Pia, Emilia: 179n
Pico della Mirandola, Giovanni: 15, 27, 44n, 46n
Plato: 9, 11n, 16, 17, 21, 31, 33-34, 45n, 46n, 49n, 126, 149, 180n, 183n, 184n, 189, 192-93, 195, 209n, 210n
Player-King, Player-Queen: 119, 179n
Plotinus: 46n, 49n
Plutarch: 45n, 184n
Polonius: 119-20
Pompey: 107-10
Pomponazzi, Pietro: 27
Popkin, Richard H.: 46n
Portia: 51-72
Priam: 117n
Primaudaye, Pierre de la: 72n
Problem Comedies: 9, 10, 70, 72, 75-117, 120-22, 131, 137, 139, 150, 172, 178, 198, 207
Prometheus Bound: 206
Prospero: 10, 186-211
Protestantism: 21-22, 43, 47n, 128
Puttenham, George: 28-29, 48n, 73n, 88
Pyrrhus: 120, 139
Pythagoreanism: 14, 17

Rabkin, Norman: 2, 11n, 13, 44n
Raleigh, Sir Walter: 28
Ramists: 45n, 46n
The Rape of Lucrece: 8
Recorde, Robert: 72n
Regan: 138-43, 149
Richard II: 42, 121-22
Richard III: 148
Romeo: 39-40, 49n

Romeo and Juliet: 7, 9, 28, 35,
36-40, 51, 64, 71, 85, 87,
121-22, 198, 200
Rose, Mark: 14, 44n, 186, 209n
Rotondi, Pasquale: 46n

St. Matthew, Gospel according
to: 127
St. Peter's Cathedral: 208-09n
Saxl, F.: 211n
Schiller, Friedrich von: 208n
Scholasticism: 23, 45n, 80
Scott, Walter: 46n
Sebastian: 186, 194, 203, 205
Seneca: 175
Sergeant (*Macbeth*): 158-59
Sextus Empiricus: 46n
Shylock: 51-54, 59-64, 68-72,
73n, 122
Sidney, Sir Philip: 17, 21-22, 28,
45n, 47n, 127, 179n, 180n
Similia similibus: 27, 29, 197-98
Singer, Dorothea Waley: 48n, 49n
Singleton, Charles: 47n, 73n, 179n,
184n
Sisk, J. P.: 72n
Skepticism: 17, 46n
Smith, Marion: 44n
Socrates: 16, 21, 33, 45n, 183n,
184n
Sol: 79-83, 99
Sonnets of Shakespeare: 134, 171,
184n, 207
—Sonnet 94: 35, 40-43, 57, 64,
71, 114, 128, 207
—Sonnet 129: 184n
—Sonnet 144: 172
Specificity, Paracelsian notion of: 24,
29-30, 36-37
Speier, Hans: 191-92, 198, 209n
Spencer, Theodore: 72n
Spenser, Edmund: 22, 128
Stensgaard, Richard K.: 88-89, 115n,
116n
Stephano: 186, 195, 205-06
Still, Colin: 11n
Stoicism; 17, 45n, 77, 123
Strauss, Leo: 148, 180n
Sudhoff, Karl: 47-50n, 115n, 183n

Sylvester, Joshua: 201-02, 211n;
quoted, 204-05

Tansillo: 181-82n
Tarquin: 207
The Tempest: 7, 8, 9, 185-211
Theobald, Lewis: 73n, 116n
Thomas, Friar: 99-104
Thrasymachus: 149
Tilley, Morris Palmer: 47n, 115n
Tillyard, E. M. W.: 72n, 115n,
203-04, 211n
Timon of Athens: 5, 7
Timon: 4, 5
Tom o' Bedlam: 145, 147, 181n
Trinculo: 186, 205
Trinkaus, Charles: 48n
Troilus: 5, 72n, 86
Troilus and Cressida: 5, 8, 9, 70, 75,
77-86, 115n, 117n, 120
The Two Noble Kinsmen: 6
Tybalt: 38

Ulysses: 75-86, 96-99, 101, 104,
109, 115n, 117n, 120, 134
Unified sensibility: 24
Urbino, ducal palace at: 18, 46n
Utopians: 191

Valla, Lorenzo: 27
Venus (*Tempest*): 187, 200-05, 208;
(*Venus and Adonis*) 139, 171,
207
Venus and Adonis: 8, 139, 171, 207
Vickers, Brian: 11n

Waller, G. F.: 45n
Warhaft, Sidney: 46n
Wells, Stanley: 11n
Wesen gegen Wesen: 22, 26-27
White, Howard B.: 11n, 14, 44n
Whytinton, R.: 116n
Wiener, Philip P.: 48n
Wilson, Dover: 196, 210n
Wind, Edgar: 46n
Wittenberg: 31

Yates, Frances: 210n

Zwingli, Huldreich or Ulrich: 30

Designer: Al Burkhardt
Compositor: Marin Typesetters
Printer: McNaughton & Gunn, Inc.
Binder: McNaughton & Gunn, Inc.
Text: MTSC Aldine
Display: Typositor Cancelleresca
Cloth: Joanna Arrestox A linen 14550
Paper: 50lb Bookmark Natural